NEW CONCEPT ENGLISH

PRACTICE AND PROGRESS

An Integrated Course For Pre-Intermediate Students

L. G. ALEXANDER

Illustrations by Michael ffolkes, Graham and Gus

LONGMAN

Addison Wesley Longman Limited
Edinburgh Gate, Harlow,
Essex CM20 2JE, England
and Associated Companies throughout the world.

© Longman Group Limited 1984

First published 1967
Seventy-nine impression 1996

Produced through Longman Malaysia, CLP

ISBN 0 – 582 – 52330 – 3

CONTENTS

v

To the Teacher

Language Learning at the Pre-Intermediate Level

General Principles

Traditional methods of learning a foreign language die hard. As long ago as 1921, Dr Harold Palmer pointed out the important difference between understanding how a language works and learning how to use it. Since that time, a great many effective techniques have been developed to enable students to learn a foreign language. In the light of intensive modern research, no one would seriously question the basic principles that have evolved since Palmer's day, though there is considerable disagreement about how these principles can best be implemented. Despite the great progress that has been made, teachers in many parts of the world still cling to old-fashioned methods and to some extent perpetuate the systems by which they themselves learnt a foreign language. It may, therefore, not be out of place to restate some basic principles and to discuss briefly how they can best be put into effect in the classroom.

Learning a language is not a matter of acquiring a set of rules and building up a large vocabulary. The teacher's efforts should not be directed at informing his students about a language, but at enabling them to use it. A student's mastery of a language is ultimately measured by how well he can use it, not by how much he knows about it. In this respect, learning a language has much in common with learning a musical instrument. The drills and exercises a student does have one end in sight: to enable him to become a skilled performer. A student who has learnt a lot of grammar but who cannot *use* a language is in the position of a pianist who has learnt a lot about harmony but cannot play the piano. The student's command of a language will therefore be judged not by how much he knows, but how well he can perform in public.

In order to become a skilled performer, the student must become proficient at using the units of a language. And the unit of a language is not, as was once commonly supposed, the word, but the sentence. Learning words irrespective of their function can be a waste of time, for not all words are equal. We must draw a distinction between *structural* words and *lexical* items. Words like *I, you, he* etc. are *structural*. Their use can be closely defined; they are part of a grammatical system. Words like *tree, plant, flower* etc. are purely *lexical* items and in no way part of a grammatical system. From the learner's point of view, skill in handling structural words is the key to mastering a language, for the meaning that is conveyed in sentence-patterns depends largely on the function of the structural words that hold them together.

It is possible, though this has yet to be proved scientifically, that every student of a foreign language has what might be called a 'language ceiling', a point beyond which he cannot improve very much. If we accept this supposition, our aim must be to enable every student to learn as much as he is capable of learning in the most efficient way. The old-fashioned translation and grammar-rule methods are extremely wasteful and inefficient, for the student is actually encouraged to make mistakes: he is asked to perform skills before he is adequately prepared. Teachers who use such methods unwittingly create the very problems they seek to avoid. At some point in the course their students inevitably become incapable of going *on*: they have to go *back*. They have become remedial students and the teacher is faced with the problem of remedying what has been incorrectly learnt. No approach could be more ineffective, wasteful and inefficient.

The student should be trained to learn by making as few mistakes as possible. He should never be required to do anything which is beyond his capacity. A well-designed course is one which takes into account what might be called the student's 'state of readiness': the point where he can proceed from easy to difficult. If the student is to make the most of his abilities, he must be trained to adopt correct learning habits.

What has to be Learnt?

The student must be trained adequately in all four basic language skills: *understanding, speaking, reading* and *writing*. In many classroom courses the emphasis is wholly on the written language. The student is trained to use his eyes instead of his ears and his inability to achieve anything like correct pronunciation, stress and intonation must be attributed largely to the tyranny of the printed word. If the teacher is to train his students in all four skills, he must make efficient use of the time at his disposal. Efficiency presupposes the adoption of classroom procedures which will yield the best results in the quickest possible time. The following order of presentation must be taken as axiomatic:

Nothing should be spoken before it has been heard.
Nothing should be read before it has been spoken.
Nothing should be written before it has been read.

Speaking and writing are the most important of these skills, since to some extent they presuppose the other two.

Learning to Speak

The traditional 'conversation lesson' is of no value at all if the student is not ready for it. It is impossible for any student at the post-elementary level to take part in discussions on topics like 'The Cinema Today', for his ideas quite outstrip his capacity for expressing them. The student must first be trained to use patterns in carefully graded aural/oral drills. Only in this way will he finally learn to speak.

Before considering how this can be done, it should be noted that the patterns in a language fall into two distinct categories: *progressive* and *static*. For instance, learning how to answer and to ask questions involves the use of *progressive* patterns. They are *progressive* because the student's skill in handling these complex forms must be developed over a long period, beginning with a simple response like 'Yes, it is' and culminating in complex responses like 'Yes, I should, shouldn't I'. A *static* pattern, on the other hand, like the comparison of adjectives can be taught in a limited number of lessons, not over a long period.

Progressive patterns should be practised through comprehension exercises which require the student to answer and to ask questions which become increasingly complex as the course proceeds. The student should be trained to give tag answers; make negative and affirmative statements to answer double questions joined by *or*; answer general questions which begin with question-words like *When, Where, How* etc.; and at each stage, the student should be trained to ask questions himself. It is obvious that these skills cannot be dealt with in one or two lessons: the student requires practice of this kind in *every* lesson.

At the same time, static patterns should be practised by means of drills which make use of language-laboratory techniques. In each of these drills, the teacher seeks to elicit a particular kind of response. He provides the student with a stimulus to elicit the new pattern in a series of oral drills until the student is able to respond accurately and automatically.

Students may also be trained to speak through oral composition exercises where they are required to reproduce orally a passage of English they are familiar with. At the outset, the student should practise reproducing narrative and descriptive pieces. At a much later stage, he will practise reproducing the substance of an argument. When he can do this well, he will be in a position to converse on set topics which deal with abstract ideas. By this time he will be able to express himself with confidence and will make relatively few mistakes.

The techniques used in speech training at the pre-intermediate level may be summarized as follows:

Drilling in progressive patterns.
Drilling in static patterns.
Practice in oral composition.

Learning to Write

The same sort of careful grading is required when we attempt to teach students to write. We must again begin with the simplest form of statement. Students are all too often plunged into composition work long before they are ready for it. At some point in a course, the teacher may decide that it is time his students attempted to write a composition, so he sets a short narrative or descriptive piece and hopes for the best. This is a random, hit-or-miss method which creates enormous remedial problems and produces disastrous results. If a student's sole experience of written English has been to fill in blank spaces in tailor-made sentences, it is wildly unreasonable to spring a composition subject on him and then expect him to produce correct and readable prose. As with premature discussions on set topics, all we are doing is to encourage him to make mistakes. And it is no good hoping that after a few years of this (involving massive correction on the part of the teacher) the student will somehow improve on his own. Very few students are sufficiently conscientious or highly motivated to examine in detail their own corrected written work. Even if they did, there is absolutely no guarantee that they will not go on making the same mistakes. Writing skill can best be developed through carefully controlled and graded comprehension/précis exercises. Précis writing is not a sterile academic exercise useful only for examination purposes. It can be used effectively to develop a student's writing ability. At the pre-intermediate stage, the student must learn how to write simple, compound, and complex sentences and to connect ideas from notes. Controlled précis writing will enable the student to master each of these difficulties and bring him to a point where he will be capable of writing a composition with a minimum of error.

The main stages in training the student in the written language at the pre-intermediate level may be summarized as follows:

Practice in writing simple sentences through controlled comprehension/précis exercises.

Practice in writing compound sentences through controlled comprehension/précis exercises.

Practice in writing complex sentences through controlled comprehension/précis exercises.

Practice in connecting ideas from notes that have been provided.

The Teaching of Grammar

In traditional textbooks, all information about sentence patterns is presented in the form of 'rules' which the student applies in a series of disconnected sentences by filling in blank spaces, or by giving the correct form of words in brackets. It has become abundantly clear that this approach to language-learning is highly ineffective. It encourages the teacher to talk *about* the language, instead of training his students to use it. The emphasis is on written exercises. The greatest weakness in this approach is that the student cannot transfer what he has learnt from abstract exercises of this kind to other language skills like understanding, speaking and creative writing.

A new pattern should not be presented as the exemplification of some abstract grammar-rule, but as a *way of saying something*. No further explanation or elucidation is necessary. The student is trained to use correct forms automatically, rather than by applying 'grammar logic'. Where explanation is necessary, it can be done by relating a new pattern to one that has already been learnt. If, for instance, the student has learnt the use of 'must', he can be taught the use of 'have to' by being made to see a meaningful relationship between the two.

Students working at the pre-intermediate level may be given exercises in recall, that is, relating language difficulties to a particular context they know well. In this way they will be trained to use correct forms instinctively. The teacher is, incidentally, saved the trouble of correcting exercises, since, for the most part, the passages do this for him.

Traditional filling-in-the-blank exercises still have a place in a modern course, but with one important difference: they should not be used as a means of teaching new patterns, but as a means of consolidating what has been learnt. They are an end, not a means to an end. In this respect, they are extremely useful in tests and can be employed for diagnostic purposes or to enable the teacher to assess terminal behaviour.

The Multi-Purpose Text

In order to do all the exercises outlined above, the student must work from specially-written texts. Each text must be used to train the student in the following skills:

Aural comprehension.
Oral practice (*progressive* and *static* patterns).
Reading aloud.
Oral composition.
Dictation.
Controlled comprehension, précis and composition practice (simple, compound and complex sentences).
Written grammar exercises in recall.

We might call these specially-written passages *multi-purpose texts*, since they are used as the basis for a variety of exercises which aim at developing a number of skills simultaneously.

If these texts are to be suitable for so many purposes, they must be specially devised. The new patterns that are to be taught must be *contextualized*, that is, they must be built into each text. These reiterated patterns should be unobtrusive: their use should strike the listener as being inevitable rather than artificially superimposed. There is also another very important requirement: the texts must be interesting or amusing so that they will entertain the student, hold his attention, and minimize the inevitable drudgery involved in drill work. If the texts are accompanied by illustrations, they will be even more appealing. At the beginner's level, illustrations are more functional than decorative. At this level, the reverse is true: the pre-intermediate stage marks a transition from audio-visual techniques to audio-lingual ones.

Speed and Intensity

Traditional courses are often divided into 'lessons', but these 'lessons' do not take into account what can be done in an average teaching period of forty-five minutes or an hour. They simply consist of 'an amount of information' and may run on for a great many pages. In the classroom, one of these 'lessons' might drag on for weeks because so much has to be done.

A lesson must be precisely what the word implies: an amount of material that can reasonably be covered in a teaching period, possibly with additional material which can be done as homework. In other words, a lesson must be considered as a unit of instruction and no more. Now it is extremely difficult for the course designer to decide what can be done in an average period. Obviously a class of bright students will cover more ground than a class of less able ones. This problem can be overcome if the lesson contains material which can be omitted at the discretion of the teacher, providing that these omissions do not hamper the students' progress.

Levels

For purely practical purposes, students attending language schools have to be classified in terms of knowledge and achievement. It might be worth noting that a full-scale course would resolve itself into three parts, each of which would consist of two stages:

Stage 1 : Pre-elementary level.
Elementary level.

Stage 2 : Pre-intermediate level.
Intermediate level.

Stage 3 : Pre-advanced level.
Advanced level.

About this Course

From Theory to Practice: Basic Aims

This course attempts to put into practice all the theories about language learning outlined above. Briefly, the aims may be stated as follows:

1. To provide a comprehensive course for post-elementary adult or secondary students. The course contains sufficient material for about one and a half academic years' work. It is assumed that the student will receive about four hours' instruction each week i.e. four one-hour lessons on four separate occasions, or two 'double periods' each consisting of two hours or ninety minutes. If we take the academic year to consist of thirty-six weeks, there will be sufficient material in this course for fifty-four weeks' work. The student will receive most of his training in the classroom and will be required to do a little extra work in his own time.

2. To train the student in all four skills: *understanding*, *speaking*, *reading*, and *writing*—in that order. In this respect, the course sets out to do two things: to provide material which will be suitable for aural/oral practice and which can at the same time be used to train the student systematically to write English.

3. To provide the student with a book which will enable him to *use* the language.

4. To provide the teacher with well-co-ordinated and graded material which will enable him to conduct each lesson with a minimum of preparation. As many of the exercises are 'self-correcting', the teacher will, incidentally, be relieved of the arduous task of correcting a great many written exercises.

5. To enable the teacher and the student to work entirely from a single volume without the need for additional 'practice books'.

6. To prepare the ground for students who might, at some future date, wish to sit for academic examinations like the Cambridge Lower Certificate. This aim must be regarded as coincidental to the main purpose of training students in the four language skills.

7. To provide the teacher with recorded material which can be used in the classroom and language-laboratory. It must be emphasized, however, that this is in no way a full-scale language-laboratory course. It is essentially a classroom course, designed primarily for teachers who have no access to a language laboratory. The recorded drills are only intended for teachers who make use of a language-laboratory at regular or irregular intervals to supplement work done in the classroom.

For Whom the Course is Intended

This course should be found suitable for:

1. Adult or secondary students who have completed *First Things First: An Integrated Course for Beginners*, or who have completed *any* other elementary course.

2. Students in need of remedial work: e.g. students who did English at school and now wish to take it up again; students who have begun English several times and never got beyond the point of no return.

3. Schools and Language Institutes where 'wastage' caused by irregular

attendance and late starters is a problem. The course is so designed that it will enable hard-pressed or erratic students to catch up on work they have missed.

4. Post-elementary students who wish to study on their own.

How Much Knowledge has been Assumed?

The material in *First Things First*, the beginners' course which precedes this one, has been designed to 'overlap' this course. Students who have completed it will have no difficulty whatever in continuing where they left off.

Students who have learnt English from other elementary courses and now wish to continue their studies with this course should have a fair working knowledge of the structures listed below. The list may look formidable, but close inspection will reveal that there is nothing in it that would not be found in the average elementary course. In any case, most of the knowledge that has been assumed is revised in the course itself.

It should be noted that a distinction has been drawn in the list between *active* and *passive* knowledge. A student has *active* command of a pattern if he can use it in speech or writing. He has *passive* command of a pattern if he can understand it when he hears or reads it, but is, as yet, incapable of using it. In the list below, this distinction is drawn by the following designations: ability to recognize and to form (*active* knowledge); ability to recognize (*passive* knowledge).

Assumed Knowledge

1. Elementary uses of the verbs *be* and *have* in the present and past.
2. The Present Continuous: ability to recognize and to form.
3. The Simple Present: ability to recognize; to form with *s*, *es*, or *ies* in the third person.
4. The Simple Past: ability to recognize and to form with common regular and irregular verbs.
5. The Past Continuous: ability to recognize.
6. The Present Perfect (Simple): ability to recognize.
7. The Past Perfect: ability to recognize.
8. The Future: ability to recognize and to form with *going to*, *shall* and *will*.
9. Auxiliary Verbs: elementary uses of *can*, *may* and *must*. The ability to recognize the forms *could*, *might* and *would*.
10. The ability to form *questions* and *negatives* with auxiliary verbs including *do/does* and *did*. The use of interrogative pronouns and adverbs.
11. The ability to answer questions beginning with auxiliary verbs and question words.
12. Adverbs: ability to form with *-ly* and *-ily*. The ability to recognize exceptions like *well*, *hard* and *fast*.
13. Articles: definite and indefinite. Elementary uses of *a/an* and *the*. The use of *some*, *any*, *no*, *much*, *many*, *a lot of* with countable and uncountable nouns.
14. Nouns: the ability to form the plural with *-s*, *-es*, *-ves*; common irregular plurals: *men*, *women*, *children*, *teeth* etc.
15. Pronouns: personal, possessive, reflexive. Apostrophe 's'.
16. Adjectives: elementary uses. Regular comparison; irregular comparison: *good*, *bad*, *much/many* and *little*.
17. Prepositions: the use of common prepositions of *place*, *time* and *direction*.

18. Relative Pronouns: the ability to recognize and to use *who/whom*, *which* and *that*.

Miscellaneous Features
19. This/that; these/those.
20. Elided forms: it's, I'm, isn't, didn't, etc.
21. There is/it is; there are/they are.
22. The imperative.
23. The days of the week, dates, seasons, numbers, points of time (today, yesterday, tomorrow, etc.).
24. Telling the time.

The Components of the Course

The course consists of the following:
- One text-book (to be used by teachers and students).
- Four $4\frac{1}{4}$ in. (11 cm.) long-playing tapes (length: 600 feet), recorded at $3\frac{3}{4}$ i.p.s. (9·5 cm. p.s.), on which the multi-purpose texts have been recorded.
  Eight 5 in. (13 cm.) long-playing tapes (length: 900 feet), recorded at $3\frac{3}{4}$ i.p.s. (9·5 cm. p.s.), on which drills have been recorded.
- Recorded drills: Tapescript.
- Supplementary written exercises: Multiple choice.

A Description of the Course

General Arrangement of Material
This course is divided into four Units each of which is preceded by a searching test. Each Unit consists of twenty-four passages which become longer and more complex as the course progresses. Detailed instructions to the student, together with worked examples, precede each Unit.

The passages are multi-purpose texts. Each passage will be used to train the student in the following: aural comprehension; oral practice (*progressive* and *static* patterns); reading aloud; oral composition; dictation; controlled comprehension, précis, and composition practice (simple, compound and complex sentences); written grammar exercises in recall.

Instructions and Worked Examples
These precede each Unit and should be read very carefully. The successful completion of this course depends entirely on the student's ability to carry out the instructions given.

Pre-Unit Tests
A searching test, based on material already studied, precedes each Unit. This will make it possible for students to find their own level and enable them to begin at any point in the book. At the same time, the student who works through the course systematically from beginning to end is not expected to make too sudden a jump between Units. The tests should enable the teacher to assess how much the students have learnt. If they are found to be too long, they should be divided into manageable compartments.

The Passages
An attempt has been made to provide the student with passages which are as

interesting and as varied in subject-matter as possible. Each passage contains examples of the language patterns the student is expected to master. It will also be used as the basis for all aural/oral and written work. The approximate length of the passages in each Unit is as follows:

Unit 1: 100 words.
Unit 2: 140 words.
Unit 3: 160 words.
Unit 4: 180 words.

Oral Exercises
Oral exercises are not included in the book itself and must be supplied by the teacher. They may be along the lines suggested in the section on *How to Use this Course*.

Comprehension and Précis
The aim has been to train the student to make statements which are based directly on the passages he has read. The student is required to derive specific information from each passage (comprehension) which he will put together to form a paragraph (précis). The amount of help he is given to do this gradually diminishes. In these exercises, the student will incidentally gain a great deal of experience in coping with one of the biggest difficulties in English: word order. Here is a brief outline of what is required in each Unit:

Unit 1: The passages contain mainly compound sentences. The comprehension questions have been designed to elicit *simple* statements which will be put together to form a précis and composition.
Unit 2: The passages contain mainly complex sentences (though not necessarily difficult ones) and the comprehension questions are designed to elicit *simple* and *compound* statements. These will be put together to form a précis of the passage.
Unit 3: The comprehension questions are designed to elicit *simple*, *compound* and *complex* statements. These will be put together to form a précis.
Unit 4: The student will practise writing all three types of statement by using connecting words to join ideas. The ideas are derived from each passage and will be joined together to form a précis.

Composition
Composition exercises, which are introduced in Unit 2, run closely parallel to work that is being done in comprehension and précis. From Unit 3 onwards, these exercises are based on ideas suggested by the passages. This will relieve the student of the added burden of having to find something to say when he is struggling to express himself. The arrangement is as follows:

Unit 2: Exercises in writing compound statements.
a Passages 25–36: selecting correct verbs and joining words.
b Passages 37–48: joining simple statements to make compound statements.
Unit 3: Alternating exercises.
a Joining ideas to make compound or complex statements.
b Joining simple statements to make compound or complex statements.
Unit 4: Joining ideas to write two short paragraphs (a total of about 150 words).

Letter-writing

Work in letter-writing is begun in Unit 2 and difficulties concerning layout and subject-matter are introduced gradually. This course deals with personal letters only. The exercises have been graded as follows:

Unit 2: The Heading.
Unit 3: The Salutation and the opening paragraph.
Unit 4: The Body, the Subscription, the Signature and the Postscript.

Key Structures and Special Difficulties

A distinction has been drawn between absolutely essential grammar (Key Structures) and difficulties in usage (Special Difficulties). No attempt has been made to deal with every aspect of grammar. All information about Key Structures and Special Difficulties is derived directly from each passage. Grammatical terminology has not been used at all. New items are presented in the form of sentence patterns. Where explanations are necessary, this has been done by relating a new pattern to one which the student already knows and by providing numerous examples, not by abstract description and 'grammar rules'.

Filling-in-the-blank exercises are given to consolidate what the student has already learnt and practised orally. They cannot be used to teach new patterns. There are also numerous exercises in recall where the student is required to relate language difficulties to a passage he knows well. These grammar exercises are presented as part of a real context, not in disconnected sentences. By referring to the passage, the student can find out immediately whether he has grasped the new patterns. The teacher is also saved the trouble of correcting exercises of this type, since, for the most part, the passages do this for him.

The way the Key Structures have been arranged is one of the most important features of this course. The Key Structures have been presented in what might be called 'concentric cycles', the basic idea being that no new concept should be introduced without reference to what has been learnt so far. This concentric arrangement makes provision for constant revision of the most difficult sentence patterns. The following outline will make this clear:

Unit 1 (Passages 1–24): Key Structures are dealt with at an elementary level.
Unit 2 (Passages 25–48): Exactly the same ground is covered at a slightly more difficult level.
Unit 3 (Passages 49–72): The same ground is covered yet again at a still more difficult level.
Unit 4 (Passages 73–96): The Key Structures are revised.

Cross-references

Cross-references have been included to enable the student to refer to material he has already learnt and to draw useful comparisons. In the text, cross-references are in heavy type and are indicated in the following manner:

a **KS** (=**KEY STRUCTURE**). These letters are followed by a page number and sometimes a paragraph reference: e.g. **KS 47b**.
b **SD** (=**SPECIAL DIFFICULTY**). These letters are also followed by a page number and sometimes a paragraph reference: e.g. **SD 52c**.

The Tapes

Two sets of tapes accompany the course for use in the classroom and the language laboratory.

(a) Four $4\frac{1}{4}$ in. (11 cm.) long-playing tapes.

On these, the ninety-six multi-purpose texts have been recorded at slightly less than normal speed (120 words per minute). These tapes are intended for use in the classroom when the teacher is carrying out the aural/oral procedure suggested for each lesson. The recorded passages may therefore be used for aural comprehension and repetition work. The teacher may, however, choose to work without these tapes if he wishes—in which case he will have to read the contextualized pieces himself.

(b) Eight 5 in. (13 cm.) long-playing tapes.

On these, selected drills have been recorded for use in the classroom and language laboratory. There are ninety-six drills in all, each of which lasts approximately for $3\frac{1}{2}$ minutes. They are intended for teachers who have access to a language laboratory and who make use of it at regular or irregular intervals. It is essential to introduce the drills in the classroom before they are practised in the laboratory.

The drills are four-phase: stimulus/*response*/correct response/*repetition*. They are based entirely on the Key Structures and Special Difficulties introduced in each lesson. The vocabulary used in the drills is drawn from the course itself.

The drills have been published in a separate book which is available to teachers. Detailed information about the drills and suggestions on how they may be used will be found in the introduction to this publication.

Vocabulary Range

Structures permitting, the vocabulary in Units 1 and 2 is based largely on the General Service List of English Words, compiled and edited by Dr Michael West. From then on, the range is unrestricted—within, of course, reasonable limits, and gradually becomes more difficult.

How to Use this Course

Allocation of Time

Ideally, two classroom lessons of approximately 50 minutes each should be spent on each text. The first lesson should be devoted to Guided Conversation; the second to Composition and Language Study. This means that there is enough material in this book for approximately 200 lessons (including tests). However, you may choose to spend only *one* classroom lesson on each text—in which case, *every* lesson may be devoted to Guided Conversation and a selection of written exercises may be set as homework. Your first task is to decide how much time you have in your programme in relation to the material available in the course.

The suggestions given below outline the basic steps in each lesson. You may decide to follow them closely, adapt them to suit your style of teaching, or reject them altogether—BUT PLEASE READ THEM FIRST!

Lesson 1: Guided Conversation

Books Required:

> *Practice and Progress* (for teachers and students)
> *Recorded Drills Tapescript* (for teachers only)

The Stages of the Lesson

1 Aural/Oral Presentation:	about 15 minutes
2 Question and Answer Practice:	about 10 minutes
3 Pattern Drill:	about 5 minutes
4 Oral Reconstruction:	about 10 minutes
5 Talking Points, Singing, Games, Story-telling, etc:	about 10 minutes

Let's see what each step involves:

1 Aural/Oral Presentation:
  a Listening (Books shut)
  b Intensive Reading (Books open)
  c Listening (Books shut)
  d Chorus, Group and Individual Repetition (Books shut) (This step is optional.)
  e Reading Aloud: Chorus, Group or Individual (Books open)

a Listening (Books shut). Play the recording or read the passage once. The students should *listen* and try to understand as much as they can.

b Intensive Reading (Books open). Read the text in small units (e.g. a sentence at a time, or less) making sure the students *really* understand it. Rather than give direct explanations, try to get as much information as possible from the students. (Think of it as 'a corkscrew operation'!) Explanations should be given entirely in

English, but don't carry direct-method teaching to absurd lengths. If your students fail to understand in spite of all your efforts, translate briefly and move on. Remember, if you don't translate a particular difficulty, then someone in the class will!

c Listening (Books shut). Play the recording or read the passage once more.

d Chorus, Group and Individual Repetition (Books shut). These are *optional* activities at this level, and in any case should be confined to (say) Unit 1 only (the first 24 texts). If you conduct repetition exercises, first ask the *whole* class to repeat the text after you. Next divide the class into three groups and repeat the text once more. Finally, ask individual students round the class to repeat the text.

e Reading Aloud: Chorus, Group or Individual (Books open). How you conduct this depends on the size of the class. If it is a very large class, chorus and group reading is appropriate; if it is a small class (up to 20 students) individual reading may be more suitable.

The entire Aural/Oral Presentation should not occupy more than about 15 minutes. DON'T SPEND TOO MUCH TIME ON ANY ONE ACTIVITY!

2 Question and Answer Practice:
Question and answer practice should be based mainly on the text. However, you may vary this with questions which relate to the student's own experience. If you find it difficult to ask questions spontaneously, prepare yourself in advance. Five types of exercise are suggested, but this is by no means a rigid pattern. Questions should be asked individually round the class—preferably at speed. About half a dozen questions relating to each type should be sufficient. The five types are as follows:

a Yes/No Tag Answers
b Questions with Who
c Negative and Affirmative Statements
d General Questions: When, Where, Why, How, etc.
e Asking Questions in Pairs

a Yes/No Tag Answers. Train the students to listen to the *first* word in your questions and to use *the same word* (where applicable) in their answers. (All examples are based on Text 4.)
Teacher: *Have* you received a letter from your sister?
Student: No, I *haven't.*
Teacher: *Have* you received a letter from your brother?
Student: Yes, I *have.* etc.

b Questions with Who. Train the students to supply the correct auxiliary verbs in their answers. Note that *Who . . . ?* is only used as a subject.
Teacher: Who's received a letter?
Student: I have. etc.

c Negative and Affirmative Statements. Train the student to make negative and affirmative statements by asking double questions joined by *or.*
Teacher: Have you received a letter from your brother or your sister?
Student: I haven't received a letter from my sister. I've received one from my
         brother. etc.

d General Questions: When, Where, Why, How, etc. Train the student to provide natural answers to general comprehension questions.
Teacher: Who've you received a letter from?

Student: My brother.   etc. (*Not:* I have received a letter from my brother.)
e Asking Questions in Pairs. In order to understand the function of question words well, the student should be trained to ask questions in pairs. In this way he will learn that the addition of a question word in no way affects the form of the question. Intensive training of this sort prevents the student from using incorrect forms like 'Where he went?' etc. The student first asks a question using an auxiliary verb. Then he asks *precisely the same question* preceding it with a question word.

Teacher: Ask me if I've received a letter from my brother.
Student: Have you received a letter from your brother?
Teacher: Who . . . (Always provide the question word.)
Student: Who have you received a letter from?   etc.

3 Pattern Drill:

Drill the main language point which has been introduced in the text. Use the publication entitled *Practice and Progress, Recorded Drills: Tapescript* for this purpose. Here, for instance, is part of the drill which relates to Text 4:

Teacher: Have your breakfast.
Student: I've already had my breakfast.
Teacher: Tell him to leave.
Student: He's already left.
Teacher: Tell her to comb her hair.
Student: She's already combed her hair.   etc.

The students may be trained to answer in chorus or groups, or the drill may be conducted a number of times rapidly round the class with individual students responding. If a language-laboratory is available, this will be adequate preparation for further practice. However, it must be stressed that a laboratory is by no means indispensable: it is quite possible to do all the drilling live in the classroom. Alternatively, teachers who have tape-recorders may choose to play the taped drills in class.

4 Oral Reconstruction:

Write a number of brief notes ('key words') on the blackboard summarizing the subject-matter of the text. Now invite individual pupils to reconstruct the text by referring to the notes. The students should be encouraged to speak without interruption for up to a minute at a time and should try to use as many as possible of the expressions, structures etc. of the original story. Here, for instance, are some notes which relate to Text 4:

1 Letter—brother—Tim.	6 Bought—Australian car—Alice
2 In Australia.	Springs—small town—centre.
3 Been there—six months.	7 Visit Darwin.
4 Engineer.	8 From there—Perth.
5 Big firm—visited different places.	9 Never before—trip—exciting.

5 Talking Points, Singing, Games, Story-telling, etc.

The final part of the Guided Conversation Lessons should be devoted to free conversation. Where the text immediately suggests a subject or subjects for general discussion, individual students should be invited to speak impromptu. Here, for instance, are a few talking points suggested by Text 4:

a Do you know anyone abroad? What can you tell me about him/her?

b What do you think (Australia) is like?

c Which country would you like to visit and why?

d Tell me about your job.

Obviously, not all texts provide suitable material for conversation. Where a general discussion is not possible, the lesson may end with any one of the following activities:

a Singing: Teach the class traditional or modern British and American songs. Any good song book may be used for this purpose. For instance:

Lee and Dodderidge: *Time for a Song* (Longman)

Dakin: *Songs and Rhymes for the Teaching of English* (Longman)

b Games: Well-known parlour games like 'Twenty Questions' are always popular with students. A book like *Language-Teaching Games and Contests* by W. R. Lee (O.U.P.) is full of excellent ideas.

c Story-telling: You may occasionally read a story to the class—providing it is roughly within the students' structural/lexical range. Many of the titles in the series Pleasant Books in Easy English Stages 1–4 (Longman) are suitable for this purpose.

Lesson 2: Composition and Language Study

As has already been indicated, this entire lesson may be omitted and a selection of written exercises may, instead, be set as homework. If this approach is adopted, then the Précis and Composition exercises *must always be set*. Needless to say, more satisfactory results will be obtained where a complete classroom lesson can be devoted to written exercises.

Books Required:

> *Practice and Progress* (for teachers and students)
> *Supplementary Written Exercises* (for teachers and students)

The Stages of the Lesson

> 1 Comprehension/Précis/Composition/Letter-writing
> 2 Key Structures
> 3 Exercises
> 4 Special Difficulties
> 5 Exercises
> 6 Dictation
> 7 Multiple Choice Questions

No specific suggestions are made regarding the amount of time to be spent on each part of the lesson as this will be found to vary greatly.

1 Comprehension/Précis/Composition/Letter-writing

These exercises must never be omitted as they are part of a carefully planned guided summary and composition scheme which evolves progressively through *Practice and Progress* and *Developing Skills*. As the exercises are largely self-correcting, it will be sufficient to check that they have been done. Go round the class while the students are writing and help individuals.

2 Key Structures

This part of the lesson should be devoted to a *brief* explanation of the main grammar points that were presented in the text. Grammatical information should be considered a means to an end, not an end in itself. Technical terms have been deliberately excluded: it has been left to the teacher to decide how to present the grammar. This, in turn, will depend wholly on the class. In the case of students who are familiar with the grammar of their own language, there is no reason why the teacher should not make use of technical terms. In the case of students who are wholly unfamiliar with grammatical concepts, no technical terms should be used at all. The aim behind all the explanation should be to reinforce theoretically what the student has already practised orally. It is best to avoid sweeping 'rules' and to confine the study of grammar to the points presented. Additional information can be obtained from any standard textbook: e.g. W. S. Allen: *Living English Structure* (Longman).

3 Exercises

These should be tackled in writing. They will provide further reinforcement of the grammar that has just been presented.

4 Special Difficulties

A brief explanation regarding the special lexical/structural difficulties should now be given. Where appropriate, you may draw a brief contrast between the problem presented in the text and a similar problem in the mother tongue.

5 Exercises

These should now be tackled in writing to reinforce what has been taught.

6 Dictation

Depending on the amount of time available, dictations should be given frequently. A few sentences taken from a passage the students have already studied may be dictated. The students may correct their own work by comparing their version with the passage.

7 Multiple Choice Exercises

These will be found in the separate publication, *Supplementary Written Exercises,* and may be tackled in class or as homework.

Homework

The written exercises become more demanding and time-consuming as the student progresses through the course. At a later stage, exercises which have not been completed in class may be set as homework.

Pre-Unit Tests

These should always be set before the students move on to a new Unit.

Additional Reading Material

It is essential for the students to read as much as possible in their own time. Students only find reading an irksome task when they attempt to read books which are too difficult for them. The books the students should read must be simplified and well within their range. Longman Structural Readers series is recommended for this purpose. A set of readers may accompany each of the Units in this book:

PRE-UNIT TEST 1

IF YOU CAN DO THIS TEST GO ON TO UNIT 1

A. Look at this example:

> I am tired.
> *He is* tired.

Write these sentences again. Begin each sentence with *He*.

1. I am busy.
2. I am learning English.
3. I have a new book.
4. I live in the country.
5. I shall see you tomorrow.
6. I can understand you.
7. I must write a letter.
8. I may come next week.
9. I do a lot of work every day.
10. I did a lot of work yesterday.
11. I played football yesterday.
12. I bought a new coat last week.
13. I have had a letter from Tom.
14. I was busy this morning.
15. I could play football very well when I was younger.
16. I always try to get up early.
17. I might see you next week.
18. I always enjoy a good film.
19. I had finished my work before you came.
20. I watch television every night.

B. Look at these examples:

> I want *a* biscuit.   I want *a* cup of coffee.
> I want *some* biscuits.   I want *some* coffee.
> Do you want *any* biscuits?   Do you want *any* coffee?
> I don't want *any* biscuits.   I don't want *any* coffee.

Write these sentences again. Put in *a, some* or *any*.

1. There are .... books on the desk.
2. I drank .... glass of beer.
3. Do you want .... butter?
4. There aren't .... people in the street.
5. Tom has just bought .... new car.
6. We have .... apple trees in our garden.
7. Can I have .... bar of chocolate, please?
8. There isn't .... bread in that tin.
9. Is there .... ink in that bottle?
10. Are there .... eggs in that basket?

3

C. Look at these examples:

> I haven't any eggs.   I haven't *got many* eggs.
> He hasn't any coffee.   He hasn't *got much* coffee.

Do these in the same way:
1. I haven't any butter.
2. You haven't any cigarettes.
3. We haven't any milk.
4. She hasn't any biscuits.
5. They haven't any stationery.

D. Look at this example:

> She goes to town every day.   She *went* to town yesterday.

Do these in the same way:
1. He buys a new car every year.   He .... a new car last year.
2. She airs the room every day.   She .... it this morning.
3. He often loses his pen.   He .... his pen this morning.
4. He always listens to the news.   He .... to the news yesterday.
5. She empties this basket every day.   She .... it yesterday.

E. Look at these examples:

> He went to the cinema yesterday.
> *Question:* Did he go to the cinema yesterday?
> *Question:* Where did he go yesterday?
> *Negative:* He didn't go to the cinema yesterday.

Do these in the same way:

1. He bought a new car.
Q. ....
Q. What ....
N. ....

2. She can come tomorrow.
Q. ....
Q. When.......................
N. ....

3. They were here yesterday.
Q. ....
Q. When.......................
N. ....

4. He must leave early.
Q. ....
Q. Why.......................
N. ....

5. He gave you a pen.
Q. ....
Q. What ....
N. ....

6. He lives next door.
Q. ....
Q. Where ....
N. ....

7. You know him well.
Q. ....
Q. How well.......................
N. ....

8. He has found his pen.
Q. ....
Q. What ....
N. ....

9. You saw that film.
Q. ....
Q. When.......................
N. ....

10. He arrived at two o'clock.
Q. ....
Q. When.......................
N. ....

4

F. Look at this example:

> She smiled .... (pleasant)
> She smiled *pleasantly*.

Do these in the same way:

1. He read the phrase .... (slow)
2. He worked .... (lazy)
3. He cut himself .... (bad)
4. He worked .... (careful)
5. The door opened .... (sudden)

G. Look at this example:

> *It will* rain tomorrow.
> *It'll* rain tomorrow.

Write these sentences again. Use short forms.

1. *He will* arrive tomorrow morning.
2. *She will* come this evening.
3. *I shall* see you the day after tomorrow.
4. He *will not* believe me.
5. We *shall not* remain here.

H. Look at this example:

> This dress belongs to my sister.   It is *hers*.

Do these in the same way:

1. These things belong to my husband. They are ....
2. This coat belongs to me. It is ....
3. These shoes belong to my wife. They are ....
4. These pens belong to Tom and Betty. The pens are ....
5. This suitcase belongs to you. It is ....

I. Look at this example:

> It is *warm* today, but it was *warmer* yesterday.

Do these in the same way:

1. It is *cool* today, but it was .... yesterday.
2. It is *wet* today, but it was .... yesterday.
3. He's *late* again today, but he was .... yesterday.
4. This test is *easy*, but that one is ....
5. This book is *expensive*, but that one is ....
6. This bookcase is *large*, but that one is ....
7. That film was *interesting*, but the other one was ....
8. Betty is *pretty*, but Jane is ....
9. Miss Green is *beautiful*, but Miss White is ....
10. Tom is *intelligent*, but Bill is ....

J. Put in the right word or phrase: *yesterday*, *last night*, *tomorrow* etc.

The date today is Monday, March 5th.

1. I saw him .... (Sunday, March 4th)
2. I shall see him .... (Tuesday, March 6th)
3. I shall see him .... (Monday, March 5th)
4. I shall see him .... (Monday, March 5th–afternoon)
5. I shall see him .... (Wednesday, March 7th)
6. I saw him .... (Saturday, March 3rd)
7. I saw him .... (Sunday, March 4th–night)
8. I shall see him .... (Tuesday, March 6th–morning)
9. I shall see him .... (Monday, March 5th–morning)
10. I saw him .... (Sunday, March 4th–afternoon)

K. Put in *at*, *in*, or *on*:
1. He is going to telephone .... five o'clock.
2. My birthday is .... May 21st.
3. It is always cold .... February.
4. My father was there .... 1942.
5. He is going to arrive .... Tuesday.

L. Put in *across*, *over*, *between*, *off*, *along*, *in*, *on*, *into*, *out of*, or *under*:
1. The aeroplane is flying .... the village.
2. The ship is going .... the bridge.
3. The boy is swimming .... the river.
4. Two cats are running .... the wall.
5. My books are .... the shelf.
6. The bottle of milk is .... the refrigerator.
7. The boy is jumping .... the tree.
8. Mary is sitting .... her mother and her father.
9. It is 9 o'clock. The children are going .... class.
10. It is 4 o'clock. The children are coming .... class.

M. Put in *Who* or *Which*:
1. .... hat did you buy?
2. .... broke this plate?
3. .... bus did you catch?
4. .... is knocking at the door?
5. .... of the two books do you want?

N. Look at these examples:

> She is the girl. *She* met me yesterday.
> She is the girl *who* met me yesterday.
> She is the girl. I met *her* yesterday.
> She is the girl *whom* I met yesterday.
> This is the book. I bought *it* yesterday.
> This is the book *which* I bought yesterday.

Join these sentences in the same way. Use *who*, *whom* or *which*.
1. This is the car. The mechanic repaired *it* yesterday.
2. He is the man. I invited *him* to the party.
3. These are the things. I bought *them* yesterday.
4. He is the man. *He* came here last week.
5. He is the policeman. *He* caught the thieves.

6. She is the nurse. *She* looked after me.
7. She is the woman. I met *her* yesterday.
8. I am the person. *I* wrote to you.
9. They are the people. I saw *them* yesterday.
10. They are the trees. We cut *them* down yesterday.

O. Look at this example:

> I can see some cups, but I can't see any *glasses*.

Do these in the same way:
1. I can see some spoons, but I can't see any .... (knife)
2. I can see some hammers, but I can't see any .... (box)
3. I can see some cupboards, but I can't see any .... (shelf)
4. I can see Mr Jones and Mr Brown, but I can't see their .... (wife)
5. I can see some cups, but I can't see any .... (dish)

P. Read this story carefully:
Last week, I took my four-year-old daughter, Sally, to a children's party. We travelled by train. Sally has never travelled by train before. She sat near the window and asked a lot of questions. Suddenly, a middle-aged lady came into our compartment and sat opposite Sally. 'Hullo, little girl,' she said. Sally did not answer, but looked at her curiously. The lady took out her powder compact. She then began to make up her face.

'Why are you doing that?' Sally asked.

'To make myself beautiful,' the lady answered. She put away her compact and smiled kindly.

'But you are still ugly,' Sally said.

Now write answers to these questions:
1. Did you take Sally to the park?
2. Did you take Sally to a children's party?
3. Where did Sally sit?
4. Who came into your compartment?
5. Was the lady young or was she middle-aged?
6. Where did the lady sit?
7. Did she say 'Hullo' to Sally, or did Sally say 'Hullo' to her?
8. Why did the lady make up her face?
9. Did Sally think the lady was beautiful?
10. What did Sally say to the lady?

Unit 1

INSTRUCTIONS TO THE STUDENT

Comprehension Précis and Composition

Précis is a test of your ability to find the important points in a piece of writing and to put them together. To write a précis, you must be able to do two things. You must be able to understand what you read, and to put ideas together. *Comprehension* is a test of your ability to understand what you read. *Composition* is a test of your ability to put ideas together. So *précis*, *comprehension* and *composition* are closely related to each other.

Unit 1 contains twenty-four short pieces. There are some questions under each piece. Your answers to these questions will be in short, simple sentences. Put your answers together. In this way, you will make a short paragraph. Your paragraph will be a précis of the piece. At the same time, it will be a composition.

Before you begin each exercise, read these instructions carefully. Read them *each time* you begin a new piece. They are very important.

How to work

1. Read the piece carefully two or three times. Make sure you understand it.
2. Write an answer to each question. Each answer must be *a complete sentence*.
3. Your answers to the questions must follow each other. Together, they will make *a complete paragraph*.
4. Read through your work and correct your mistakes.
5. Count the number of words in your paragraph. Words like 'the', 'a' etc. count as single words. Words which are joined by a hyphen (e.g. 'living-room') also count as single words. Do not go over the word limit. At the end of your paragraph write the number of words that you have used.

Example

Work through this example carefully and then try to do the exercises in Unit 1 in the same way.

Granny Forbes

Mrs Forbes was very old and very poor. Everybody in the neighbourhood called her Granny Forbes and tried to help her. Some neighbours came in each day and cooked meals for her. Others came and cleaned her room. There was little furniture in her room. It was small, dark, and almost empty. There was a bed and a
5 table, and there were two chairs. In winter, neighbours sometimes brought coal and lit a fire, but Granny's room was often very cold. Granny lived in poverty all her life. She died at the age of eighty-four. Then her neighbours got a big surprise. She left £50,000!

Comprehension Précis and Composition

Answer these questions *in not more than 50 words*.
1. Did Granny Forbes live in poverty all her life or not?
2. Did her neighbours help her, or did her relations help her?
3. Did they cook meals for her every day or not?
4. Did they clean her small, poorly-furnished room or not?

5. Did they sometimes light a fire for her in winter or not?
6. Did Granny Forbes die at the age of eighty-one, or did she die at the age of eighty-four?
7. Did everyone get a surprise or not?
8. How much did she leave?

Answer

Granny Forbes lived in poverty all her life. Her neighbours helped her. They cooked meals for her every day. They cleaned her small, poorly-furnished room. They sometimes lit a fire for her in winter. Granny Forbes died at the age of eighty-four. Everyone got a surprise. She left £50,000!   (49 words)

Key Structures and Special Difficulties

When you finish the exercise in Comprehension Précis and Composition, go on to the language exercises that follow. The information under the title **Key Structures** gives you advice about important problems in grammar. The information under the title **Special Difficulties** gives you advice about particular problems. The twenty-four passages in Unit 1 will help you to understand these problems and to do the language exercises.

1 A Private Conversation

Last week I went to the theatre. I had a
very good seat. The play was very interesting. I did not enjoy it. A young man
and a young woman were sitting behind
5 me. They were talking loudly. I got very
angry. I could not hear the actors. I
turned round. I looked at the man and the
woman angrily. They did not pay any
attention. In the end, I could not bear it.
10 I turned round again. 'I can't hear a
word!' I said angrily.

'It's none of your business,' the young
man said rudely. 'This is a private conversation!'

'It's none of your business'

Comprehension Précis and Composition

Answer these questions *in not more than 55 words.*
1. Where did the writer go last week?
2. Did he enjoy the play or not?
3. Who was sitting behind him?
4. Were they talking loudly, or were they talking quietly?
5. Could the writer hear the actors or not?
6. Did he turn round or not?
7. What did he say?
8. Did the young man say, 'The play is not interesting.' or did he say, 'This is a
private conversation!'?

Key Structures

Word Order in Simple Statements.
a A statement tells us about something. All the sentences in the passage are statements.
Each of these statements contains one idea. Each statement tells us about *one thing*.
A statement that tells us about one thing is a *simple statement.*
b The order of the words in a statement is very important. Look at these two statements. They both contain the same words but they do not mean the same thing:
   The policeman arrested the thief.
   The thief arrested the policeman.
c A simple statement can have six parts, but it does not always have so many. Study
the order of the words in the columns on page 14. Note that column 6 (When?) can be
at the beginning or at the end of a statement.

Exercises
A. Rule seven columns on a double sheet of paper. At the top of each column, write
the numbers and the words given in the Table. Copy out the rest of the passage. Put the
words of each statement in the correct column in the way shown in the Table.

6	1	2	3	4	5	6
When?	Who? Which? What?	Action	Who? Which? What?	How?	Where?	When?
Last week	I	went			to the theatre.	
	I	had	a very good seat.			
	The play	was	very interesting.			
	I	did not enjoy	it.			
	A young man and a young woman	were sitting			behind me.	
	They	were talking		loudly.		

B. You will use the seven columns again for this exercise. There is a line under each word or group of words in the statements below. The words are not in the right order. Arrange them correctly in the seven columns. Look at this example:

I   last year   to America   went.

The correct order is: I (*who*) went (*action*) to America (*where*) last year. (*when*)
Or: Last year I went to America.

1. The film I enjoyed yesterday.
2. The news listened to I carefully.
3. Well the man the piano played.
4. Games played yesterday in their room the children quietly.
5. Quietly the door he opened.
6. Immediately left he.
7. A tree in the corner of the garden he planted.
8. Before lunch the letter in his office quickly he read.
9. This morning a book I from the library borrowed.
10. The soup spoilt the cook.
11. We at home stay on Sundays.
12. There a lot of people are at the bus-stop.
13. The little boy an apple this morning ate greedily in the kitchen.
14. She beautifully draws.
15. Music I like very much.
16. A new school built they in our village last year.
17. The match at four o'clock ended.
18. She a letter from her brother last week received.

2 Breakfast or Lunch?

It was Sunday. I never get up early on Sundays. I sometimes stay in bed until lunch time. Last Sunday I got up very late. I looked out of the window. It was
5 dark outside. 'What a day!' I thought. 'It's raining again.' Just then, the telephone rang. It was my aunt Lucy. 'I've just arrived by train,' she said. 'I'm coming to see you.'
10 'But I'm still having breakfast,' I said. 'What are you doing?' she asked. 'I'm having breakfast,' I repeated. 'Dear me,' she said. 'Do you always get up so late? It's one o'clock!'

I never get up early

Comprehension Précis and Composition

Answer these questions *in not more than 50 words.*
1. Does the writer always get up early on Sundays, or does he always get up late?
2. Did he get up early last Sunday, or did he get up late?
3. Who telephoned then?
4. Had she arrived by train, or had she come on foot?
5. Was she coming to see him or not?
6. Did he say, 'I'm still having breakfast', or did he say, 'I am still in bed'?
7. Was his aunt very surprised or not?
8. What was the time?

Key Structures

Now, Often and Always.
Study these statements and questions:

Now

These sentences are from the passage:
It's raining.
I'm coming to see you.
I'm still having breakfast.
What are you doing?

Here are some more sentences:
He is still sleeping.
We are enjoying our lunch.

I am reading in bed.

Often and Always

I never get up early on Sundays.
I sometimes stay in bed until lunch time.
Do you always get up so late?

He rarely gets up before 10 o'clock.
We frequently have lunch at this restaurant.

Do you ever read in bed?

Exercises
A. Write out these two paragraphs again. Give the right form of the words in brackets:
1. I am looking out of my window. I can see some children in the street. The children (play) football. They always (play) football in the street. Now a little boy (kick) the ball. Another boy (run) after him but he cannot catch him.

2. I carried my bags into the hall.

'What you (do)?' my landlady asked.

'I (leave), Mrs Lynch,' I answered.

'Why you (leave)?' she asked. 'You have been here only a week.'

'A week too long, Mrs Lynch,' I said. 'There are too many rules in this house. My friends never (come) to visit me. Dinner is always at seven o'clock, so I frequently (go) to bed hungry. You don't like noise, so I rarely (listen) to the radio. The heating doesn't work, so I always (feel) cold. This is a terrible place for a man like me. Goodbye, Mrs Lynch.'

B. Note the position of the words in italics in these sentences:

My friends *never* come to visit me.

I *frequently* go to bed hungry.

I *rarely* listen to the radio.

I *always* feel cold.

I *never* get up early on Sundays.

I *sometimes* stay in bed until lunch time.

Write these sentences again. Put the words in brackets in the right place:

1. She answers my letters. (rarely)
2. We work after six o'clock. (never)
3. The shops close on Saturday afternoons. (always)
4. Do you go to work by car? (always)
5. Our teacher collects our copybooks. (frequently)
6. We spend our holidays abroad. (sometimes)
7. I buy gramophone records. (often)
8. Do you buy gramophone records? (ever)

Special Difficulties

What a day! (l. 5)

Instead of saying:	*We can say:*
It is a terrible day!	What a terrible day!
This is a beautiful picture!	What a beautiful picture!
	Or: What a beautiful picture this is!

Exercise

Write these sentences again. Each sentence must begin with *What*.

1. This is a wonderful garden!
2. This is a surprise!
3. He is causing a lot of trouble!
4. They are wonderful actors!
5. She is a hard-working woman!
6. It is a tall building!
7. It's a terrible film!
8. You are a clever boy!
9. She is a pretty girl!
10. He is a strange fellow!

3 Please Send Me a Card

Postcards always spoil my holidays. Last
summer, I went to Italy. I visited
museums and sat in public gardens. A
friendly waiter taught me a few words of
5 Italian. Then he lent me a book. I read
a few lines, but I did not understand a
word. Every day I thought about postcards. My holidays passed quickly, but I
did not send any cards to my friends. On
10 the last day I made a big decision. I got
up early and bought thirty-seven cards.
I spent the whole day in my room, but I
did not write a single card!

I bought thirty-seven cards

Comprehension Précis and Composition

Answer these questions *in not more than 50 words.*
1. Do postcards always spoil the writer's holidays or not?
2. Where did he spend his holidays last summer?
3. What did he think about every day?
4. Did he send any cards to his friends or not?
5. How many cards did he buy on the last day?
6. Where did he stay all day?
7. Did he write any cards or not?

Key Structures

What happened?
Read this short conversation. Pay close attention to the verbs in italics. Each of these
verbs tells us *what happened.*

POLICEMAN: Did you see the accident, sir?
MAN: Yes, I did. The driver of that car *hit* that post over there.
POLICEMAN: What happened?
MAN: A dog *ran* across the road and the driver *tried to avoid* it. The car suddenly *came*
towards me. It *climbed* on to the pavement and *crashed* into that post.
POLICEMAN: What did you do?
MAN: I *ran* across the street after the dog.
POLICEMAN: Why did you do that? Were you afraid of the car?
MAN: I wasn't afraid of the car. I was afraid of the driver. The driver *got out* of the car
and *began shouting* at me. He was very angry with me. You see, it was my dog.

Exercises
A. Look at the passage 'Please Send Me A Card'. Put a line under all the verbs which
tell us what happened to the writer when he was on holiday in Italy.

B. Give the correct form of all the verbs in brackets. Do not refer to the passage until you finish the exercise:

Last summer, I (go) to Italy. I (visit) museums and (sit) in public gardens. A friendly waiter (teach) me a few words of Italian. Then he (lend) me a book. I (read) a few lines, but I (not understand) a word. Every day I (think) about postcards. My holidays (pass) quickly, but I (not send) any cards to my friends. On the last day, I (make) a big decision. I (get) up early and (buy) thirty-seven cards. I (spend) the whole day in my room, but I (not write) a single card!

C. Give the correct form of the verbs in brackets in the passage below. Each verb must tell us *what happened*:

My friend, Roy, (die) last year. He (leave) me his record player and his collection of gramophone records. Roy (spend) a lot of money on records. He (buy) one or two new records every week. He never (go) to the cinema or to the theatre. He (stay) at home every evening and (listen) to music. He often (lend) records to his friends. Sometimes they (keep) them. He (lose) many records in this way.

Special Difficulties

He lent me a book. (l. 5)

Instead of saying:	*We can say:*
He lent me a book.	He lent a book to me.
He sent me a card.	He sent a card to me.
He passed me the salt.	He passed the salt to me.
She bought me a tie.	She bought a tie for me.
She made me a cake.	She made a cake for me.

Exercise

Write each of the following sentences in a different way:

1. He paid the shop-keeper some money.
2. He handed me the prize.
3. The waiter brought a bottle of beer to the man.
4. He sold all his books to me.
5. The shop-assistant chose some curtain material for me.
6. He did me a big favour.
7. She showed her husband her new hat.
8. She promised a reward to the finder.
9. He gave his son some advice.
10. His uncle left him some money.
11. He is teaching English to us.
12. I bought this bunch of flowers for you.
13. Bring that book to me please.
14. He offered me a cigarette.
15. Read me the first paragraph.
16. I've ordered some soup for you.
17. I owe him a lot of money.
18. Pass the mustard to your father.

4 An Exciting Trip

I have just received a letter from my brother, Tim. He is in Australia. He has been there for six months. Tim is an engineer. He is working for a big firm and he has already visited a great number of different places in Australia. He has just bought an Australian car and has gone to Alice Springs, a small town in the centre of Australia. He will soon visit Darwin. From there, he will fly to Perth. My brother has never been abroad before, so he is finding this trip very exciting.

an engineer in Australia

Comprehension Précis and Composition

Answer these questions *in not more than 50 words.*
1. What has the writer just received from his brother, Tim?
2. Is Tim an engineer, or is he a doctor?
3. How long has he been in Australia?
4. Has he already visited many places or not?
5. Where is he now?
6. Has Tim ever been abroad before or not?
7. Is he enjoying his trip very much or not?

Key Structures

What has happened?
These sentences are from the passage. Study them carefully. Pay close attention to the words in italics:
I have *just* received a letter from my brother, Tim.
He has *just* bought an Australian car and has gone to Alice Springs.
He has been there *for six months*.
He has *already* visited a great number of different places.
My brother has *never* been abroad before.

Here are some more sentences:
He has retired *now*.
Have you *ever* been to Australia?
Have you read any good books *lately*?
I haven't been very successful *so far*.
The train has not arrived *yet*.

Exercises
A. Write these sentences again. Put the words in brackets in the right place:
1. I have had breakfast. (just)
2. He has been in prison. (for six months)
3. The police have not caught the thief. (yet)
4. You have asked that question three times. (already)
5. Have you been to Switzerland? (ever)

6. I have been to Switzerland. (never)
7. He is a wonderful runner. He has broken two records. (so far)
8. I haven't seen George. (lately)

B. Give the correct form of the verbs in brackets. Do not refer to the passage until you finish the exercise:
I just (receive) a letter from my brother Tim. He is in Australia. He (be) there for six months. Tim is an engineer. He is working for a big firm and he already (visit) a great number of different places in Australia. He just (buy) an Australian car and (go) to Alice Springs. My brother never (be) abroad before, so he is finding this trip very exciting.

C. What is happening? What has happened?
Read these two statements: The bell is ringing.
                                  The bell has just rung.
Complete the following in the same way:
1. He is leaving the house.　　He has just . . .
2. He is having breakfast.　　He has . . .
3. She is writing a letter.
4. My sister is turning on the radio.
5. My mother is making the bed.
6. She is buying a new hat.

D. Read these two statements: He is still having breakfast.
                                  He hasn't had breakfast yet.
Complete the following in the same way:
1. She is still washing the dishes.　　She hasn't . . .
2. She is still making the beds.　　She . . .
3. He is still combing his hair.
4. She is still sweeping the carpet.
5. We are still reading 'Macbeth'.

E. Read these two sentences: I've already had lunch.
                               Have you had lunch yet?
Ask questions in the same way:
1. I've already seen the new play at 'The Globe'. Have you . . .
2. I've already taken my holidays.
3. I've already read this book.
4. I've already done my homework.
5. I've already finished my work.

Special Difficulties

Words Often Confused
Receive and Take.
Receive: I have just received a letter from my brother. (ll. 1-2)
Take: Someone has taken my pen.

Exercise
Choose the correct words in the following:
1. Yesterday I (took) (received) a present from Aunt Jane.
2. Have you (taken) (received) a letter from him yet?
3. I (took) (received) the letter with me.
4. He has (taken) (received) some flowers to her.
5. Why did you (receive) (take) this book off the shelf?

5   No Wrong Numbers

Mr James Scott has a garage in Silbury
and now he has just bought another
garage in Pinhurst. Pinhurst is only five
miles from Silbury, but Mr Scott cannot
5 get a telephone for his new garage, so he
has just bought twelve pigeons. Yesterday, a pigeon carried the first message
from Pinhurst to Silbury. The bird
covered the distance in three minutes.
10 Up to now, Mr Scott has sent a great
many requests for spare parts and other
urgent messages from one garage to the
other. In this way, he has begun his own
private 'telephone' service.

... private 'telephone' service

Comprehension Précis and Composition

Answer these questions *in not more than 50 words.*
1. Where has Mr Scott opened his second garage?
2. Where is his first garage?
3. How far away is Silbury?
4. Can Mr Scott get a telephone for his new garage or not?
5. What has he bought?
6. In how many minutes do they carry messages from one garage to the other?

Key Structures

What happened? What has happened?
Study these sentences. Pay close attention to the words in italics.
What happened? (**KS 17**)
I wrote to him *last month.*
I bought this car *last year.*
He came to see me *this morning.*
I saw him *ten minutes ago.*

What has happened? (**KS 19**)
The train has *just* left the station.
I've *already* seen that film.
He has been abroad *for six months.*
Have you *ever* met him *before?*
I have *never* met him *before.*
I have not finished work *yet.*
There have been a great number of accidents *lately.*
Up till now he has won five prizes.

Exercises
A. Underline all the verbs in the passage which tell us *what happened* and *what has happened.*

B. Give the correct form of the verbs in brackets. Do not refer to the passage until you finish the exercise:

Mr James Scott has a garage in Silbury and now he just (buy) another garage in Pinhurst. Pinhurst is only five miles from Silbury, but Mr Scott cannot get a telephone for his new garage, so he just (buy) twelve pigeons. Yesterday, a pigeon (carry) the first message from Pinhurst to Silbury. The bird (cover) the distance in three minutes. Up to now, Mr Scott (send) a great many requests for spare parts and other urgent messages from one garage to the other. In this way, he (begin) his own private 'telephone' service.

C. Give the correct form of the verbs in brackets:
1. What . . . you (buy) yesterday?
2. Up till now, he never (lend) me anything.
3. . . . you (burn) those old papers yet?
4. He (fight) in Flanders in the first World War.
5. They already (leave).
6. When . . . you (lose) your umbrella?
7. . . . you (listen) to the concert last night?
8. We just (win) the match.

Special Difficulties

Words Often Confused or Misused

a Phrases with the word 'way'. (In this way, he has begun his own private 'telephone' service. ll. 13–14)

In the way: Please move this chair. It is in the way.
　　　　　　　Do your work in the way I have shown you.
On the way: On the way to the station, I bought some cigarettes.
In this way: He saves old envelopes. In this way, he has collected a great many stamps.
By the way: By the way, have you seen Harry recently?
In a way: In a way, it is an important book.

Exercise

Supply the correct phrases with 'way' in the following:
1. . . . from Athens to London, the plane stopped at Rome.
2. I cooked this . . . you showed me.
3. . . ., where is my coat?
4. Yes, . . . he has been very successful.
5. Children get . . . during the holidays.

b Spare and To Spare. ('spare parts' l. 11)

Note the following:
I cannot spare the time.
I have no time to spare.
I cannot buy spare parts for this car.
There is a spare room in this house.
Caligula spared the slave's life.

Exercise

Rewrite these sentences using *spare* or *to spare* in place of the words or phrases in italics. Make any other necessary changes.
1. There is *an extra* wheel in the back of the car.
2. I always go on excursions in my *free* time.
3. 'Have you any old clothes *that you do not want?*' he asked.
4. The guest slept in the room *we do not use.*
5. '*Do not kill* me!' begged the prisoner.

22

6 Percy Buttons

I have just moved to a house in Bridge Street. Yesterday a beggar knocked at my door. He asked me for a meal and a glass of beer. In return for this, the beggar
5 stood on his head and sang songs. I gave him a meal. He ate the food and drank the beer. Then he put a piece of cheese in his pocket and went away. Later a neighbour told me about him. Everybody
10 knows him. His name is Percy Buttons. He calls at every house in the street once a month and always asks for a meal and a glass of beer.

... stood on his head and sang songs

Comprehension Précis and Composition

Answer these questions *in not more than 55 words.*
1. Has the writer just moved to a house in Bridge Street or not?
2. Who knocked at her door yesterday?
3. Did he sing songs, or did he ask for money?
4. What did the writer give him in return for this?
5. What is the beggar's name?
6. Does he call at every house once a week or once a month?

Key Structures

A, The and Some

a A and *Some*
We can say: a pen, some pens; a book, some books; a picture, some pictures; a glass of milk, some milk; a bag of flour, some flour; a bar of soap, some soap. We can also use these words without *a* or *some*. Read these sentences carefully:

Yesterday I bought *a book. Books* are not very expensive.
I have just drunk *a glass of milk. Milk* is very refreshing.
Mrs Jones bought *a bag of flour, a bag of sugar* and *some tea.*
She always buys *flour, sugar* and *tea* at the grocer's.

b A and *The*
Read this paragraph. Pay close attention to the words *a* and *the.*
A man is walking towards me. *The* man is carrying *a* parcel. *The* parcel is full of meat. *The* man has just bought some meat. *A* dog is following *the* man. *The* dog is looking at *the* parcel.

c Names
We cannot put *a* or *the* in front of names:
John lives in England. He has a house in London. His house is in Duke Street. Last year he went to Madrid. John likes Spain very much. He goes there every summer.

Exercises
A. Write these words again. Put in *a* or *some* in front of each one.
meat, desk, tobacco, tin of tobacco, comb, city, cloth, oil, bottle of ink, day, word, student, sugar, rain, orange, rubber.

B. Read the passage again. Put a line under the words *a* and *the*.

C. Put in the words *a* or *the* where necessary. Do not refer to the passage until you finish the exercise:

I have just moved to . . . house in . . . Bridge Street. Yesterday . . . beggar knocked at my door. He asked me for . . . meal and . . . glass of beer. In return for this, . . . beggar stood on his head and sang . . . songs. I gave him . . . meal. He ate . . . food and drank . . . beer. Then he put . . . piece of cheese in his pocket and went away. Later . . . neighbour told me about him. Everybody knows him. His name is . . . Percy Buttons. He calls at every house in . . . street once . . . month and always asks for . . . meal and . . . glass of beer.

D. Write sentences using *a*, *the* or *some* with the following:

1. found/coin/garden. 2. put/sugar/my tea. 3. cut/wood/fire.
4. bought/newspaper. 5. made/coffee. 6. like/curtains in this room.

Special Difficulties

Some verbs change in meaning when we put short words after them. Read these sentences. The verbs are in italics. Do you know what these verbs mean?
I *put* your book on the shelf.
I *put on* my hat and left the house.
Who *took* my umbrella?
It was very hot, so I *took off* my coat.
Come and *look at* my photograph album.
I am *looking for* my pen. I lost it this morning.
Will you *look after* the children for me please?

Read these sentences. Each one contains the verb *knock*. The verb has a different meaning in each sentence:
A beggar *knocked at* my door. (ll. 2–3)
I *knocked* the vase *off* the table and broke it.
He always *knocks off* at six o'clock. (He finishes his work.)
The shop-assistant *knocked* 10% *off* the bill. (He reduced the price.)
A car *knocked* the boy *over*. (It hit him hard and made him fall.)
In the fight, the thief *knocked out* the policeman. (The policeman was unconscious for three minutes.)

Exercise

A. Put in the right words:

1. He did not know how to fight, but he knocked . . . the boxer.
2. This flower-pot is broken. Who knocked it . . . ?
3. I knocked . . . early yesterday and went to a football match.
4. Listen! Someone is knocking . . . the window!

B. Rewrite the following sentences using the correct form of the verb *knock* in place of the words in italics:

1. The old lady hit the thief over the head with a candlestick and *now he is unconscious*.
2. At what time do you *finish work* every day?
3. The shop-keeper *reduced* the price of all his goods *by 20%*.

7 Too Late

The plane was late and detectives were waiting at the airport all morning. They were expecting a valuable parcel of diamonds from South Africa. A few hours
5 earlier, someone had told the police that thieves would try to steal the diamonds. When the plane arrived, some of the detectives were waiting inside the main building while others were waiting on the
10 airfield. Two men took the parcel off the plane and carried it into the Customs House. While two detectives were keeping guard at the door, two others opened the parcel. To their surprise, the precious
15 parcel was full of stones and sand!

Two men took the parcel

Comprehension Précis and Composition

Answer these questions *in not more than 50 words.*
 1. How long were detectives waiting at the airport?
 2. What were they expecting from South Africa?
 3. Where did two men take the parcel after the arrival of the plane?
 4. How many detectives opened it?
 5. What was the parcel full of?

Key Structures

What were you doing when I telephoned?
Study these sentences carefully. Pay close attention to the words in italics.
When I was watering the garden, it began to rain.
I was having breakfast *when* the telephone rang.
While we were having a party, the lights went out.
George was reading *while* his wife was listening to the radio.
As I was getting on the bus, I slipped and hurt my foot.
Someone knocked at the door *just as* I was getting into the bath.
The plane was late and detectives were waiting at the airport *all morning.*

Exercises
A. Underline the verbs in the passage which tell us what *was happening.*

B. What was happening when . . . ?
Read the passage again then answer these questions. Write a complete sentence in answer to each question.
 1. What was happening when the plane arrived?
 2. What was happening when two of the detectives opened the parcel?

C. Write sentences of your own in answer to these questions. Each answer must begin with 'I was . . .'
 1. What were you doing when I telephoned you?
 2. What were you reading when I saw you in the library this morning?
 3. What were you saying when I interrupted you?

D. What was happening? What happened?
Give the correct form of the verbs in brackets:
1. As my father (leave) the house, the postman (arrive).
2. Tom (work) in the garden while I (sit) in the sun.
3. As I (walk) down the street, I (meet) Charlie.
4. While he (read) the letter, he (hear) a knock at the door.
5. While mother (prepare) lunch, Janet (set) the table.
6. She (drop) the tray when I (speak) to her.

Special Difficulties

Two men took the parcel off the plane. (ll. 10–11)
Do you remember these sentences? (**SD 24**)
Come and *look at* my photograph album.
I am *looking for* my pen. I lost it this morning.
Will you *look after* the children for me please?

Now read these sentences:

Instead of saying:	*We can say:*
He took off his coat.	He took his coat off.
	He took it off.
He put out the fire.	He put the fire out.
	He put it out.
She put on her hat.	She put her hat on.
	She put it on.

Exercise
We can change the position of the words in italics in some of the sentences below. For instance, we can change the position of the word *out* in this sentence: He put *out* the fire. But we cannot change the position of the word *for* in this sentence: He is looking *for* his pen. Where possible, change the position of the words in italics in the sentences below:
1. He gave *away* all his books.
2. She woke *up* the children early this morning.
3. He is looking *for* his umbrella.
4. They cut *off* the king's head.
5. Put *on* your hat and coat.
6. Give it *back* to your brother.
7. Help me to lift *up* this table.
8. Take *off* your shoes and put *on* your slippers.
9. He is looking *at* the picture.
10. Send her *away* or she will cause trouble.
11. They have pulled *down* the old building.
12. Make *up* your mind.
13. He asked *for* permission to leave.
14. She threw *away* all those old newspapers.

8 The Best and the Worst

Joe Sanders has the most beautiful garden
in our town. Nearly everybody enters for
'The Nicest Garden Competition' each
year, but Joe wins every time. Bill Frith's
5 garden is larger than Joe's. Bill works
harder than Joe and grows more flowers
and vegetables, but Joe's garden is more
interesting. He has made neat paths and
has built a wooden bridge over a pool. I
10 like gardens too, but I do not like hard
work. Every year I enter for the garden
competition too, and I always win a little
prize for the worst garden in the town!

Joe wins every time

Comprehension Précis and Composition

Answer these questions *in not more than 45 words.*
1. Who has the best garden in town?
2. What does he win each year?
3. Who else has a fine garden?
4. Is Joe's better or not?
5. Is the writer's garden beautiful, or is it terrible?
6. What does he always win a prize for?

Key Structures

The best and the worst
I want to tell you something about three girls in our class. The girls' names are Mary,
Jane and Betty. Read these sentences carefully:

Mary is tall, but Jane is taller. Jane is taller than Mary. Betty is very tall. She is the
tallest girl in the class.

Jane's handwriting is bad, but Mary's is worse. Betty's handwriting is very bad. It
is the worst handwriting I have ever seen.

The three girls collect photos of film stars. Mary hasn't many photos, but Jane has
more. Jane has more photos than Mary. Betty has very many. She has the most.

Mary's collection of photos is not very good. Jane's is better. Betty's collection is
the best.

Last week the three girls bought expensive dresses. Betty's dress was more expensive than Jane's. Mary's was more expensive than Betty's. Mary's dress was the most
expensive.

Exercises
A. How do they compare?
These questions are about Mary, Jane and Betty. Answer each question with a complete sentence:
1. How does Mary's handwriting compare with Jane's?
2. How does Betty's handwriting compare with Mary's and Jane's?
3. How does Betty's dress compare with Jane's?
4. How does Mary's dress compare with Jane's and Betty's?

B. In the passage 'The Best and the Worst' there are seven comparisons. Can you find them?

C. Give the correct form of the words in brackets and make other necessary changes. Do not refer to the passage until you finish the exercise:

Joe Sanders has the (beautiful) garden in our town. Nearly everybody enters for 'The (Nice) Garden Competition' each year, but Joe wins every time. Bill Frith's garden is (large) Joe's. Bill works (hard) Joe and grows (many) flowers and vegetables, but Joe's garden is (interesting). He has made neat paths and has built a wooden bridge over a pool. I like gardens too, but I do not like hard work. Every year I enter for the garden competition too, and I always win a little prize for the (bad) garden in the town!

D. Put in *of* or *in*:
1. Which is the longest river . . . the world?
2. This is the finest picture . . . them all.
3. This radio is the most expensive . . . all the ones in the shop.
4. He is the best boxer . . . our town.

Special Difficulties

a Everyone, everybody, everything. Everybody enters for 'The Nicest Garden Competition'. (ll. 2–3)
Read these sentences:
Everything is ready.
Everybody has come.
Everyone likes ice-cream.

Exercise
Choose the correct verbs in the following sentences:
1. Everybody (believe) (believes) he will win.
2. I heard a noise and went downstairs. I found that everything (were) (was) in order.
3. Everyone (try) (tries) to earn more and work less.

b Enter. Everybody enters for the competition. (ll. 2–3)
Read these sentences:
Everyone stood up when he entered the room.
Did you enter for this examination?
The lights went out just as we entered the cinema.
How many people have entered for the race?

Exercise
Put in the word *for* where necessary:
1. He is very ill. No one is allowed to enter . . . his room.
2. Will you enter . . . this week's crossword competition?
3. Many athletes have entered . . . the Olympic Games this year.
4. No one saw the thief when he entered . . . the building.
5. I have entered . . . the examination but I don't want to take it.

9 A Cold Welcome

On Wednesday evening, we went to the
Town Hall. It was the last day of the year
and a large crowd of people had gathered
under the Town Hall clock. It would
5 strike twelve in twenty minutes' time.
Fifteen minutes passed and then, at five
to twelve, the clock stopped. The big
minute hand did not move. We waited
and waited, but nothing happened. Sud-
10 denly someone shouted, 'It's two minutes
past twelve! The clock has stopped!' I
looked at my watch. It was true. The big
clock refused to welcome the New Year.
At that moment, everybody began to
15 laugh and sing.

the clock stopped

Comprehension Précis and Composition

Answer these questions *in not more than 50 words.*
1. Where did we go on New Year's Eve?
2. Were there many people there or not?
3. In how many minutes would the Town Hall clock strike twelve?
4. At what time did it stop?
5. Did it refuse to welcome the New Year or not?
6. What did the crowd do then?

Key Structures

When did you arrive? I arrived at 10 o'clock.
Read these sentences carefully. Pay close attention to the phrase in italics. We can use
phrases like these to answer questions beginning with *When.*
a Phrases with *at*:
I always leave home *at 8 o'clock.* I begin work *at 9 o'clock.* I work all day and often get
home late *at night.*
b Phrases with *in*:
I'm going out now. I'll be back *in ten minutes* or *in half an hour.*
The second World War began *in 1939* and ended *in 1945.*
Many tourists come here *in summer.* They usually come *in July* and *in August.* It is
very quiet here *in winter.* The hotels are often empty *in January, February* and *in
March.*
I'll see you *in the morning.* I can't see you *in the afternoon* or *in the evening.*
c Phrases with *on*:
I shall see him *on Wednesday.* I'm not free *on Tuesday or Thursday.*
My brother will arrive from Germany *on April 27th.* He will return *on May 5th.*
d Other phrases:
The shops are open *from 9 till 5.*
It rained heavily *during the night.*
He will not arrive *until 10 o'clock.*

Exercises

A. Answer these questions on the passage:
1. When did we go to the Town Hall?
2. When would the clock strike twelve?
3. When did the clock stop?

B. Supply the correct words in the following sentences:
1. He has gone abroad. He will return . . . two years' time.
2. . . . Saturdays I always go to the market.
3. I never go to the cinema . . . the week.
4. He ran a hundred metres . . . thirteen seconds.
5. I can't see him . . . the moment. I'm busy.
6. My birthday is . . . November 7th. I was born . . . 1948.
7. The days are very short . . . December.
8. We arrived at the village late . . . night. We left early . . . the morning.
9. I shall not hear from him . . . tomorrow.

C. Write sentences using the following:
1. begin/3 o'clock. 2. bought/1960. 3. shop/from . . . till.
4. children/school/morning. 5. finish/two years' time. 6. go for a walk/evening.
7. went to church/Sunday.

Special Difficulties

Any, Not . . . Any and No
We can answer these questions in two ways. Both answers mean the same thing:

Question	*Answer*
Is there any tea in the pot?	There isn't any tea in the pot.
	There's no tea in the pot.
Is there anyone at the door?	There isn't anyone at the door.
	There's no one at the door.
Is there anybody at the door?	There isn't anybody at the door.
	There's nobody at the door.
Is there anything in the box?	There isn't anything in the box.
	There's nothing in the box.
Did you go anywhere yesterday?	I didn't go anywhere yesterday.
	I went nowhere yesterday.

Exercise

A. Write negative answers to these questions in two different ways:
1. Have you any money?
2. Did you go anywhere in the holidays?
3. Did you buy anything this morning?
4. Was there anybody present when the accident happened?

B. Change the form of these sentences:
He hasn't any hobbies. He does not go anywhere. He does not see anybody. He is not interested in anything—except food!

10 Not For Jazz

We have an old musical instrument. It is called a clavichord. It was made in Germany in 1681. Our clavichord is kept in the living-room. It has belonged to our
5 family for a long time. The instrument was bought by my grandfather many years ago. Recently it was damaged by a visitor. She tried to play jazz on it! She struck the keys too hard and two of the
10 strings were broken. My father was shocked. Now we are not allowed to touch it. It is being repaired by a friend of my father's.

My father was shocked

Comprehension Précis and Composition

Answer these questions *in not more than 45 words*.
1. Do we own an old clavichord, or do we own a new piano?
2. When was it made?
3. Who bought the instrument many years ago?
4. Who damaged it recently?
5. What did she try to do?
6. What did she break?
7. Who is repairing it now?

Key Structures

It was made in Germany in 1681.
a Read these two questions and answers:

Who built this bridge?
Prisoners of war built this bridge in 1942.

When was this bridge built?
This bridge was built in 1942.

In the first question we want to know *who* built the bridge. In the second question we want to learn about *the bridge*. We can still say *who* built it. We can say:
This bridge was built *by prisoners of war* in 1942.

b Now read these pairs of sentences carefully. The first sentence in each pair tells us about *a person*. (Who) The second tells us about *a thing*. (What or Which)

Workmen are building a new road outside my house. (Who)
A new road is being built outside my house. (What)

The newsagent delivers our papers every morning. (Who)
Our papers are delivered every morning. (What)

The postman delivered a letter this morning. (Who)
A letter was delivered this morning. (What)

c Now read these sentences:

Instead of saying:	*We can say:*
The police arrested the thief.	The thief was arrested (by the police).
He gave me a present.	I was given a present.
The headmaster has punished the boy.	The boy has been punished (by the headmaster).

Exercises

A. Answer these questions on the passage. Write a complete answer to each question:
1. What is our old musical instrument called?
2. Where was it made?
3. Where is it kept?
4. When was it bought?
5. When was it damaged?
6. How many strings were broken?
7. How did my father feel about this?
8. What aren't we allowed to do?
9. What is being done to the clavichord?

B. Change the form of the phrases in italics. Do not refer to the passage until you finish the exercise:

We have an old musical instrument. *We call it a clavichord. Someone made it* in Germany in 1681. *We keep our clavichord* in the living-room. *My grandfather bought the instrument* many years ago. Recently *a visitor damaged it.* She struck the keys too hard and *broke two of the strings. This shocked my father. He does not allow us* to touch it. *A friend of my father's is repairing it.*

Special Difficulties

a Made in, made of, made from, made by.

Made in (a country): It was made in Germany. (ll. 2–3)
Made of (a material): The tea-pot is made of silver.
Made from (a number of materials): Glass is made from sand and lime.
Made by (someone): This cake was made by my sister.

Exercise

Supply the correct words in the following:
1. Is your watch made . . . gold?
2. These knives were made . . . Sheffield.
3. This cake was made . . . sugar, flour, butter and eggs.

b A friend of my father's. (ll. 12–13)

Instead of saying:	*We can say:*
He is one of my father's friends.	He is a friend of my father's.
Tom lent me one of his books.	Tom lent me a book of his.
He is one of my friends.	He is a friend of mine.

Change the form of the phrases in italics:
1. He borrowed *one of my records.*
2. She showed me *one of John's pictures.*
3. It was *one of her ideas.*
4. *One of your letters* was found on my desk.
5. *Some of their friends* came to see me.

11 One Good Turn Deserves Another

I was having dinner at a restaurant when
Harry Steele came in. Harry worked in a
lawyer's office years ago, but he is now
working at a bank. He gets a good salary,
5 but he always borrows money from his
friends and never pays it back. Harry saw
me and came and sat at the same table.
He has never borrowed money from me.
While he was eating, I asked him to lend
10 me £2. To my surprise, he gave me the
money immediately. 'I have never borrowed any money from you,' Harry said,
'so now you can pay for my dinner!'

'*you can pay for my dinner!*'

Comprehension Précis and Composition

Answer these questions *in not more than 50 words.*
1. Where were you having dinner?
2. Did you see Harry Steele after a while or not?
3. What does he always borrow from his friends?
4. Did Harry sit at your table, or did he sit somewhere else?
5. How much did you ask him to lend you?
6. Did he give you the money at once or not?
7. What did he want you to do?

Key Structures

Review **KS 15–31**
Now, Often and Always. (**KS 15**)
What happened? (**KS 17**)
What has happened? (**KS 19**)
What were you doing when I telephoned? (**KS 25**)
It was made in Germany. (**KS 31**)

Exercises
A. Which verbs in the passage tell use *a* what is happening now; *b* what always
happens; *c* what happened; *d* what has happened; *e* what was happening when/
while . . . ?

B. Give the correct form of the verbs in brackets. Do not refer to the passage until
you finish the exercise:
I (have) dinner at a restaurant when Harry Steele (come) in. Harry (work) in a lawyer's
office years ago, but he now (work) at a bank. He (get) a good salary, but he always
(borrow) money from his friends and never (pay) it back. Harry (see) me and (come)
and (sit) at the same table. He never (borrow) money from me. While he (eat), I (ask)
him to lend me £2. To my surprise, he (give) me the money immediately. 'I never
(borrow) any money from you,' Harry (say), 'so now you can pay for my dinner!'

33

C. Give the correct form of the verbs in brackets:

1. He usually (get) up at 7 o'clock, but this morning he (get) up at 6 o'clock.
2. So far, we not (have) a reply.
3. While he (write) on the blackboard, the children (talk).
4. I can't come now. At the moment I (type) a letter.
5. As the royal visitors (pass), the people cheered.

D. Supply the correct form of the verbs in brackets. Refer to **KS 31** if you have difficulty:
The Taj Mahal (build) in the seventeenth century for the emperor Shah Jehan. A few years after he (become) ruler, his wife, Mumtaz-i-Mahal, (die). The Taj Mahal (build) in her honour. Experts (call) in from many parts of the world to construct the domes and to decorate the walls. The Taj Mahal which (begin) in 1632 and (complete) in 1654 (cost) a fortune. Up to the present day, it (visit) by millions of people.

Special Difficulties

a I asked him to lend me £2. (ll. 9–10)
Study the word order in these sentences:
He wants *me* to ask you a question.
Frank helped *Tom* to dig this hole.
She taught *her son* to read.
We advised *them* to stay at home.
They did not allow *us* to enter the museum before 9 o'clock.

Exercises
A. Put the words in brackets in their correct order:
1. The officer ordered (to fire, at the enemy, the men).
2. He wants (his wife, this dress, to wear).
3. She wants (us, it, to explain).
4. I cannot allow (the room, him, to enter).

B. Write similar sentences using the following:
1. He asked ... 2. We prefer ... 3. He taught ... 4. My mother wished ... 5. Do you want ... ?

b Words Often Confused.
Salary (l. 4) and Wages.
Salary: He collects his salary at the end of each month.
Wages: The workmen collected their wages at the end of the week.

c Borrow and Lend.
Borrow: He has never borrowed money from me. (l. 8)
Lend: I asked him to lend me £2. (ll. 9–10)
I asked him to lend £2 to me. (See **SD 18**)

Exercise
Use any of the above words in the following sentences:
1. He is a bank manager and he gets a good ...
2. I ... him some money and he said he would give it back to me when he got his ...
3. Yesterday he ... my typewriter. I hope he returns it soon.
4. The postmen are on strike again. They want higher ...
5. Workmen's ... have gone up since the war.

34

12 Goodbye and Good Luck

Our neighbour, Captain Charles Alison, will sail from Portsmouth tomorrow. We shall meet him at the harbour early in the morning. He will be in his small boat, 5 *Topsail*. *Topsail* is a famous little boat. It has sailed across the Atlantic many times. Captain Alison will set out at eight o'clock, so we shall have plenty of time. We shall see his boat and then we shall say good-10 bye to him. He will be away for two months. We are very proud of him. He will take part in an important race across the Atlantic.

We shall say goodbye to him

Comprehension Précis and Composition

Answer these questions *in not more than 45 words*.
1. Whom shall we meet at Portsmouth Harbour early tomorrow morning?
2. Where will he be?
3. At what time will he leave?
4. Shall we say goodbye to him, or shall we travel with him?
5. What will he take part in?

Key Structures

I'll see you tomorrow.
These sentences tell us about the future. Read them carefully. Note that the word *shall* is often used with *I* and *We*. Pay close attention to the words in italics:
I shall see you tomorrow. *I'll see* you at 3 o'clock.
We shall travel by air. *We'll be* at the airport tomorrow morning.
George will be here this evening. *He'll come* by train.
Alice will meet him at the station. *She'll be* there at 5 o'clock.
The train will arrive at 4.55. *It'll be* here soon.
You will miss the train. *You'll be* late.
They will come here on foot. *They'll walk* from the station.

Exercises
A. Underline all the verbs in the passage which tell us what will happen.

B. Give the correct form of the verbs in brackets. Do not refer to the passage until you finish the exercise.
Our neighbour, Captain Charles Alison, (sail) from Portsmouth tomorrow. We (meet) him at the harbour early in the morning. He (be) in his small boat, *Topsail*. *Topsail* is a famous little boat. It has sailed across the Atlantic many times. Captain Alison (set out) at eight o'clock, so we (have) plenty of time. We (see) his boat and then we (say) goodbye to him. He (be) away for two months. We are very proud of him. He (take part) in an important race across the Atlantic.

C. In the paragraph below, the verbs in italics tell us *what happened*. Write the passage again. Change the verbs in italics so that they tell us *what will happen*.

I *went* to the theatre with my friend Reg. Reg and I *saw* the first performance of a play called 'The End of the Road'. After the play, the producer *gave* a short speech. He *spoke* to the audience about the play. The play *was* very successful and I think a great many people *enjoyed* it very much.

D. Put in *shall* or *will*:

1. The plane . . . arrive in two hours' time.
2. I . . . wait here until he comes.
3. When . . . we see you again?
4. I . . . send you a telegram from Nassau.
5. My secretary . . . write to you shortly.

Special Difficulties

a Read these sentences. Each sentence contains the verb *be*. This verb has a different meaning in each sentence:

He *will be away* for two months. (ll. 10–11)
I'm going out now. *I'll be back* at six o'clock.
If anyone telephones, tell them *I'll be out* all morning.
I went to Ted's house and asked to see him but he *wasn't in*.
Why don't you forget about it? *It's all over*. (It has finished.)
What's on at the local cinema this week?
She is very ill. She can't start work yet. She *is not up to* it. (She is not capable of it.)

b Now look at the verb *set* in these sentences:

Captain Alison will *set out* at eight o'clock. (l. 7) (He will start his journey.)
Tom and I *set off* early in the morning. (We started our journey.)
Jansen *set up* a new world record for the 400 metres.

Exercise

Replace the words in italics by the correct form of *be* or *set*.

1. He *has not yet returned*. He will *return* in ten minutes.
2. A new play is *being performed* at the Globe Theatre.
3. When the concert *ended*, we went home.
4. They will *leave* very early tomorrow morning.
5. You can't take the exam yet. You are not *capable of* it.
6. He will be *absent* from home for two months.
7. She swam across the English Channel and *created* a new world record.

13 The Greenwood Boys

The Greenwood Boys are a group of popular singers. At present, they are visiting all parts of the country. They will be arriving here tomorrow. They will be
5 coming by train and most of the young people in the town will be meeting them at the station. Tomorrow evening they will be singing at the Workers' Club. The Greenwood Boys will be staying for five
10 days. During this time, they will give five performances. As usual, the police will have a difficult time. They will be trying to keep order. It is always the same on these occasions.

a group of popular singers

Comprehension Précis and Composition
Answer these questions *in not more than 50 words.*
1. Are the Greenwood Boys popular singers, or are they popular dancers?
2. When will they be coming here?
3. Who will be meeting them at the station?
4. How many performances will they give?
5. What will the police be trying to do as usual?

Key Structures
What will you be doing tomorrow?
a Read these sentences carefully. Pay close attention to the verbs in italics:

Now	*Tomorrow*
I *am writing* letters now.	I *shall be writing* letters all day tomorrow.
We *are decorating* this room.	We *shall be decorating* this room tomorrow.
He *is working* in the garden.	He *will be working* in the garden tomorrow.
She *is getting ready* for the party.	She *will be getting ready* for the party tomorrow.
Are you washing your car?	*Will you be washing* your car tomorrow?
They *are playing* football.	They *will be playing* football tomorrow.

b Now read these pairs of sentences. Each pair has the same meaning:

Instead of:	*We can say:*
I'll come to your house tomorrow.	*I'll be coming* to your house tomorrow.
He'll arrive in a minute.	*He'll be arriving* in a minute.
He'll catch the 4 o'clock train.	*He'll be catching* the 4 o'clock train.
I'll see you next week.	*I'll be seeing* you next week.
She'll meet him at the station.	*She'll be meeting* him at the station.

Exercises

A. Underline all the verbs in the passage which tell us what *will be happening.*

B. Give the correct form of the verbs in brackets. Do not refer to the passage until you finish the exercise:

The Greenwood Boys are a group of popular singers. At present, they are visiting all parts of the country. They (arrive) here tomorrow. They (come) by train and most of the young people in the town (meet) them at the station. Tomorrow evening they (sing) at the Workers' Club. The Greenwood Boys (stay) for five days. During this time they will give five performances. As usual, the police will have a difficult time. They (try) to keep order. It is always the same on these occasions.

C. Change the form of the verbs in italics so that they tell us what will be happening:
1. I *am ironing* the clothes.
2. The train *will arrive* in a few minutes.
3. *We'll see* you in the morning.
4. We *are watching* the match.
5. He *is correcting* copybooks.

Special Difficulties

The Workers' Club. (l. 8) Compare **SD 150**
Read these questions and answers. Pay close attention to the position of the apostrophe (') in each answer:
Whose is this car? It is Tom's. It belongs to Tom.
Whose is this handbag? It is Susan's. It belongs to Susan.
Whose is this hammer? It is the workman's. It belongs to the workman.
Whose are these copybooks? They are the students' copybooks. They belong to the students.
Whose are these toys? They are the children's. They belong to the children.
Whose are these tools? They are the workmen's. They belong to the workmen.
Whose is this car? It is James' (*or* James's) car. It belongs to James.
When will he arrive? He will arrive in three hours' time.
How much petrol do you want? I want two pounds' worth of petrol.

Exercise
Answer these questions. The words you must use in your answers are given in brackets. Put the apostrophe in the right place:
1. Whose is this umbrella? (George)
2. Whose is this idea? (Jean)
3. Whose is this handbag? (That woman)
4. Whose poetry do you like best? (Keats)
5. Whose are these clothes? (The children)
6. Whose are these uniforms? (The soldiers)
7. When will you leave? (In six hours time)
8. How much damage was there? (A hundred pounds worth)

14 Do You Speak English?

I had an amusing experience last year.
After I had left a small village in the south
of France, I drove on to the next town.
On the way, a young man waved to me. I
5 stopped and he asked me for a lift. As
soon as he had got into the car, I said
good morning to him in French and he
replied in the same language. Apart from
a few words, I do not know any French
10 at all. Neither of us spoke during the
journey. I had nearly reached the town,
when the young man suddenly said, very
slowly, 'Do you speak English?' As I
soon learnt, he was English himself!

'*Do you speak English?*'

Comprehension Précis and Composition

Answer these questions *in not more than 55 words.*
1. Whom did the writer give a lift to in the south of France last year?
2. Did they greet each other in English or in French?
3. Does the writer speak any French or not?
4. Did they sit in silence, or did they talk to each other?
5. What did the young man say at the end of the journey?
6. Was he English himself, or was he French?

Key Structures

After he had finished work he went home.
Read these two sentences:
He finished work. He went home.
We can join these two sentences together with the word *after*. We can say:
After he had finished work he went home.
Note how these sentences have been joined. Pay close attention to the words in italics:
The children ran away. They broke the window.
The children ran away *after they had broken* the window.
The sun set. We returned to our hotel.
As soon as the sun had set we returned to our hotel.
He finished lunch. He asked for a glass of water.
When he had finished lunch he asked for a glass of water.
I did not understand the problem. He explained it.
I had not understood the problem until he explained it.

Exercises
A. These questions are about the passage. Write a complete sentence in answer to each
question:
1. When did you drive on to the next town?
2. When did you say good morning to him in French?
3. When did the young man say 'Do you speak English?'?

B. Join these sentences together. Do not refer to the passage until you finish the exercise:

1. I left a small village in the south of France. I drove on to the next town.
2. He got into the car. I said good morning to him in French.
3. I nearly reached the town. The young man said, 'Do you speak English?'

C. Join these pairs of sentences with the words given in brackets:

1. (After) She wrote the letter. She went to the post-office.
2. (After) He had dinner. He went to the cinema.
3. (When) I fastened my seat-belt. The plane took off.
4. We did not disturb him. (until) He finished work.
5. (As soon as) He left the room. I turned on the radio.
6. He was very ill. (before) He died.

D. Give the correct form of the verbs in brackets:

1. The moment he had said this, he (regret) it.
2. It (begin) to rain before she took a taxi.
3. When all the guests had left, Derek (arrive).

Special Difficulties

Words Often Confused
a Ask and Ask for. He asked me for a lift. (l. 5)
Ask (a question): After the lesson, he asked me a question.
Ask for (something): He asked for an apple.

b Except, except for, apart from. Apart from a few words . . . (ll. 8–9)
When *except* is used at the beginning of a sentence, it is usually followed by *for*. Read these sentences:
I invited everyone except George.
Except for/Apart from this, everything is in order.

c Which of, either of, neither of, both of. Neither of us . . . (l. 10)
We use these words when we refer to *two* persons or things.
Which of the two do you want?
Either of them will do.
I like neither of them.
I bought both of them.

Exercise
Choose the correct words in these sentences:

1. (Except) (Except for) a slight headache, I feel all right now.
2. I liked them very much so I bought (neither of) (both of) them.
3. (Except) (Apart from) the fact that he drank too much, he was rude to everybody present.
4. I (asked) (asked for) a question. I did not (ask for) (ask) an answer.
5. He could not answer (neither of) (either of) the questions I (asked) (asked for).

15 Good News

The secretary told me that Mr Harmsworth would see me. I felt very nervous when I went into his office. He did not look up from his desk when I entered. After I had sat down, he said that business was very bad. He told me that the firm could not afford to pay such large salaries. Twenty people had already left. I knew that my turn had come.

'Mr Harmsworth,' I said in a weak voice.

'Don't interrupt,' he said.

Then he smiled and told me I would receive an extra £100 a year!

business was very bad

Comprehension Précis and Composition

Answer these questions *in not more than 55 words.*
1. Who wanted to see you?
2. How did you feel about this?
3. Where did you go?
4. Did he say that business was bad, or did he say that it was good?
5. Could the firm pay such large salaries or not?
6. How many people had left already?
7. Did he ask you to leave as well or not?
8. What did he offer you?

Key Structures

He said that . . . He told me . . .
Study these sentences carefully:
'I am busy,' he said.
He says that he is busy.
He said that he was busy.
He told me that he was busy.

'I never work on Sundays,' she said.
She says that she never works on Sundays.
She said that she never worked on Sundays.
She told Mr Harmsworth that she never worked on Sundays.

'I have just finished work,' Mr Jones said.
Mr Jones says that he has just finished work.
Mr Jones said that he had just finished work.
Mr Jones told his wife that he had just finished work.

'I broke that plate,' he said.
He says that he broke that plate.
He said that he had broken that plate.
He told me that he had broken that plate.

'Mr Jones will see you now,' she said.
She says that Mr Jones will see you now.
She said that Mr Jones would see you now.
She told me that Mr Jones would see you now.

'You can go now,' the teacher said.
The teacher says that you can go now.
The teacher said that you could go now.
The teacher told the pupil that he could go now.

Exercises

A. These questions are about the passage. Write a complete sentence in answer to each question:
1*a* What did the secretary tell me?
 b What were the secretary's exact words?
2*a* What did Mr Harmsworth say after I had sat down?
 b What were Mr Harmsworth's exact words?
3*a* What did Mr Harmsworth tell me about the firm?
 b What were Mr Harmsworth's exact words?

B. Supply *said* or *told* in the following sentences. Give the correct form of the verbs in brackets:
1. He . . . me that she (come) tomorrow.
2. The gardener . . . that he (cut) that tree down yesterday.
3. I . . . you I (have) never played tennis before.
4. What . . . he . . . that he (do)?
5. When . . . he . . . you that he (buy) this car?
6. He . . . he (cannot) understand me.
7. He . . . that he (work) all day yesterday.
8. He . . . me he never (write) letters to anybody.
9. Why . . . you . . . that you (be) busy?
10. He . . . that he (will wait) for me.

Special Difficulties

Words Often Confused and Misused
a Nervous and Irritable. I felt very nervous. (l. 2)
Nervous (restless or uneasy): Examinations make me nervous.
Irritable (easily made angry): He is such an irritable person, you can hardly speak to
    him.
b Office (l. 3), Study, Desk (l. 4).
Study these examples:
There are six typists in our office.
The living-room is next to the study. I often read in the study when I want peace and quiet.
My desk is covered with books.

c Afford (l. 7)
Study these examples:
Will you buy this car? I can't afford it. I can't afford £700.
You can afford this model. It's not very expensive.
I haven't been to the cinema lately. I can't afford the time.

Exercise
Supply any of the above words in the sentences below:
1. We shall use the spare room in our new house as a . . .
2. Smith works in a lawyer's . . .
3. She felt very . . . before the plane took off.
4. I can only . . . to pay £5 a week rent.
5. Since his illness he has been very . . . He is always losing his temper.

16 A Polite Request

If you park your car in the wrong place, a traffic policeman will soon find it. You will be very lucky if he lets you go without a ticket. However, this does not al-
5 ways happen. Traffic police are sometimes very polite. During a holiday in Sweden, I found this note on my car: 'Sir, we welcome you to our city. This is a "No Parking" area. You will enjoy your stay
10 here if you pay attention to our street signs. This note is only a reminder.' If you receive a request like this, you cannot fail to obey it!

If you receive a request
like this . . .

Comprehension Précis and Composition

Answer these questions *in not more than 55 words.*
1. Do traffic police usually give you a ticket if you park your car in the wrong place or not?
2. When did the writer find a polite note on his car?
3. What did the traffic police want him to do?
4. Can anyone fail to obey a request like this or not?

Key Structures

If you open the door you will get a surprise.
Study these sentences. Pay close attention to the words in italics:
a If he is out, I'll call tomorrow.
If it rains tomorrow, we shall stay at home.
You'll miss the train *if you don't hurry*.
If you see him, will you tell him about it?
If he is working I shall not disturb him.
If I have time, I shall be writing to him tomorrow.
He will come tomorrow *if he can*.
If they can help you they will.

b If you make a mistake, correct it.
If you don't like the food, don't eat it.
Please don't disturb him *if he is busy*.

Exercises
A. How many times has the word *if* been used in the passage?

B. Give the correct form of the verbs in brackets. Do not refer to the passage until you finish the exercise:
1. If you (park) your car in the wrong place, a traffic policeman soon (find) it.
2. You (be) very lucky if he (let) you go without a ticket.
3. You (enjoy) your stay here if you (pay) attention to our street signs.
4. If you (receive) a request like this, you (cannot) fail to obey it.

C. Supply the correct form of the verbs in brackets in these sentences:
1. If it (rain) I shall take an umbrella with me.
2. You never (pass) this test if you don't work hard.
3. If he (be) here before 10 o'clock, I shall see him.
4. If he plays well, he (get) into the team.
5. If he (enjoy) concerts, why doesn't he come with us?
6. Tell him to wait for me if he (be) not in a hurry.

D. Supply the correct form of the verbs in brackets in this paragraph:
A mother received a letter from her eight-year-old daughter. Here is part of it: 'If I (listen) to the radio, don't tell me to do my homework. If I (do) something wrong, (not shout) at me. If the house (be) untidy, (not blame) me. If you (want) me to do something, (not forget) to say "please". If I (play) a nice game, (not send) me to bed. If I (ask) for something, don't always say "No!" If it (be) cold (not put) the cat out. Don't say "don't" so often!'

Special Difficulties

Words Often Confused and Misused
a Police. Traffic police are sometimes very polite. (ll. 5–6)
Study these examples:
The police *are looking* for him.   *They have* not found him.
There were police everywhere.

b Pay attention to, Care, Take care of, Look after.
Compare the following:
Please *pay attention to* the blackboard.
I don't care if he breaks his neck!
Don't worry about the garden. I'll *take care of* it while you are on holiday.
Please *look after* the children for me when I am out.

c Remind and Remember. This note is only a reminder. (l. 11)
Remind: I reminded him to post my letter.
Remember: I remembered to post your letter.
             Remember me to your mother.

d You. If you receive a request like this . . . (ll. 11–12)
Instead of saying:	*We can say:*
One must be careful these days.	You must be careful these days.
One must never tell lies.	You must never tell lies.

'You' can have the sense of 'anyone'.

Exercise
Choose the correct words in the following sentences:
1. You can only learn if you (look after) (pay attention).
2. Don't forget to (remind) (remember) me about it tomorrow.
3. The police (is knocking) (are knocking) at the door.
4. Our neighbours will (pay attention to) (look after) our house when we are away.
5. (Remind me) (Remember me) to your wife.

17 Always Young

My aunt Jennifer is an actress. She must
be at least thirty-five years old. In spite
of this, she often appears on the stage as
a young girl. Jennifer will have to take
5 · part in a new play soon. This time, she
will be a girl of seventeen. In the play, she
must appear in a bright red dress and
long black stockings. Last year in another
play, she had to wear short socks and a
10 bright, orange-coloured dress. If anyone
ever asks her how old she is, she always
answers, 'My dear, it must be *terrible* to
be grown up!'

*. . . often appears as a
young girl*

Comprehension Précis and Composition

Answer these questions *in not more than 50 words.*
1. Is your aunt Jennifer an actress or a nurse?
2. Is she over thirty years old or is she under thirty years old?
3. Does she often appear on the stage as a young girl or not?
4. Will Jennifer act the part of a girl of seventeen in a new play soon or not?
5. Does she ever tell anyone how old she really is or not?

Key Structures

Must
Study these sentences:
(*a*) *Instead of saying:*
I must leave now.

We can say:
   I have to leave now.
Or: I have got to leave now.

He must leave now.

   He has to leave now.
Or: He has got to leave now.

Must you leave now?

   Do you have to leave now?
Or: Have you got to leave now?

We must leave early tomorrow.

   We have to leave early tomorrow.
Or: We have got to leave early tomorrow.
Or: We shall have to leave early tomorrow.

He said he must leave early.

He said he would have to leave early.
    (KS 41)

b We cannot use *must* in this sentence:
She had to go shopping yesterday.

c Instead of saying:
I, personally, think he is a fool.
I, personally, think he is mad.
I, personally, think she is over forty.

We can say:
He must be a fool.
He must be mad.
She must be over forty.

45

Exercises

A. Underline the verbs *must* or *have to* in the passage.

B. Supply *must* or the correct form of *have to* in the spaces below. Do not refer to the passage until you finish the exercise.

My aunt Jennifer is an actress. She . . . be at least thirty-five years old. In spite of this, she often appears on the stage as a young girl. Jennifer will . . . take part in a new play soon. This time, she will be a girl of seventeen. In the play, she . . . appear in a bright red dress and long black stockings. Last year in another play, she . . . wear short socks and a bright, orange-coloured dress. If anyone ever asks her how old she is, she always answers, 'My dear, it . . . be terrible to be grown up!'

C. Write these sentences again using *must* or *have to* in place of the words in italics. Example:

 It is necessary for you to work hard.
 You must (or 'have to') work hard.

1. *It will be necessary for you to* see a doctor.
2. *Is it necessary for you to* make so much noise?
3. She said *it would be necessary for us to* stay here.
4. *It is necessary for me to* have some help.
5. *It was necessary for him to* go out last night.

Special Difficulties

Words Often Confused and Misused

a As. She often appears on the stage as a young girl. (ll. 3–4)
As can have a number of meanings:
 I cannot come as I am busy. (because)
 As I was leaving the house, the postman brought a letter. (at the time when) **KS 25**
 Do as you are told. (the thing that)
 He works as an engineer. (in the position of)

b Dress, Suit, Costume. She must appear in a bright red dress. (ll. 6–7)
Study these examples:
My sister bought a new dress yesterday.
My brother never wears ready-made suits.
All the actors wore fifteenth-century costumes.

c Grow and Grow up. It must be terrible to be grown up! (ll. 12–13)
Study these examples:
Children grow quickly. The grass has grown very high.
Some people never grow up. (mature in mind)

Exercises

A. What does *as* mean in these sentences:
1. He works as a pilot.
2. You mustn't shout so loudly as you'll wake up the baby.
3. As we were listening to the radio, someone knocked at the door.

B. Choose the correct words in the following sentences:
1. Trees take a long time to (grow) (grow up).
2. My father bought a new (suit) (costume) recently.
3. She hired a (suit) (costume) for the fancy dress party.
4. Do you like my sister's new (dress) (costume)?

18 He Often Does This!

After I had had lunch at a village inn, I looked for my bag. I had left it on a chair beside the door and now it wasn't there! As I was looking for it, the inn-keeper
5 came in.

'Did you have a good meal?' he asked.

'Yes, thank you,' I answered, 'but I can't pay the bill. I haven't got my bag.'

The inn-keeper smiled and imme-
10 diately went out. In a few minutes he returned with my bag and gave it back to me.

'I'm very sorry,' he said. 'My dog had taken it into the garden. He often does
15 this.'

'He often does this.'

Comprehension Précis and Composition

Answer these questions *in not more than 40 words.*
1. Did the writer have lunch at a village inn or not?
2. Could she find her bag after her meal or not?
3. Could she pay the bill or not?
4. Who soon found it for her?
5. Where had his dog taken it?

Key Structures

Have
Study these uses of *have*:
a Have you had lunch yet? **(KS 19)**
    After he had finished work he went home. **(KS 39)**

b Instead of saying:	*We can say:*
He owns a new house.	He has a new house.
	Or: He has got a new house.
He possesses a lot of money.	He has a lot of money.
	Or: He has got a lot of money.
Does he possess a lot of money?	Has he a lot of money?
	Or: Has he got a lot of money?
He doesn't possess a lot of money.	He hasn't a lot of money.
	Or: He hasn't got a lot of money.

c Instead of saying:	*We can say:*
I took a bath before dinner.	I had a bath before dinner.
Take a cigarette.	Have a cigarette.
I enjoyed myself at the party.	I had a good time at the party.
I received a letter from him yesterday.	I had a letter from him yesterday.

Exercises
A. These questions are on the passage. Write a complete sentence in answer to each question:
1. When did you look for your bag?
2. What had you done with your bag?
3. What did the inn-keeper ask you?
4. Why can't you pay the bill?
5. What had the dog done with the bag?

B. Supply the correct form of *have* in the following. Do not refer to the passage until you finish the exercise:
1. After I . . . lunch at the village inn, I looked for my bag.
2. I . . . left it on a chair beside the door.
3. '. . . a good meal?' he asked.
4. I can't pay the bill. I . . . got my bag.
5. I'm very sorry. My dog . . . taken it into the garden.

C. In which of these sentences can we put the verb *got* after *have*?
1. He had a drink before dinner.
2. Mrs Sullivan has a lot of money.
3. He had to leave early.
4. We have had a long conversation.
5. My mother has a headache.
6. They had a good time at the party.
7. This sock has a hole in it.
8. She has to be patient with him.
9. I have a bath every day.
10. This room has four windows.
11. He has a farm.
12. We had a letter from Jill yesterday.

Special Difficulties

a Read these sentences. Each one contains the verb *give*. The verb has a different meaning in each sentence:
He returned with my bag and *gave it back* to me. (ll. 10–12)
Give in your copybooks to me.
He can't continue fighting. He will soon *give in*. (He will surrender.)
I *gave away* my collection of stamps to the little boy.
I have *given up* smoking. (I have stopped.)
Three of our officers *gave themselves up* to the enemy. (They surrendered.)

b Words Often Confused: Beside (l. 3), Besides.
Beside : Come and sit beside me. (next to me)
Besides : Besides this photograph, I have a number of others. (in addition to)

Exercises
A. Supply the missing words in the following sentences:
1. Will the person who took my ruler please give it . . . to me.
2. When my children grew up, I gave all their toys . . .
3. When do we have to give . . . our compositions?
4. We were losing the battle but we did not give . . .

B. Supply *beside* or *besides* in the following:
1. . . . football he plays tennis.
2. Can you see that boy standing . . . the tree?

19 Sold Out

'The play may begin at any moment,' I said.

'It may have begun already,' Susan answered.

5 I hurried to the ticket-office. 'May I have two tickets please?' I asked.

'I'm sorry, we've sold out,' the girl said.

'What a pity!' Susan exclaimed.

10 Just then, a man hurried to the ticket-office.

'Can I return these two tickets?' he asked.

'Certainly,' the girl said.

15 I went back to the ticket-office at once.

'Could I have those two tickets please?' I asked.

'Certainly,' the girl said, 'but they are for next Wednesday's performance. Do you still want them?'

'I might as well have them,' I said sadly.

a man hurried to the ticket-office

Comprehension Précis and Composition

Answer these questions *in not more than 45 words.*
1. When was the play going to begin?
2. How many tickets did you ask for?
3. Were there any left or not?
4. Were Susan and you disappointed or not?
5. Who hurried to the ticket-office just then?
6. How many tickets did he return?
7. Were they for that day's performance, or were they for next Wednesday's performance?
8. Did you buy them or not?

Key Structures

Can and May
Study these uses of *can* and *may*:

a Instead of saying:
Will you let me use your telephone please?

We can say:
Can I use your telephone please?
Or: Could I use your telephone please?
Or: May I use your telephone please?
Or: Might I use your telephone please?

b Instead of saying:
Perhaps he will come tomorrow.

We can say:
He may come tomorrow.
Or: He might come tomorrow.

Perhaps he telephoned last night, but I'm not sure.

He may have telephoned last night, but I'm not sure.
Or: He might have telephoned last night, but I'm not sure.

c Now study these expressions:
Do you want to come to the cinema with me?
I haven't got anything to do, so I *may as well* (or: I *might as well*) come with you.
Do you think he'll pass that exam?
He'll never pass. He *might as well* give up.

Exercises
A. Read the passage again. Put a line under the verbs *can*, *could*, *may* and *might*.

B. Use phrases with *can*, *could*, *may* or *might* in place of the words in italics. Do not refer to the passage until you finish the exercise.
   '*Perhaps the play will begin* at any moment,' I said.
   '*Perhaps it has begun already*,' Susan answered.
   I hurried to the ticket-office. '*Will you let me have* two tickets, please?' I asked.
   'I'm sorry, we've sold out,' the girl said.
   Just then, a man hurried to the ticket-office.
   '*Will you let me return* these two tickets?' he asked.
   I went back to the ticket-office at once. '*Will you let me have* those two tickets please?' I asked.
   'Certainly,' the girl said, 'but they are for next Wednesday's performance. Do you still want them?'
   '*Not really, but I'll have them*,' I said sadly.

Special Difficulties

Instead of saying:	*We can say:*
I am sorry.	I'm sorry. (l. 7)
We have sold out.	We've sold out. (l. 7)

Exercise
Change the form of the verbs in italics:
   1. I *haven't* seen him for three years.
   2. There *are not* many people here.
   3. He *doesn't* understand what *you're* saying.
   4. She *did not* tell me she *had not* seen you.
   5. I *shall not* stay a moment longer.
   6. He *will not* do as *he is* told.
   7. *When'll* I see you?
   8. *What've* you done? *You've* broken that bottle!
   9. *He's* in the living room. *He's* just come home.
   10. I *cannot* understand why he *hasn't* arrived.
   11. You *mustn't* believe him.
   12. I *wasn't* expecting you. You *weren't* supposed to arrive until 6 o'clock.
   13. That *man's* been in prison.
   14. They *hadn't* seen the film before.

20 One Man in a Boat

Fishing is my favourite sport. I often fish for hours without catching anything. But this does not worry me. Some fishermen are unlucky. Instead of catching fish, they
5 catch old boots and rubbish. I am even less lucky. I never catch anything—not even old boots. After having spent whole mornings on the river, I always go home with an empty bag. 'You must give up
10 fishing!' my friends say. 'It's a waste of time.' But they don't realize one important thing. I'm not really interested in fishing. I am only interested in sitting in a boat and doing nothing at all!

I never catch anything

Comprehension Précis and Composition

Answer these questions *in not more than 50 words.*
1. What is the writer's favourite sport?
2. What do some unlucky fishermen catch?
3. Is the writer as lucky as they are, or is he not so lucky?
4. Does he ever catch anything?
5. Is he really interested in fishing?
6. What is the only thing that interests him?

Key Structures

You must give up fishing.
Study these sentences carefully. Pay close attention to the verbs in italics. All these verbs end in *-ing*.
a *Eating* is always a pleasure.
  Watching television is my favourite pastime.
  Reading in bed is something I always enjoy.
b I am very keen on *cycling*.
  She is afraid of *staying* in that house alone.
  He is capable of *doing* anything.
c Note how these sentences have been joined:
  He sat there. He did not say anything.
  He sat there without *saying* anything.
  He turned off the radio. He left the room.
  Before *leaving* the room, he turned off the radio.
  He looked at his watch. He hurried to the station.
  After *looking* at his watch, he hurried to the station.
  Or: After *having looked* at his watch, he hurried to the station.
  I must apologize. I interrupted you.
  I must apologize for *interrupting* you.
  Or: I must apologize for *having interrupted* you.
  I must apologize. I did not let you know earlier.
  I must apologize for *not letting* you know earlier.

Or: I must apologize for *not having let* you know earlier.
He congratulated me. I won the competition.
He congratulated me on *winning* the competition.
Or: He congratulated me on *having won* the competition.

Exercises
A. Underline all the verbs in the passage that end in *-ing*.

B. Give the correct form of the verbs in brackets. Do not refer to the passage until you finish the exercise:

(Fish) is my favourite sport. I often fish for hours without (catch) anything. But this does not worry me. Some fishermen are unlucky. Instead of (catch) fish, they catch old boots and rubbish. I am even less lucky. I never catch anything—not even old boots. After (have spend) whole mornings on the river, I always go home with an empty bag. 'You must give up (fish)!' my friends say. 'It's a waste of time.' But they don't realize one important thing. I'm not really interested in (fish). I am only interested in (sit) in a boat and (do) nothing at all!

C. Join these pairs of sentences with the words given in brackets. Make any other necessary changes.
1. He went out of the restaurant. (without) He did not pay the bill.
2. She bought a pair of boots. (instead of) She did not get a pair of shoes.
3. She was afraid. (of) She did not spend the night alone.
4. (After) She heard the news. She fainted.
5. Think carefully. (before) Answer my question.
6. (On) I saw the plane coming towards me. I dashed for cover.

Special Difficulties

Words Often Confused
a Interested and Interesting. Excited and Exciting.
Study these examples:
Fishing is not interesting. I am not really interested in fishing. (l. 12)
The match was very exciting. The crowd got very excited.

b It's and Its. It's a waste of time. (ll. 10–11)
Study these examples:
It's (=it is) cold today. It's raining too.
The cat drank its milk.
This engine has lost its power.

c Realize and Understand. They don't realize . . . (l. 11)
Study these examples:
I realized he was mad.
He didn't realize that he had made a mistake.
I don't understand English.

Exercise
Choose the correct words in the following:
1. I (realized) (understood) he was not telling me the truth.
2. This poem is difficult. (It's) (Its) impossible for you to (understand) (realize) (its) (it's) meaning.
3. There was some (excited) (exciting) news on the radio.
4. He is not an (interesting) (interested) person.
5. He is an explorer. He leads an (excited) (exciting) life.
6. I am not (interesting) (interested) in other people's affairs.

52

21 Mad or Not?

Aeroplanes are slowly driving me mad. I
live near an airport and passing planes
can be heard night and day. The airport
was built during the war, but for some
5　reason it could not be used then. Last
year, however, it came into use. Over a
hundred people must have been driven
away from their homes by the noise. I am
one of the few people left. Sometimes I
10　think this house will be knocked down by
a passing plane. I have been offered a
large sum of money to go away, but I am
determined to stay here. Everybody says
I must be mad and they are probably
15　right.

Everybody says I must be mad

Comprehension Précis and Composition

Answer these questions *in not more than 50 words.*
1. Is the writer slowly going mad or not?
2. Where does he live?
3. What can be heard night and day?
4. Have most of his neighbours left their homes or not?
5. Has he been offered money to leave or not?
6. What is he determined to do?
7. What does everyone say?
8. Are they probably right or wrong?

Key Structures

Passing planes can be heard night and day. See **KS 31**
a Read these pairs of sentences carefully. The first sentence in each pair tells us about *a
person.* (Who) The second tells us about *a thing.* (What or Which)
He will repair your watch. (Who)
Your watch will be repaired. (What)
He can repair your watch. (Who)
Your watch can be repaired. (What)
They must test this new car. (Who)
This new car must be tested. (What)
You have to write this letter again. (Who)
This letter has to be written again. (What)
I told you *he could do it.* (Who)
I told you *it could be done.* (What)
I told you *he would do it.* (Who)
I told you *it would be done.* (What)
I can't find my bag. *Someone has stolen* it. (Who)
I can't find my bag. *It has been stolen.* (What)
I can't find my bag. *Someone must have stolen* it. (Who)
I can't find my bag. *It must have been stolen.* (What)

b Instead of saying:

b Instead of saying:	*We can say:*
The police will arrest the thieves.	The thieves will be arrested (by the police).
You must pay me for this.	I must be paid for this.
They cannot find him.	He cannot be found.

Exercises

A. There are some verbs in the passage which are like the examples given above. Can you find them?

B. Change the form of the phrases in italics. Do not refer to the passage until you finish the exercise:

I live near an airport and *I can hear passing planes* night and day. *They built the airport* during the war, but for some reason *they could not use it* then. Last year, however, it came into use. *The noise must have driven over a hundred people away* from their homes. I am one of the few people left. Sometimes I think *a passing plane will knock down this house. They have offered me* a large sum of money to go away, but I am determined to stay here.

C. Change the form of these sentences. Your sentences must begin with the words in italics:

1. I will send *a message* immediately.
2. We must sell *all these goods.*
3. I told you he would receive *the parcel* in time.
4. He has to deliver *the letter* by hand.
5. They must have lost *your letter* in the post.

Special Difficulties

Words Often Confused and Misused

a Drive.
This verb can be used in many ways. Study these examples:
Aeroplanes are slowly driving me mad. (l. 1)
He drives his car very badly.
The farmer drove the cattle into the field.
Our army drove the enemy back.
During the war, many people were driven out of their homes.

b Home and House. (ll. 8 and 10)
Study these examples:
After work I always go home. I stay at home during the week-end. There is no place like home.
They are building many new houses in our district. Houses are very expensive. I paid a lot of money for a new house.

Exercises

A. Write sentences using: drive out of, drive back and drive into.

B. Supply *house(s)* or *home* in the following:
1. It was raining heavily and I was glad to get ...
2. The government plans to build thousands of ... next year.
3. He is very rich. He owns a ... in the country.
4. Most people like to spend their Christmas holidays at ...

22   A Glass Envelope

My daughter, Jane, never dreamed of receiving a letter from a girl of her own age in Holland. Last year, we were travelling across the Channel and Jane put a
5   piece of paper with her name and address on it into a bottle. She threw the bottle into the sea. She never thought of it again, but ten months later, she received a letter from a girl in Holland. Both girls write to
10   each other regularly now. However, they have decided to use the post-office. Letters will cost a little more, but they will certainly travel faster.

ten months later, she received a letter

Comprehension Précis and Composition

Answer these questions *in not more than 55 words.*
1. When did Jane cross the Channel?
2. What did she throw into the sea?
3. What did it contain?
4. What did she receive ten months later?
5. Do they write to each other regularly now or not?
6. Do they send their letters by post, or do they send them in bottles?

Key Structures

Verbs followed by Of, From, In and On
We can put *of, from, in,* or *on* after certain verbs:

Jane never dreamed *of* receiving a letter . . . (ll. 1–2)
She never thought *of* it again. (l. 7)
She received a letter *from* a girl in Holland. (ll. 8–9)

Use this list for reference:
a OF: accuse, approve, assure, beware, boast (or about), complain (or about), consist, convince (or about), cure, despair, dream (or about), expect (or from), hear (or from), be/get rid, smell, suspect, think (or about), tire(d), warn (or against).

b FROM: borrow, defend (or against), demand (or of), differ, dismiss, draw (SD 158), emerge, escape, excuse (or for), hinder, prevent, prohibit, protect (or against), receive, separate, suffer.
c IN: believe, delight, employ(ed), encourage, engage(d), experience(d), fail, help (or with), include, indulge, instruct, interest(ed), invest, involve(d), persist, share.

d ON: act, base(d), call (SD 90), comment, concentrate, congratulate, consult (or about), count, decide, depend, economize, embark, experiment, insist, lean (or against), live, operate, perform (or in), pride (oneself), rely, vote (*on* a motion; *for* someone), write (or about).

Exercise

Supply the missing words (*of, from, in* or *on*) without referring to the above lists as far as possible:

1. I drew a lot of money . . . the bank yesterday. 2. I refuse to comment . . . his work. 3. It's no use complaining . . . the cold. 4. The waiter's tip is included . . . the bill. 5. He congratulated me . . . having got engaged. 6. This warm coat will protect you . . . the cold. 7. Did anything emerge . . . your discussion? 8. I dreamt . . . you last night. 9. You can never rely . . . him to be punctual. 10. Nothing will prevent him . . . succeeding. 11. Are you interested . . . music? 12. I suppose I can count . . . you for help . . . this matter? 13. Beware . . . the dog. 14. He persisted . . . asking questions. 15. I insist . . . your telling me the truth. 16. It took me a long time to get rid . . . him. 17. Do you mean to say you have never heard . . . Beethoven? 18. I separated them . . . each other because they were fighting. 19. They can only cure him . . . his illness if they operate . . . him. 20. You can depend . . . me. 21. I haven't accused him . . . anything, but I suspect him . . . having taken it. 22. Whatever made you think . . . such a thing? 23. We expect a great deal . . . you, Smith. 24. My hands smell . . . soap. 25. They differ . . . each other so much. 26. He invested a lot of money . . . shipping. 27. The film was based . . . a novel by Dickens. 28. Don't lean . . . that shelf! You'll regret it. 29. She often suffers . . . colds. 30. We have embarked . . . a new scheme. 31. I believe . . . taking my time. 32. Jones was dismissed . . . the firm. 33. They began by experimenting . . . rats. 34. Please concentrate . . . what you are doing. 35. She prides herself . . . her clean house. 36. The climber failed . . . his attempt to reach the summit. 37. Many people escaped . . . prison camps during the last war. 38. We must economize . . . fuel. 39. He's never done any work. He lives . . . his mother. 40. He was employed . . . a factory before he joined the army. 41. And what does this delightful drink consist . . . ? 42. I shall certainly act . . . your advice. 43. Don't write . . . the desk! 44. You should not boast . . . your success. 45. You must encourage him . . . his efforts. 46. I was instructed . . . drawing once upon a time. 47. Two or three people were involved . . . the accident. 48. Children should be prohibited . . . smoking. 49. It is unreasonable to demand this . . . him. 50. I can assure you . . . my support. 51. Do you approve . . . hunting? 52. I despair . . . ever teaching him anything! 53. He performs beautifully . . . the piano. 54. I warned him . . . the danger, but he wouldn't listen to me. 55. How much have you borrowed . . . me already? 56. Everyone shared . . . his happiness. 57. He delights . . . annoying me.

23 A New House

I had a letter from my sister yesterday. She lives in Nigeria. In her letter, she said that she would come to England next year. If she comes, she will get a surprise.
5 We are now living in a beautiful new house in the country. Work on it had begun before my sister left. The house was completed five months ago. In my letter, I told her that she could stay with us. The
10 house has many large rooms and there is a lovely garden. It is a very modern house, so it looks strange to some people. It must be the only modern house in the district.

the only modern house in the district

Comprehension Précis and Composition

Answer these questions *in not more than 50 words.*
1. What will your sister do next year?
2. Will she get a surprise if she comes or not?
3. Have you a new house in the country or not?
4. Have you invited your sister to stay with you or not?
5. Is it a very modern house, or is it an old house?
6. Has it got many large rooms and a lovely garden or not?

Key Structures

Review **KS 35-53**
I'll see you tomorrow. (**KS 35**)
What will you be doing tomorrow? (**KS 37**)
After he had finished work he went home. (**KS 39**)
He said that . . . He told me . . . (**KS 41**)
If you open the door you will get a surprise. (**KS 43**)
Must. (**KS 45**)
Have. (**KS 47**)
Can and May. (**KS 49**)
Passing planes can be heard night and day. (**KS 53**)

Exercises
A. Underline all the verbs in the passage. Revise any Key Structures you have forgotten.

B. Give the correct form of the verbs in brackets. Do not refer to the passage until you finish the exercise:
I (have) a letter from my sister yesterday. She (live) in Nigeria. In her letter, she (say) that she (come) to England next year. If she (come), she (get) a surprise. We now (live) in a beautiful new house in the country. Work on it (begin) before my sister (leave). The house (complete) five months ago. In my letter, I (tell) her that she (can stay) with us. The house (have) many large rooms and there (be) a lovely garden. It (be) a very modern house, so it (look) strange to some people.

C. Give the correct form of the verbs in brackets:
1. After he had read the book, he (write) a review of it.
2. He did not leave his office until he (finish) work.
3. If he (break) his promise, I shall never speak to him again.
4. If the weather is fine we (go) for a picnic.

D. Supply *said* or *told* in the following sentences. Give the correct form of the verbs in brackets:
1. She . . . me she (will) be absent from work.
2. I . . . my mother that I (lose) the key.
3. The manager . . . that he (not like) my work.

E. Which verbs can we use in place of the verbs or phrases in italics?
1. He *owns* a new house.
2. He *possesses* a lot of money.
3. I *took* a bath before dinner.
4. *Take* a cigarette.
5. *Will you let me* use your telephone please?
6. *Perhaps the play will* begin at any moment.
7. *Perhaps it has* begun already.
8. *It is necessary for me* to take a taxi.

Special Difficulties

There is and It is.
The house has many large rooms and *there is* a lovely garden. *It is* a very modern house, so it looks strange to some people. (ll. 9–12)
Study these examples:
There is
There is a fine new school in our neighbourhood. It was only built last year. *There are* 250 pupils at the school. Last year *there were* only 180. Next year *there will be* over 300.
It is
What's the time? *It is* five o'clock.
How far away is the station from here? *It is* five miles away.
What's the weather like? *It is* very cold.

Exercise
Supply *it* or *there* in the following sentences:
1. . . . is a pity that he could not come.
2. . . . is a bus that leaves in ten minutes.
3. . . . were some men digging up the road outside my house.
4. Look at those clouds. I think . . . will be a thunderstorm.
5. . . . is unusual for him to be late.
6. . . . has been very cold this year.
7. . . . has been no news of him.
8. I am sure . . . will be fine tomorrow.
9. After dinner . . . will be a long discussion on politics.
10. When will . . . be convenient for you to come?

24 It Could be Worse

I entered the hotel manager's office and sat down. I had just lost £50 and I felt very upset. 'I left the money in my room,' I said, 'and it's not there now.' The
5 manager was sympathetic, but he could do nothing. 'Everyone's losing money these days,' he said. He started to complain about this wicked world but was interrupted by a knock at the door. A girl
10 came in and put an envelope on his desk. It contained £50. 'I found this outside this gentleman's room,' she said. 'Well,' I said to the manager, 'there is still some honesty in this world!'

The manager was sympathetic

Comprehension Précis and Composition

Answer these questions *in not more than 55 words.*
1. How much money had you just lost?
2. How did you feel?
3. Did you tell the manager about it or not?
4. Could he do anything or not?
5. What did he begin complaining about?
6. Who came in with the money just then?
7. Where had she found it?
8. Is there still some honesty in this world or not?

Special Difficulties

Review **SD 16–58**

Exercises
A. Words Often Confused.
Choose the correct words in the following sentences:
1. I (took) (received) a letter from him yesterday. (**SD 20**)
2. I met Harry (in the) (on the) way to the station. (**SD 22a**)
3. (In the) (On the) way from Athens to London the plane stopped at Rome. (**SD 22a**)
4. Everybody (believe) (believes) he will win. (**SD 28a**)
5. Is your watch made (of) (from) gold? (**SD 32a**)
6. At the end of the month I received my (salary) (wages). (**SD 34b**)
7. Can you (borrow) (lend) me £5? (**SD 34c**)
8. I (asked) (asked for) an explanation. (**SD 40a**)
9. (Except) (Apart from) that, everything is all right. (**SD 40b**)
10. He is such a(n) (irritable) (nervous) person. He is always bad tempered. (**SD 42a**)
11. The police (is) (are) looking for him. (**SD 44a**)
12. Please (look after) (pay attention to) the blackboard. (**SD 44b**)
13. (Remind) (Remember) me to your mother. (**SD 44c**)
14. Father bought a new (suit) (costume) yesterday. (**SD 46b**)
15. When I (grow) (grow up) I shall be an engine driver. (**SD 46c**)

16. He was standing (besides) (beside) the window. (SD 48b)
17. (It's) (Its) a very (excited) (exciting) film. (SD 52a/b)
18. He does not (realize) (understand) English. (SD 52c)
19. It was raining heavily so I was glad to get (house) (home). (SD 54b)
20. (It is) (There is) someone at the door. (SD 58).

B. What a day! (SD 16)
Write these sentences again. Each sentence must begin with *What*.
1. This is a wonderful garden!
2. He is causing a lot of trouble!
3. It is a tall building!
4. You are a clever boy!

C. He lent me a book. He lent a book to me. (SD 18)
  She bought me a tie. She bought a tie for me. (SD 18)
Write each of the following sentences in a different way:
1. He handed me the prize.
2. The waiter brought a bottle of beer to the man.
3. I've ordered some soup for you.
4. Bring that book to me please.
5. She promised a reward to the finder.

D. Is there any tea in the pot?
  There isn't any tea in the pot.
  There's no tea in the pot. (SD 30)
Write negative answers to these questions in two different ways:
1. Have you any money?
2. Did you go anywhere in the holidays?
3. Was there anybody present when the accident happened?

E. Answer these questions. Put the apostrophe in the right place: (SD 38)
1. Whose umbrella is this? (George)
2. Whose is this handbag? (That woman)
3. Whose poetry do you like best? (Keats)
4. Whose are these clothes? (The children)
5. Whose are these uniforms? (The soldiers)

F. Knock (SD 24); Be (SD 36a); Give (SD 48a).
Complete these sentences by adding any of the following words: up, off, over, back, on, or away.
1. He usually knocks . . . at 6 o'clock, but today he's working late.
2. I'm going out now, but I'll be . . . in half an hour.
3. I gave . . . smoking last year but I have just started again.
4. The concert was . . . and everybody left the hall.
5. A new play is . . . at the Phoenix.
6. I've given . . . all my old furniture.

G. Change the position of the words in italics. (SD 24/26)
1. I put *on* my hat.
2. I took *off* my coat.
3. He put *out* the fire.
4. They cut *off* the king's head.

IF YOU CAN DO THIS TEST GO ON TO UNIT 2

Key Structures

A. Word Order in Simple Statements.

a There is a line under each word or group of words in the statements below. The words are not in the right order. Arrange them correctly:
1. The film I enjoyed yesterday.
2. My mother to market went.
3. The children asked continuously questions in class this morning.
4. We at home stay on Sundays.
5. This morning a book I from the library borrowed.

b Write these sentences again. Put the words in brackets in the right place:
1. She answers my letters. (rarely)
2. The shops close on Saturday afternoons. (always)
3. We work after six o'clock. (never)
4. We spend our holidays abroad. (sometimes)
5. Do you buy gramophone records? (ever)

B. Verbs.

a Now and Always.
The verbs in brackets tell us what is happening *now* and what *always* happens. Give the correct form of each verb:
I am looking out of my window. I can see some children in the street. The children (play) football. They always (play) football in the street. Now a little boy (kick) the ball. Another boy (run) after him but he cannot catch him.

b What happened?
The verbs in brackets tell us *what happened*. Give the correct form of each verb:
My friend, Roy, (die) last year. He (leave) me his record player and his collection of records. Roy (spend) a lot of money on records. He (buy) one or two new records every week. He never (go) to the cinema or to the theatre. He (stay) at home every evening and (listen) to music. He often (lend) records to his friends. Sometimes they (keep) them. He (lose) many records in this way.

c What has happened?
The verbs in brackets tell us *what has happened*. Give the correct form of each verb:
I just (receive) a letter from my brother Tim. He is in Australia. He (be) there for six months. Tim is an engineer. He is working for a big firm and he already (visit) a great number of different places in Australia. He just (buy) an Australian car and (go) to Alice Springs.

d What happened? What has happened?
The verbs in brackets tell us *what happened* and *what has happened*.
Give the correct form of each verb:
1. What . . . you (buy) yesterday?
2. Up till now, he never (lend) me anything.
3. . . . you (burn) those old papers yet?
4. He (fight) in Flanders in the First World War.
5. We just (win) the match.

e What was happening? What happened?
The verbs in brackets tell us *what was happening* and *what happened*. Give the correct form of each verb:
1. As my father (leave) the house, the postman (arrive).
2. Tom (work) in the garden while I (sit) in the sun.
3. As I (walk) down the street, I (meet) Charlie.
4. While he (read) the letter, he (hear) a knock at the door.
5. She (drop) the tray when I spoke to her.

f What will happen?
In the paragraph below, the verbs in italics tell us *what happened*. Write the passage again. Change the verbs in italics so that they tell us *what will happen*.
I *went* to the theatre with my friend Reg. Reg and I *saw* the first performance of a play called 'The End of the Road.' After the play, the producer *gave* a short speech. He *spoke* to the audience about the play. The play *was* very successful and I think a great many people *enjoyed* it very much.

g What will be happening?
Change the form of the verbs in italics so that they tell us *what will be happening*:
1. I *am ironing* the clothes.
2. The train *will arrive* in a few minutes.
3. *We'll see* you in the morning.
4. We *are watching* the match.
5. He *is correcting* copybooks.

h After he had finished work he went home.
Join these pairs of sentences with the words given in brackets:
1. (After) She wrote the letter. She went to the post-office.
2. (After) He had dinner. He went to the cinema.
3. (When) I fastened my seat belt. The plane took off.
4. We did not disturb him. (until) He finished work.
5. (As soon as) He left the room. I turned on the radio.

i It was made in Germany in 1681.
Supply the correct form of the verbs in brackets:
The Taj Mahal (build) in the seventeenth century for the emperor Shah Jehan. A few years after he (become) ruler, his wife, Mumtaz-i-Mahal, (die). The Taj Mahal (build) in her honour. Experts (call) in from many parts of the world to construct the domes and to decorate the walls. The Taj Mahal which (begin) in 1632 and (complete) in 1654 (cost) a fortune. Up to the present day, it (visit) by millions of people.

j He said that ... He told me ...
Supply *said* or *told* in the following sentences. Give the correct form of the verbs in brackets:
1. He ... me that she (come) tomorrow.
2. The gardener ... that he (cut) that tree down yesterday.
3. I ... you I (have) never played tennis before.
4. What ... he ... that he (do)?
5. When ... he ... you that he (buy) this car?

k If.
Give the correct form of the verbs in brackets:
1. If it (rain) I shall take an umbrella with me.
2. You never (pass) this test if you don't work hard.
3. If he (be) here before 10 o'clock, I shall see him.

4. If he plays well, he (get) into the team.
5. If he (enjoy) concerts, why doesn't he come with us?

l Give the correct form of the verbs in brackets:
(Fish) is my favourite sport. I often fish for hours without (catch) anything. But this does not worry me. Some fishermen are unlucky. Instead of (catch) fish, they catch old boots and rubbish. I am even less lucky. I never catch anything—not even old boots. After (have spend) whole mornings on the river, I always go home with an empty bag. 'You must give up (fish)!' my friends say. 'It's a waste of time.' But they don't realize one important thing. I'm not really interested in (fish). I am only interested in (sit) in a boat and (do) nothing at all!

C. Must, Have, Can and May.
a Write these sentences again using *must* or *have to* in place of the words in italics:
1. *It will be necessary for you to* see a doctor.
2. *Is it necessary for you to* make so much noise?
3. She said *it would be necessary for us to* stay here.
4. *It is necessary for me to* have some help.
5. *It was necessary for him to* go out last night.

b Write these sentences again in a different way using *must be* in place of the words in italics:
1. *I, personally, think he is* a fool.
2. *I, personally, think he is* mad.
3. *I, personally, think she is* over forty.

c Write these sentences again in a different way using *can* or *may* in place of the words in italics:
1. *Will you let me* use your telephone please?
2. *Perhaps he will* telephone tomorrow.
3. *Will you let me* have two tickets please?
4. *Perhaps the play has* begun already.
5. *Will you let me* leave the table please?

D. A, The and Some.
a Write these words again. Put in *a* or *some* in front of each one:
soap, picture, milk, money, woman, window, bus, sand, rice, newspaper, water, cloud, son, coal, secretary, oil.

b Put in *a* or *the* where necessary in the passage below:
I have just moved to . . . house in . . . Bridge Street. Yesterday . . . beggar knocked at my door. He asked me for . . . meal and . . . glass of beer. In return for this, . . . beggar stood on his head and sang . . . songs. I gave him . . . meal. He ate . . . food and drank . . . beer. Then he put . . . piece of cheese in his pocket and went away. Later . . . neighbour told me about him. Everybody knows him. His name is . . . Percy Buttons. He calls at every house in . . . street once . . . month and always asks for . . . meal and . . . glass of beer.

E. The best and the worst.
Give the correct form of the words in brackets. Supply *than* where necessary:
1. It is . . . (unusual) film I have ever seen.
2. Mr Jones is a . . . (good) teacher . . . Mr Brown.
3. This book is . . . (interesting) . . . that one.
4. She is . . . (lazy) pupil in the class.
5. The weather today is . . . (bad) . . . it was yesterday.

F. When did you arrive? I arrived at ten o'clock.
Supply the correct words in the following sentences:
1. He has gone abroad. He will return . . . two years' time.
2. . . . Saturdays I always go to the market.
3. I never go to the cinema . . . the week.
4. I can't see him . . . the moment. I'm busy.
5. My birthday is . . . November 7th. I was born . . . 1948.
6. The days are very short . . . December.
7. We arrived at the village late . . . night. We left early . . . the morning.

G. Verbs followed by *of*, *from*, *in* and *on*.
Supply the missing words in the sentences below:
1. Is this included . . . the bill?
2. I received a telephone call . . . him yesterday.
3. You can rely . . . me.
4. I am thinking . . . going abroad next year.
5. Are you interested . . . music?
6. I am tired . . . telling you the same thing again and again.

Special Difficulties

a Words Often Confused.
Choose the correct words in the following sentences:
1. (By the way) (On the way) have you seen Tom lately?
2. I (borrowed) (lent) this book from the library.
3. Can you (ask) (ask for) questions in English?
4. That tree has (grown) (grown up) a lot since I last saw it.
5. (Besides) (Beside) being a teacher, he is also a novelist.
6. The cat has drunk (it's) (its) milk.
7. Have you seen Tom (yet) (still)?
8. I put the papers on your (desk) (office).
9. You can't jump over that fence. (It is) (There is) impossible.
10. I like staying at (house) (home) during the week-end.

b Knock, Give and Be.
Supply the missing words in the following:
1. Someone is knocking . . . the door.
2. The doctor told him to give . . . smoking.
3. What's . . . at the cinema this week?
4. You can't see Mr Jones. He is . . . at the moment. He will be . . . in ten minutes.
5. The soldier hit the guard very hard and knocked him . . .

c Where possible, change the position of the words in italics:
1. Who knocked *over* this vase?
2. She is looking *after* the children.
3. Put *on* your jacket.
4. Bring it *back* quickly.
5. The thieves woke *up* the night-watchman.

d Put the words in brackets in their correct order:
1. The officer ordered (to fire, at the enemy, the men).
2. He wants (his wife, this dress, to wear).
3. She wants (us, it, to explain).
4. I cannot allow (the room, him, to enter).
5. She taught (to read, her son).

c Write these sentences in a different way. Omit the words in italics.
1. She made this dress *for* me.
2. I lent my typewriter *to* him.
3. I showed the letter *to* George.
4. Pass that cup *to* your mother.
5. Johnny gave the doll *to* his sister.

Unit 2

INSTRUCTIONS TO THE STUDENT

In Unit 1 you learned how to write simple statements. In Unit 2 you will learn how to join simple statements together with words like 'and', 'but' and 'so'. You will learn how to write sentences which contain more than one idea.

Before you begin each exercise, read these instructions carefully. Read them *each time* you begin a new piece. They are very important.

How to work—Comprehension and Précis

Unit 2 contains twenty-four short passages. There are questions under each piece. Your answers to these questions will often contain more than one idea. Put your answers together to make a short paragraph.

1. Read the passage carefully two or three times. Make sure you understand it.
2. Write a full answer to each question. When you find two or three questions together, join up your answers with the joining words given in brackets. Each answer you write must be *a complete sentence*.
3. Your answers to the questions must follow each other. All your answers together will then make *a complete paragraph*.
4. Read through your work and correct your mistakes.
5. Count the number of words in your paragraph. Words like 'the', 'a' etc. count as single words. Words which are joined by a hyphen (e.g. 'living-room') also count as single words. Do not go over the word limit. At the end of your paragraph write the number of words that you have used.

Example

Work through this example carefully and then try to do the exercises in Unit 2 in the same way.

What's the Time?

People often collect things. Stamps, books and records are fairly common. But the strangest collection I have ever seen belongs to a man who possesses 1500 clocks. There are clocks in every room of his house. The living-room is surrounded by shelves which have been filled with clocks. As there is not enough room
5 for so many clocks, the man has filled several trunks and stored them in the garage. His wife complains every day about the work she has to do, for it is not easy to dust several hundred clocks. She also complains about the noise. Each clock keeps its own time, so chimes can be heard almost any time during the day and night. In her opinion, however, there is something even worse than dust
10 and noise. Even with so many clocks around, she never knows what time it is!

Comprehension and Précis

Answer these questions *in not more than 70 words*.
1. How many clocks has a man collected? Has he put them in every room of his house
15 or not? (*and*)

2. Has he surrounded his living-room with them or not? What else has he filled? (*not only . . . but . . . as well*)
3. Does his wife have to dust hundreds of clocks or not?
4. Does she complain about the work and the noise or not?
5. Does each clock keep the correct time, or does it keep its own time?
6. What does she hear day and night? Does she ever know the correct time or not? (*Because of this . . . not only . . . but*)

Answer

A man has collected 1500 clocks *and* has put them in every room of his house. He has *not only* surrounded his living-room with them, *but* has filled several trunks *as well*. His wife has to dust hundreds of clocks. She complains about the work and noise. Each clock keeps its own time. *Because of this*, she *not only* hears chimes day and night, *but* never knows the correct time. (70 words)

Composition

In Unit 2 Composition has been dealt with separately. This Unit contains two types of composition exercise:
1. Learning how to select correct verbs and joining words. (Passages 25–36.)
2. Joining simple sentences together. (Passages 37–48.)

Examples

Work through these examples carefully and then try to do the composition exercises in the same way.

1. Composition

Rewrite these sentences using the correct verbs and joining words:
He never (knows) (understands) the correct time (and) (but) is often late for work. It was his birthday last week (so) (yet) his wife (took) (bought) him a present. She (brought) (bought) him an alarm clock (but) (and) he was (delighted) (enjoyed) with it.

Answer

He never *knows* the correct time *and* is often late for work. It was his birthday last week *so* his wife bought him a present. She *bought* him an alarm clock *and* he was *delighted* with it.

2. Composition

Rewrite the following sentences using the joining words in brackets:
1. His wife tells him he must sell the clocks. He must give them away to a museum. (*either . . . or*)
2. He refuses to do so. He spends even more money on clocks. (*not only . . . but*)
3. He says he will not sell them. He will not give them away. (*neither . . . nor*)

Answer

His wife tells him he must *either* sell the clocks *or* give them away to a museum. He *not only* refuses to do so *but* spends even more money on clocks. He says he will *neither* sell them *nor* give them away.

Letter-writing

This is begun in Unit 2. Carefully follow the instructions given under each passage.

Key Structures and Special Difficulties

When you finish the Letter-writing exercise, go on to the language exercises that follow. The **Key Structures** deal with exactly the same problems that were considered in Unit 1. You may refer back if you have forgotten anything. A little more new information about the Key Structures is added here. **Special Difficulties** are dealt with after the Key Structures. The work you do in grammar is based on material contained in the passages. Refer to the passages frequently. They will help you to understand the grammar and to do the exercises.

25 Do the English Speak English?

I arrived in London at last. The railway station was big, black and dark. I did not know the way to my hotel, so I asked a porter. I not only spoke English very
5 carefully, but very clearly as well. The porter, however, could not understand me. I repeated my question several times and at last he understood. He answered me, but he spoke neither slowly nor
10 clearly. 'I am a foreigner,' I said. Then he spoke slowly, but I could not understand him. My teacher never spoke English like that! The porter and I looked at each other and smiled. Then he said
15 something and I understood it. 'You'll

Then he spoke slowly

soon learn English!' he said. I wonder. In England, each man speaks a different language. The English understand each other, but *I* don't understand *them*! Do they speak English?

Comprehension and Précis

Answer these questions *in not more than 70 words*.
1. Did you arrive at a railway station in London or not? Did you ask a porter the way to your hotel or not? Could he understand you or not? (*and . . . but*)
2. Did he understand you at last or not? Could you understand his answer? (*but*)
3. Did your teacher ever speak English like that or not?
4. What did the porter say to you?
5. Does each man speak a different language in England or not?
6. Do they understand each other or not? Do you understand them? (*but*)

Letter-writing

The address appears at the top right-hand corner of the page. It is called 'The Heading'. The address is always followed by the date:

> 14 Grafton St.,
> Croydon,
> Surrey,
> England.
> 24th April, 19—

Exercise
Write your home address. Follow the above pattern carefully.

Key Structures

Word Order in Compound Statements
a Do you remember the six parts of a simple statement? Refer to **KS 13c** if you have forgotten them.
b We can join simple statements together to make *compound-statements*. Here are some of the joining words we use: and, but, so, yet, or, both . . . and, either . . . or, neither . . . nor, not only . . . but . . . as well (or also).

Study these sentences carefully. Pay close attention to the way they have been joined:
He finished lunch. He went into the garden.
He finished lunch *and went* into the garden.

I ran to the station. I missed the train.
I ran to the station *but missed* the train.

I saw him yesterday. He did not greet me.
I saw him yesterday *but he* did not greet me.

He teaches English. I teach English.
Both he and I teach English.

He teaches English. He teaches French.
He teaches *both English and French.*

You must tell him. I must tell him.
Either you or I must tell him.

He plays soccer. He plays rugby.
He plays *either soccer or rugby.*

He does not speak English. I do not speak English.
Neither he nor I speak English.

He does not speak English. He does not speak French.
He speaks *neither English nor French.*

He cannot read. He cannot write.
He can *neither read nor write.*

You must wash the dishes. You must sweep the floor.
You must *not only* wash the dishes *but* sweep the floor *as well.*

Exercises
A. Underline the joining words in the passage.

B. Join these pairs of sentences. Use the joining words in brackets. Do not refer to the passage until you finish the exercise.
1. I did not know the way to my hotel. I asked a porter. (*so*)
2. I spoke English very carefully. I spoke very clearly. (*not only . . . but . . . as well*)
3. I repeated my question several times. At last he understood. (*and*)
4. He answered me. He did not speak slowly. He did not speak clearly. (*but . . . neither . . . nor*)
5. Then he spoke slowly. I could not understand him. (*but*)
6. Then he said something. I understood it. (*and*)
7. The English understand each other. I don't understand them. (*but*)

C. Join these sentences with the words in brackets:
1. I knocked at the door. He did not open it. (*but*)
2. He went on holiday. I went on holiday. (*Both . . . and*)
3. He must be mad. He must be very wise. (*either . . . or*)

Composition

Join the following sentences using the words in brackets:
1. My sister went shopping. I went shopping. (*Both . . . and*)
2. We got very tired. We got very hungry. (*not only . . . but . . . as well*)
3. It was three o'clock. We could not get lunch. We had a cup of tea. (*and . . . so*)

26 The Best Art Critics

I am an art student and I paint a lot of pictures. Many people pretend that they understand modern art. They always tell you what a picture is 'about'. Of course, 5 many pictures are not 'about' anything. They are just pretty patterns. We like them in the same way that we like pretty curtain material. I think that young children often appreciate modern pictures 10 better than anyone else. They notice more. My sister is only seven, but she always tells me whether my pictures are good or not. She came into my room yesterday.

She looked at it critically

15 'What are you doing?' she asked.

'I'm hanging this picture on the wall,' I answered. 'It's a new one. Do you like it?'

She looked at it critically for a moment. 'It's all right,' she said, 'but isn't it upside-down?'

I looked at it again. She was right! It was!

Comprehension and Précis
Answer these questions *in not more than 70 words*.

1. Does the writer study art, or does he study music? Does he paint a lot of pictures or not? (*and*)
2. Do many people really understand modern art or not?
3. Do paintings always have a meaning or not?
4. Are they sometimes pretty patterns or not?
5. Do young children appreciate modern paintings better than others or not? Do they notice more or not? (*not only . . . but*)
6. When did the writer's young sister go into his room? Did she examine his new picture or not? (*and*)
7. Had he hung it upside-down, or had he hung it the right way up? Did she notice this immediately or not? (*and*)

Composition
Rewrite these sentences using the correct verbs and joining words:

I (looked at) (watched) the picture (but) (and) I could not (understand) (realize) it. It was in black and white and was (called) (named) 'Trees and Snow'. I could see (neither) (not only) trees (or) (nor) snow.

Letter-writing
Which of the following addresses is correct?

John Madgewick,	Grafton St., 14,	14 Grafton St.,
14 Grafton St.,	Croydon,	Croydon,
Croydon,	Surrey,	Surrey,
Surrey,	England.	England.
England.	24th April, 19—	24th April, 19—

Key Structures

These things always happen.

a I am having breakfast. Do you always get up so late? (Now and Always **KS 15**)

b These things always happen:

The earth *goes* round the sun.

The sun *rises* in the east and *sets* in the west.

c We rarely put *-ing* at the end of these verbs: appear, appreciate, believe, feel, forget, hear, know, like, look like, notice, remember, resemble, see, think (that), understand. These verbs tell us what *always* happens:

I *hear* that you *like* classical music.

I *remember* Tom very well. *Do you know* him?

Exercises

A. Underline the verbs in the passage that tell us what *always* happens and those which tell us what is happening *now*.

B. What is happening? What always happens?

Give the correct form of the verbs in brackets:

'Some people still (believe) the world is flat,' he said.

'You (joke),' I replied. 'I (not know) anyone who does.'

'Well, you (know) me,' he replied. 'I (believe) that the earth is flat. I met a man the other day. I (forget) his name now. He said that the earth (look) like a flat dish.'

'. . . you (try) to tell me that you (believe) him?' I asked.

'I certainly do,' he answered. 'I (think) that he is right.'

'And which side of the dish . . . you (live) on?'

'Oh, I (not know). He didn't tell me that!'

Special Difficulties

Speech Marks

In written conversation, we put speech marks ('. . .') or (". . .") round the words that are actually spoken. Read this carefully:

'What are you doing?' she asked.

'I'm hanging this picture on the wall,' I answered. 'It's a new one. Do you like it?'

She looked at it critically for a moment. 'It's all right,' she said, 'but isn't it upside-down?' (ll. 14–18)

Some things to notice:

a The speech marks are above the line. They go outside all other marks like commas (,) full stops (.) and question marks (?).

b The speaker's first word begins with a capital letter.

c Words like 'said' and 'asked' are followed by a comma. We put a full stop after them only when they come at the end of a sentence.

d When words like 'said' or 'asked' interrupt the speaker, the second half of the sentence begins with a small letter.

e We begin a new paragraph each time a new speaker is introduced.

Exercise

Write this piece of conversation again using speech marks:

Look! she said, isn't that man drunk? I think we should cross the road, answered her husband. It's too late now, she replied. Eh, you two. Look where you're going, called the drunk. Can't you walk in a straight line?

27   A Wet Night

Late in the afternoon, the boys put up their tent in the middle of a field. As soon as this was done, they cooked a meal over an open fire. They were all hungry and
5 the food smelt good. After a wonderful meal, they told stories and sang songs by the camp fire. But some time later it began to rain. The boys felt tired so they put out the fire and crept into their tent.
10 Their sleeping-bags were warm and comfortable, so they all slept soundly. In the middle of the night, two boys woke up and began shouting. The tent was full of water! They all leapt out of their sleep-
15 ing-bags and hurried outside. It was raining heavily and they found that a stream

a stream had formed in the field

had formed in the field. The stream wound its way across the field and then flowed right under their tent!

Comprehension and Précis

Answer these questions *in not more than 70 words.*
1. Where did the boys put up their tent? What did they cook? (*and*)
2. What did they do after their meal? Did it begin to rain or not? Did they creep into their tent or not? (*but . . . so*)
3. Did the boys wake up in the middle of the night or not?
4. Was the tent full of water or not? Did they rush outside or did they stay in their tent? (*so*)
5. Where had a stream formed? Where did it flow? (*and*)

Composition

Rewrite these sentences using the correct verbs and joining words:
I am very tall (so) (but) I must be careful. Doorways are often low (and) (but) I usually (beat) (knock) my head against them. My head always (hurts) (pains). I have never (met) (recognized) a tall architect. Have you?

Letter-writing

The order of the heading is as follows: the number of the house, the name of the street, the town or city, the area, the country and the date. Put in the name of the country only when you are writing to someone who lives abroad.

Exercise
Arrange the following heading in the correct order:
California, Woodside, 21st Feb., 19—, U.S.A., 21 Brook St.,

Key Structures

What happened? (KS 17)
Read these sentences carefully. The verbs in italics tell us what happened:
I *lost* my umbrella a few days ago.
I *bought* this coat yesterday.
I *dreamt* of you last night.
She *paid* the bill and *left* the shop.

Exercises
A. Underline the verbs in the passage that tell us *what happened*.

B. Give the correct form of the verbs in brackets. Do not refer to the passage until you finish the exercise:
Late in the afternoon, the boys (put) up their tent in the middle of a field. As soon as this (do), they (cook) a meal over an open fire. They were all hungry and the food (smell) good. After a wonderful meal, they (tell) stories and (sing) songs by the camp fire. But some time later it (begin) to rain. The boys (feel) tired so they (put) out the fire and (creep) into their tent. Their sleeping-bags were warm and comfortable, so they all (sleep) soundly. In the middle of the night, two boys (wake) up and (begin) shouting. The tent (be) full of water! They all (leap) out of their sleeping-bags and (hurry) outside. It was raining heavily and they (find) that a stream had formed in the field. The stream (wind) its way across the field and then (flow) right under their tent!

Special Difficulties

(See SD 24, 26)
Study these sentences. Each one contains the verb *put*. The verb has a different meaning in each sentence:
The boys *put up* their tent in the middle of a field. (ll. 1–2)
They *put out* the fire and crept into their tent. (ll. 8–9)
I *put on* my coat and left the house.
You needn't go back to London tonight. We can *put you up* for the night. (We can provide you with a bed.)
The teacher sent the boy to the headmaster. He could not *put up with* him any longer. (He could not stand him.)
Take out your note-books. *Put down* all the sentences that are on the blackboard. (Write all the sentences . . .)
We cannot have the meeting tonight. We shall have to *put it off* until tomorrow. (We shall have to postpone it.)
Close your books and *put them away*.

Exercise
Use the correct expression with *put* in each of the following:
1. Mrs Bowers told her children to . . . their toys and go to bed.
2. You can stay here tonight. We can . . . you . . . in the spare room.
3. I'm not ready yet. I haven't . . . my shoes . . .
4. 'Open your copy books and . . . the following,' the teacher said.
5. Father is . . . the fire he lit in the garden.
6. When they have . . . that new building, it will spoil the view.
7. I have . . . my trip to Japan until next month.
8. I am getting a divorce. I can't . . . him any longer.

28 No Parking!

Jasper White is one of those rare people who believes in ancient myths. He has just bought a new house in the city, but ever since he moved in, he has had
5 trouble with motorists. When he returns home at night, he always finds that someone has parked a car outside his gate. Because of this, he has not been able to get his own car into his garage even once.
10 Jasper has put up 'No Parking' signs outside his gate, but these have not had any effect. Now he has put an ugly stone head over the gate. It is one of the ugliest faces I have ever seen. I asked him what it was
15 and he told me that it was Medusa, the Gorgon. Jasper hopes that she will turn motorists to stone. But none of them has been turned to stone yet!

hopes she will turn motorists to stone

Comprehension and Précis

Answer these questions *in not more than 65 words.*
1. What does Jasper White believe in?
2. Where do motorists always park their cars? Has he put up 'No Parking' signs or not? Have they paid any attention to them or not? (*so . . . but*)
3. What has he put over his gate now?
4. Whose head is it?
5. What does he want her to do? Has she done so yet or not? (*but*)

Composition

Rewrite these sentences using the correct verbs and joining words:
My wife (drives) (leads) a car. She has (driven) (ridden) a car for many years (and) (but) she says that women drivers (do not deserve) (are not worth) their bad reputation. Yet, on the road, she often (criticizes) (judges) other women drivers.

Letter-writing

I am writing to someone who lives in the same country as I do. Which of these two headings would be correct?

19 High Lane,	19 High Lane,
Newton,	Newton,
Middlesex.	Middlesex,
10th September, 19—	England.
	10th September, 19—

Key Structures

What has happened?
Study these sentences carefully. Pay close attention to the words in italics:
I have *just* received a letter from my brother, Tim. (KS 19)
I have not seen Tim *since* last January.

77

I have not seen Tim *since* 1964.
I have not seen Tim *for* three years.
Tim has been abroad *for* three years.
Up till now he has won five prizes.
Up till now I have been to New York *three times*.
I have been to New York *three times so far*.
Have you been to New York?
Have you seen this film?
Have you read this book?

Exercises

A. Underline the verbs in the passage that tell us *what has happened*.

B. Give the correct form of the verbs in brackets. Do not refer to the passage until you finish the exercise:

Jasper White is one of those rare people who believes in ancient myths. He just (buy) a new house in the city, but ever since he moved in, he (have) trouble with motorists. When he returns home at night, he always finds that someone (park) a car outside his gate. Because of this, he (not be) able to get his own car into his garage even once. Jasper (put) up 'No Parking' signs outside his gate, but these (not have) any effect. Now he (put) an ugly stone head over the gate. It is one of the ugliest faces I ever (see). I asked him what it was and he told me that it was Medusa, the Gorgon. Jasper hopes that she will turn motorists to stone. But none of them (turn) to stone yet!

Special Difficulties

Who, Which, That, and Whose

Instead of saying:	*We can say:*
The man *whom* you met yesterday is an actor.	The man you met yesterday is an actor.
The book *which* you lent me is not very interesting.	The book you lent me is not very interesting.
The flowers *that* I love best are roses.	The flowers I love best are roses.

We *cannot* leave out *who, which, that* or *whose* in these sentences:
Jasper White is one of those rare people *who* believes in ancient myths. (ll. 1–2)
This is the hotel *which* was built last year.
This is the island *that* was bought by a millionaire.
The pilot *whose* plane landed in a field was not hurt.

Exercise

Supply *who, which, that* or *whose* only where necessary:
1. The only games . . . I play are football and tennis.
2. He is the only student . . . understands English well.
3. He is a writer . . . books are seldom read.
4. This is the hotel at . . . we are staying.
5. Is this the money . . . you lost?
6. That is the horse . . . won the race.
7. He is the sort of person . . . everyone admires.

29 Taxi!

Captain Ben Fawcett has bought an unusual taxi and has begun a new service.
The 'taxi' is a small Swiss aeroplane
called a 'Pilatus Porter'. This wonderful
5 plane can carry seven passengers. The
most surprising thing about it, however,
is that it can land anywhere: on snow,
water, or even on a ploughed field. Captain Fawcett's first passenger was a doctor
10 who flew from Birmingham to a lonely
village in the Welsh mountains. Since
then, Captain Fawcett has flown passengers to many unusual places. Once he
landed on the roof of a block of flats and
15 on another occasion, he landed in a deserted car park. Captain Fawcett has just
refused a strange request from a businessman. The man wanted to fly to Rockall,
a lonely island in the Atlantic Ocean, but Captain Fawcett did not take him
because the trip was too dangerous.

landed in a deserted car-park

Comprehension and Précis

Answer these questions *in not more than 60 words.*
1. Has Captain Ben Fawcett bought a small Swiss aeroplane, or has he bought an
   ordinary taxi? Does he use it as a taxi or not? (*and*)
2. What is it called?
3. How many passengers can it carry? Can it land anywhere or not? (*not only . . . but*)
4. Has Captain Fawcett taken passengers to many strange places in his plane or not?
5. Did he refuse to fly a businessman to Rockall or not?
6. Was the journey too dangerous or not?

Composition

Rewrite these sentences using the correct verbs and joining words:
The plane (not only) (neither) (flew) (threw) close to the river, (but) (or) also flew
under a bridge. (Then) (However) it (climbed) (ran) into the air. The people on the
bridge (waved) (shook) to the pilot (and) (yet) he did not (notice) (look after) them.

Letter-writing

I am writing to someone who lives abroad. Which of these two headings would be
correct?

19 High Lane,
Newton,
Middlesex.
10th September, 19—

19 High Lane,
Newton,
Middlesex,
England.
10th September, 19—

Key Structures

What happened? What has happened? (KS 21)
Study these pairs of sentences. Pay close attention to the words in italics:
I saw him *in 1964*.
I have not seen him *since 1964*.

I saw him *three years ago*.
I have not seen him *for three years*.

He stayed at this hotel *last month*.
Have you *ever* stayed at this hotel?

I went abroad last year.
Up till now, I have never been abroad *before*.

Exercises
A. Underline the verbs in the passage which tell us *what happened* and *what has happened*.

B. Give the correct form of the verbs in brackets. Do not refer to the passage until you finish the exercise:
Captain Ben Fawcett (buy) an unusual taxi and (begin) a new service. The 'taxi' is a small Swiss aeroplane called a 'Pilatus Porter'. This wonderful plane can carry seven passengers. Captain Fawcett's first passenger (be) a doctor who (fly) from Birmingham to a lonely village in the Welsh mountains. Since then, Captain Fawcett (fly) passengers to many unusual places. Once he (land) on the roof of a block of flats and on another occasion, he (land) in a deserted car park. Captain Fawcett just (refuse) a strange request from a businessman. The man (want) to fly to Rockall, but Captain Fawcett (not take) him because the trip (be) too dangerous.

Special Difficulties

Words Often Confused
a Refuse and Deny.
Refuse (a request or something offered): Captain Fawcett has just refused a strange request from a businessman. (ll. 16–17)
Deny (an accusation): He denied that he had stolen the money.

b Bring, Take, and Fetch. He did not take him. (ll. 18–19)
Bring (come from somewhere with something): He brought the book with him when he came to see me.
Take (away from somewhere or someone): He took the book with him when he left. (Compare SD 20)
Fetch (go somewhere, pick something up and bring it back): I asked him to go to my room and fetch my glasses.

c Very and Too. The trip was too dangerous. (l. 19)
Very: I arrived very late but I caught the train.
Too: I arrived too late and I missed the train.

Exercise
Choose the correct words in the following:
1. When you go to the kitchen, please (fetch) (bring) me a glass of water.
2. The ball went over the fence and the football player asked a boy to (fetch) (bring) it.
3. When I asked him he (refused) (denied) to tell me.
4. Do you (deny) (refuse) that you have told me a lie?
5. How are you? (Too) (Very) well thank you.

30 Football or Polo?

The Wayle is a small river that cuts across the park near my home. I like sitting by the Wayle on fine afternoons. It was warm last Sunday, so I went and
5 sat on the river bank as usual. Some children were playing games on the bank and there were some people rowing on the river. Suddenly, one of the children kicked a ball very hard and it went to-
10 wards a passing boat. Some people on the bank called out to the man in the boat, but he did not hear them. The ball struck him so hard that he nearly fell into the water. I turned to look at the children,
15 but there weren't any in sight: they had all run away! The man laughed when he realized what had happened. He called out to the children and threw the ball back to the bank.

nearly fell into the water

Comprehension and Précis

Answer these questions *in not more than 70 words.*
1. Did the writer sit by the river last Sunday or not?
2. Were some children playing games nearby or not?
3. Who kicked a ball hard? Where did it go? (*and*)
4. Did the man in the boat see the ball? Did he hear people shouting? (*neither . . . nor*)
5. Did the ball hit the man or not? What did the children do? (*and*)
6. Was the man angry or not? Where did he throw the ball? (*However, . . . and*)

Composition

Rewrite these sentences using the correct verbs and joining words:
The wind (threw) (blew) his hat into the river. He (put) (took) out his hand (and) (but) tried to (reach) (catch) it (so) (but) he could not (so) (but) he (jumped) (fell) into the river (and) (but) got it.

Letter-writing

Arrange the following heading in the correct order:
Middlesex, England, 10th September, 19—, 19 High Lane, Newton.

Key Structures

A, The, Some and Any (KS 23)
a *Some* and *Any* (Compare SD 30)
Note the use of *some* and *any* in these sentences:
Is there any milk in the bottle?
There isn't any milk in the bottle, but there is some in this jug.
Is there any soap in the bathroom?
There isn't any soap in the bathroom, but there's some in the cupboard.

Are there any nails in that tin?
There aren't any in the tin, but there are some in this box.

b Names

We cannot put *a* or *the* in front of names. (**KS 23c**)
John lives in England. He has a house in London.
But we must put *the* in front of the names of oceans, seas, rivers, mountain ranges and certain countries:
Who was the first person to sail across *the* Pacific?
It can get very rough in *the* Mediterranean.
Many great cities are built on rivers. Paris is on *the* Seine, London is on *the* Thames and Rome is on *the* Tiber.
I know a man who has been on climbing expeditions in many parts of the world. He has climbed in *the* Alps, *the* Himalayas, and *the* Rocky Mountains.

Instead of saying:	*We can say:*
I went to America last year.	I went to *the* United States of America last year
Would you like to live in Russia?	Would you like to live in *the* Soviet Union?

Exercises

A. Underline the words *a*, *the*, *some* and *any* in the passage.

B. Put in the words *a*, *the*, *some* and *any* where necessary. Do not refer to the passage until you finish the exercise.
... Wayle is ... small river that cuts across ... park near my home. I like sitting by ... Wayle on fine afternoons. It was warm last Sunday, so I went and sat on ... river bank as usual. ... children were playing ... games on ... bank and there were ... people rowing on ... river. Suddenly, one of ... children kicked ... ball very hard and it went towards ... passing boat. ... people on ... bank called out to ... man in ... boat, but he did not hear them. ... ball struck him so hard that he nearly fell into ... water. I turned to look at ... children, but there weren't ... in sight.

C. Answer these questions in two ways using *some* and *any*:
1. Did you take any photographs? Yes, ... No, ...
2. Did you buy any bread? Yes, ... No, ...
3. Did you see any people outside the cinema? Yes, ... No, ...

D. Put in *a* or *the* where necessary:
1. ... refrigerators are necessary in ... hot countries.
2. Which river is ... longest, ... Nile, ... Amazon, or ... Mississippi?
3. Heyerdahl crossed ... Pacific on ... raft.
4. Why is ... Britain sometimes called ... United Kingdom?
5. We sailed up ... Red Sea and then went through ... Suez Canal.

31 Success Story

Yesterday afternoon Frank Hawkins was telling me about his experiences as a young man. Frank is now the head of a very large business company, but as a boy he used to work in a small shop. It was his job to repair bicycles and at that time he used to work fourteen hours a day. He saved money for years and in 1938 he bought a small work-shop of his own. During the war Frank used to make spare parts for aeroplanes. At that time he had two helpers. By the end of the war, the small work-shop had become a large factory which employed seven hundred and twenty-eight people. Frank smiled when he remembered his hard early years and the long road to success. He was still smiling when the door opened and his wife came in. She wanted him to repair their son's bicycle!

experiences as a young man

Comprehension and Précis

Answer these questions *in not more than 80 words.*
1. What was Frank Hawkins telling the writer about?
2. Where did Frank use to work as a boy?
3. What did he use to do there?
4. When did he buy his own shop? What did he make during the war? (*and*)
5. Did he employ a lot of people by the end of the war or not?
6. Who came into the room after a while?
7. What did she want him to repair?

Composition

Rewrite these sentences using the correct verbs and joining words:
Frank (not only) (neither) (repaired) (made) his son's bicycle, (but) (also) went for a ride on it (as well) (both). He (said) (told) me later: ' I (make) (do) aeroplanes, (and) (but) I prefer bicycles.'

Letter-writing

Which of the following headings is correct:

Mr Bill Howard,	214 Duke St.,	Duke St. 214,
214 Duke St.,	Perth,	14th May, 19—,
Perth,	Western Australia.	Perth,
Western Australia.	14th May, 19—	Western Australia.

Key Structures

He used to work fourteen hours a day.
Do you remember these sentences? (**KS 25**)
When I *was watering* the garden, it *began* to rain.
As I *was getting on* the bus, I *slipped* and *hurt* my foot.

Now compare them with these sentences:

I *used to go* to work by bus. Now I go by car.

He *used to be* a postman a long time ago. He's a taxi driver now.

I have given up smoking. I *used to smoke* very heavily.

I *used to collect* stamps when I was a boy.

My uncle *used to live* in New Zealand but he's now living in Australia.

Exercises

A. Underline the verbs in the passage which tell us *what was happening, what happened* and *what used to happen.*

B. Give the correct form of the verbs in brackets. Do not refer to the passage until you finish the exercise:

1. Frank is now the head of a very large business company, but as a boy he (work) in a small shop. It (be) his job to repair bicycles and at that time he (work) fourteen hours a day. He (save) money for years and in 1938 he (buy) a small work-shop.
2. Frank (smile) when he (remember) his hard early years. He still (smile) when the door (open) and his wife (come) in.

C. What was happening? What happened? What used to happen?

Give the correct form of the verbs in brackets:

While my wife (work) in the kitchen, I (sit) in the garden. I (look) at cars which (pass) in the street, when a small car (stop) outside my gate and a man (get) out. I was most surprised to see that the man was Ted Hale. We (be) at the same school years ago. In those days, Ted (come) to our house nearly every day and we often (go) out together. We (be) great friends, but one day we (quarrel) and I never (see) him again. As he (get) out of his car, I (call) my wife and we both (hurry) out to greet an old friend.

Special Difficulties

Words Often Misused and Confused

a Experience. Note the following:

Frank Hawkins was telling me about his experiences. (ll. 1–2)

This job requires a lot of experience.

He is an experienced worker.

b Save. Note the following:

He saved money for years. (l. 8)

The young man dived into the river and saved the boy's life.

c Work and Job. Note the following:

It was his job to repair bicycles. (ll. 5–6)

I've just found a new job. I begin work on Monday.

Exercise

Choose the correct words in the following sentences:

1. He is a very (experience) (experienced) doctor.
2. My father enjoys doing (jobs) (works) about the house.
3. I am looking for a new (work) (job).
4. The government is trying to persuade people to (economize) (save) money.

32 Shopping Made Easy

People are not so honest as they once were. The temptation to steal is greater than ever before—especially in large shops. A detective recently watched a
5 well-dressed woman who always went into a large store on Monday mornings. One Monday, there were fewer people in the shop than usual when the woman came in, so it was easier for the detective
10 to watch her. The woman first bought a few small articles. After a little time, she chose one of the most expensive dresses in the shop and handed it to an assistant who wrapped it up for her as quickly as
15 possible. Then the woman simply took the parcel and walked out of the shop

A detective watched a well-dressed woman

without paying. When she was arrested, the detective found out that the shop-assistant was her daughter. The girl 'gave' her mother a free dress once a week!

Comprehension and Précis

Answer these questions *in not more than 70 words.*
1. Whom did a detective watch in a large store one Monday?
2. What did she buy? Did she choose an expensive dress or not?   (*and then*)
3. Did the assistant wrap it up for her or not? Did the woman take it with her or not? (*and*)
4. Did she pay for it or not? Did the detective arrest her or not? (*so*)
5. Who was the assistant?
6. What did she give her mother once a week?

Composition

Rewrite these sentences using the correct verbs and joining words:
I (came) (arrived at) the office late as usual (so) (but) Mr Blake (saw) (understood) me (and) (or) he was very angry. 'This is your last day here, Jones,' he said. 'You can (neither) (either) (stay) (sit) here (or) (nor) go home!'

Letter-writing

Each line of the address is followed by a comma. The last line is followed by a full stop. We do not put a comma or a full stop after the date.

Exercise
Arrange the following heading in the correct order. Put in full stops or commas where necessary:
New York/504 West 94th St./N.Y./24th June, 19—/U.S.A.

Key Structures

People are not so honest as they once were.
Do you remember these sentences? (**KS 27**)

Mary is tall, but Jane is taller. Jane is taller than Mary. Betty is very tall. She is the tallest girl in the class.

Now study these sentences carefully:

a   He is *as old as* I am.
    He unlocked the door *as quickly as* he could.
    She is not *as intelligent as* we think.
Or: She is not *so intelligent as* we think.

b Instead of saying:	*We can say:*
There isn't much I can do to help him.	*There is little* I can do to help him.
He hasn't got as much work to do *as* I have.	*He's got less* work to do *than* I have.
There weren't many people in the shop.	*There were very few* people in the shop.
He hasn't as many books *as* I have.	*He has fewer* books *than* I have.
There isn't much whisky in this bottle, but you can have *some* if you want it.	There isn't much whisky in this bottle, but you can have *a little* if you want it.
There aren't many apples on the tree, but you can pick *some* if you want to.	There aren't many apples on the tree, but you can pick *a few* if you want to.

Exercises

A. How many comparisons can you find in the passage? Underline them.

B. Supply the missing words and give the correct form of the words in brackets. Do not refer to the passage until you finish the exercise.
People are not . . . honest . . . they once were. The temptation to steal is (great) than ever before—especially in large shops. A detective recently watched a well-dressed woman who always went into a large store on Monday mornings. One Monday, there were (few) people in the shop than usual when the woman came in, so it was (easy) for the detective to watch her. The woman first bought a . . . small articles. After a . . . time, she chose one of the (expensive) dresses in the shop and handed it to an assistant who wrapped it up for her . . . quickly . . . possible.

Special Difficulties

Words Often Confused
A and One. (**KS 23**)
Study these examples:
A detective watched a well-dressed woman . . . (ll. 4–5)
One Monday, there were fewer people in the shop . . . (ll. 7–8)
Compare:
There is a boy in the classroom.
There is only one boy in the classroom. (And not two or more.)

Exercise
Put in *a/an* or *one*:
. . . day I received . . . postcard from Harry. He invited me to go on . . . excursion. As he was setting out that afternoon, there was only . . . thing to do. I had to send . . . telegram. I went to . . . post-office and asked for . . . form. I wrote . . . telegram of . . . word: NO.

33 Out of the Darkness

Nearly a week passed before the girl was able to explain what had happened to her. One afternoon she set out from the coast in a small boat and was caught in a storm.
5 Towards evening, the boat struck a rock and the girl jumped into the sea. Then she swam to the shore after spending the whole night in the water. During that time she covered a distance of eight miles.
10 Early next morning, she saw a light ahead. She knew she was near the shore because the light was high up on the cliffs. On arriving at the shore, the girl struggled up the cliff towards the light she had seen.
15 That was all she remembered. When she woke up a day later, she found herself in hospital.

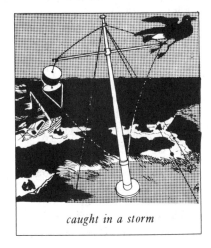

caught in a storm

Comprehension and Précis

Answer these questions *in not more than 65 words.*
1. When did the girl set out from the coast? Was she caught in a storm or not? (*and*)
2. Did her boat strike a rock or not? Did she jump into the sea, or did she remain in the boat? (*so*)
3. How many miles did she swim that night?
4. When did she reach the shore?
5. What had she seen high up on the cliffs? Did she climb up or not? (*and*)
6. Where did she find herself a day later?

Composition

Rewrite these sentences using the correct verbs and joining words:
On Saturday I (wanted) (needed) to go to a football match. It (not only) (neither) rained all day (or) (but) it was cold as well, (but) (so) I (stayed) (waited) at home (and) (but) (watched) (looked) the match on television.

Letter-writing

Arrange the following heading in the correct order. Put in full stops or commas where necessary:
Grimsby/Lincs./17 Howland St./England/18th May, 19—

Key Structures

Where did he go? He went to the cinema. (Compare **KS 29**)
Read these sentences carefully. Pay close attention to the words in italics. We can often use phrases like these to answer questions beginning with *Where*, or *Which direction*.
a Phrases with *to* and *from*:
He flew *to Washington* last night. He will be flying *from Washington to Chicago* on Wednesday.

b Phrases with *into* and *out of*:

Where is Betty? She has just gone *into the kitchen*.

Where did you throw that piece of paper? I threw it *out of the* window.

c Phrases with *for*:

We set out *for the village* at six o'clock next morning.

George has left *for Scotland*.

d Phrases with *towards*:

The car came *towards me*.

She swam *towards the shore*.

e Phrases with *at*:

The boy threw a stone *at a dog*.

It is rude to point *at people*.

Exercises

A. Answer these questions about the passage:

1. Where did the girl set out from?
2. Where did she jump?
3. Where did she swim?

B. Supply the missing words in the following sentences:

1. Tell him to come . . . my office. I want to speak to him.
2. The ship sailed . . . the harbour and disappeared from sight.
3. We climbed . . . the top of the mountain.
4. The team set out . . . Australia yesterday.
5. This ship sails . . . Venice . . . London once a week.
6. He aimed . . . the bird, fired, and missed.
7. Please bring these things . . . the kitchen for me.
8. Have you received a letter . . . Alan yet?

C. Write sentences using the following:

1. bird/flew/the room. 2. parachutist/jumped/aeroplane.
3. child/pointed/fat lady. 4. put/milk/refrigerator.

Special Difficulties

Words Often Confused and Misused.

a Passed and Past. A week passed . . . (l. 1)

Study these examples:

He passed my house this morning. ('Passed' is a verb.)

He walked past my house.

He told me about his past experiences.

He seems to live in the past.

b Next and Other.

Study these examples:

Early next morning she saw a light ahead. (l. 10)

We arrived in Paris on Tuesday evening. The next day we went sight-seeing. (The day after.)

I saw Mary the other day. (A few days ago.)

Exercise

Choose the correct expressions in the following:

1. I tried to telephone you (the other day) (the next day). You must have been out.
2. Have you (past) (passed) your driving test?
3. On the first day all went well. But on the (next) (other) day there was a storm.
4. The crowd cheered as the soldiers marched (past) (passed).

34 Quick Work

Ted Robinson has been worried all the
week. Last Tuesday he received a letter
from the local police. In the letter he was
asked to call at the station. Ted wondered
5 why he was wanted by the police, but he
went to the station yesterday and now he
is not worried any more. At the station,
he was told by a smiling policeman that
his bicycle had been found. Five days
10 ago, the policeman told him, the bicycle
was picked up in a small village four hundred miles away. It is now being sent to
his home by train. Ted was most surprised when he heard the news. He was
15 amused too, because he never expected
the bicycle to be found. It was stolen
twenty years ago when Ted was a boy of fifteen!

a letter from the local police

Comprehension and Précis

Answer these questions *in not more than 55 words.*
1. Was Ted Robinson worried or not?
2. Whom had he received a letter from?
3. Where did he go yesterday?
4. Is he worried any more or not?
5. What have the police found?
6. Was Ted surprised or not? Was he amused or not? (*not only . . . but . . . as well*)
7. When was his bicycle stolen?
8. How old was he then?

Composition

Rewrite these sentences using the correct verbs and joining words:
The man was (not only) (neither) tired (nor) (but) hungry (as well) (either). (However)
(Therefore) all the hotels in the town (existed) (were) full, (but) (so) he went to the
police station. The police (put) (gave) him a meal (and) (but) a bed for the night.

Letter-writing

In the address we usually write 'St.' for 'Street'; 'Rd.' for 'Road'; 'Sq.' for 'Square';
'Ave.' for 'Avenue'; 'Pl.' for 'Place'. We write words like 'Lane' and 'Drive' in full.

Exercise
Write these words in the way shown above:
Place, Avenue, Street, Road, Square.

Key Structures

He was asked to call at the station.
Do you remember these sentences? (**KS 31**)
Prisoners of war built this bridge in 1942. (Who)
This bridge was built (by prisoners of war) in 1942. (What)

Now study these sentences:

They asked me to make a speech. (Who)
I was asked to make a speech. (Who)

You will notice that the form of the verb depends on the person or thing we mention first. We mention the most important person or thing first.

Instead of saying:	*We can say:*
They are sending *him* abroad.	*He* is being sent abroad.
The police were questioning *the man.*	*The man* was being questioned (by the police).
He told *me* to wait for him.	*I* was told to wait for him.
They have found *your wallet.*	*Your wallet* has been found.
He never expected them to find *the bicycle.*	He never expected *the bicycle* to be found.

Exercises

A. Answer these questions on the passage. Write a complete sentence in answer to each question:

1. Who has been worried all the week?
2. What was Ted asked to do?
3. What did Ted wonder?
4. What was Ted told at the station?
5. Where was Ted's bicycle picked up?
6. Where is the bicycle being sent?
7. What did Ted feel when he heard the news?
8. Why was Ted amused?
9. How long ago was the bicycle stolen?

B. Change the form of the phrases in italics. Do not refer to the passage until you finish the exercise:

1. *Something has worried Ted* all the week.
2. In the letter *they asked him* to call at the station.
3. Ted wondered why *the police wanted him.*
4. At the station, *a smiling policeman told him* that *they had found his bicycle.*
5. *They picked up the bicycle* in a small village.
6. *They are sending it* to his home by train.
7. *This amused him* because he never expected *them to find the bicycle. Someone stole it* twenty years ago.

Special Difficulties

Read these sentences. Each sentence contains the verb *call*. The verb has a different meaning in each sentence:

He was asked to *call at* the station. (ll. 3-4)
He *called out* to me but I did not hear him.
I *called on* George yesterday. (I paid him a short visit.)
She'll *call you up* tomorrow. (She will telephone you.)
It began to rain so we *called off* the match. (We cancelled it.)

Exercise

Supply the missing words in the following sentences:

1. I called you . . . five times yesterday. Were you out?
2. It's too late to go to the pictures. Why don't we call the whole thing . . .?
3. We called . . . to him but he could not hear us.
4. I called . . . the post-office on my way to work.

35 Stop Thief!

Roy Trenton used to drive a taxi. A short while ago, however, he became a bus-driver and he has not regretted it. He is finding his new work far more exciting.
5 When he was driving along Catford Street recently, he saw two thieves rush out of a shop and run towards a waiting car. One of them was carrying a bag full of money. Roy acted quickly and drove the bus
10 straight at the thieves. The one with the money got such a fright that he dropped the bag. As the thieves were trying to get away in their car, Roy drove his bus into the back of it. While the battered car was
15 moving away, Roy stopped his bus and telephoned the police. The thieves' car was badly damaged and easy to recognize. Shortly afterwards, the police stopped the car and both men were arrested.

He is finding his new work exciting

Comprehension and Précis

Answer these questions *in not more than 70 words.*
1. Is Roy finding his new job as a bus-driver exciting or not?
2. In which street did he see two thieves recently?
3. Were they running out of a shop, or were they running out of a bank? Where did Roy drive his bus? Did they drop the stolen money or not? Did they get into a car, or did they run away? (*and . . . so . . . and*)
4. Where did Roy drive his bus then? Did he damage their car or not? (*and*)
5. Whom did he telephone after this?
6. Were both men arrested later or did they get away?

Composition

Rewrite these sentences using the correct verbs and joining words:
The politician tried to (do) (make) a speech in the park (so) (but) no one (listened to) (heard) him. The audience shouted (and) (or) threw things (so) (but) the speaker got into his car and (drove) (ran) away.

Letter-writing

Supply commas or full stops where necessary in this heading:

20 Crawford Ave
Cranley
Dorset
England
October 4th 19—

Key Structures

Review **KS 74–89**
These things always happen. (**KS 74**)
What happened? (**KS 76**)
What has happened? (**KS 77**)
He used to work fourteen hours a day. (**KS 83**)
He was asked to call at the station. (**KS 89**)

Exercises
A. Underline all the verbs in the passage.

B. Give the correct form of the verbs in brackets. Do not refer to the passage until you finish the exercise.
Roy Trenton (drive) a taxi. A short while ago, however, he (become) a bus-driver and he (not regret) it. He (find) his new work far more exciting. When he (drive) along Catford Street recently, he (see) two thieves rush out of a shop and run towards a waiting car. One of them (carry) a bag full of money. Roy (act) quickly and (drive) the bus straight at the thieves. The one with the money (get) such a fright that he (drop) the bag. As the thieves (try) to get away in their car, Roy (drive) his bus into the back of it. While the battered car (move) away, Roy (stop) his bus and (telephone) the police. The thieves' car badly (damage) and easy to recognize. Shortly afterwards, the police (stop) the car and both men (arrest).

C. Give the correct form of the verbs in brackets:
1. This is what I (mean). (. . . you understand) me?
2. Years ago, he (smoke) but he (not smoke) any more.
3. The new Town Hall (complete) last week.
4. I (not see) him since 1961.
5. She (drop) her handkerchief as she (cross) the road.

Special Difficulties

So and Such
Study these examples:
The one with the money got such a fright that he dropped the bag. (ll. 10–12)
He was so tired that he could not wake up.
You should not speak to such people. (People of this sort.)
You mustn't be so impatient.

Exercise
Supply *so*, *such*, or *such a* in these sentences:
1. He ran . . . quickly that I could not catch him.
2. Whoever told you . . . thing?
3. You should not make . . . many mistakes.
4. You should not say . . . things.
5. This picture is . . . beautiful that I shall hang it in my room.
6. It was . . . good book that it was bought by a film company.
7. It was . . . extraordinary exhibition that I went twice.
8. He is . . . lazy boy that he never does anything.

36 Across the Channel

Erna Hart is going to swim across the English Channel tomorrow. She is going to set out from the French coast at five o'clock in the morning. Erna is only four-
5 teen years old and she hopes to set up a new world record. She is a strong swim-mer and many people feel that she is sure to succeed. Erna's father will set out with her in a small boat. Mr Hart has trained
10 his daughter for years. Tomorrow he will be watching her anxiously as she swims the long distance to England. Erna in-tends to take short rests every two hours. She will have something to drink but she
15 will not eat any solid food. Most of Erna's school friends will be waiting for her on the English coast. Among them will be Erna's mother, who swam the Channel herself when she was a girl.

short rests every two hours

Comprehension and Précis

Answer these questions *in not more than 55 words.*
1. Who is going to swim across the English Channel tomorrow?
2. How old is she? Is she a strong swimmer or not? (*and*)
3. Whom has Erna been trained by?
4. Will he follow her in a small boat or not?
5. Where will Erna's mother be waiting?
6. What did she do as a girl?

Composition

Rewrite these sentences using the correct verbs and joining words:
The man on the raft saw the boat (so) (but) he tried to send a signal. He (took off) (put out) his shirt (or) (and) (waved) (shook) it (but) (so) the men on the boat (neither) (either) saw (or) (nor) (heard) (listened to) him.

Letter-writing

We do not always write the names of areas or postal districts in full when writing the address. Sometimes we write part of a name or only capital letters. For instance: 'Berks.' stands for 'Berkshire'; 'Calif.' for 'California'; 'N.W. 3' for 'North West 3'; 'N.Y.' for 'New York'.

Exercise
Write these words again in the way they might appear in an address:
Street, Road, Avenue, Square, Place, New York, West 8, South West 3.

Key Structures

She is going to swim across the Channel tomorrow.

Instead of saying: (**KS 35**)	*We can say:*
I shall travel by air.	I am going to travel by air.
He will sell his car.	He is going to sell his car.

They will move to a new house.   They are going to move to a new house.
I intend to write to him.   I am going to write to him.
She means to ask for an explanation.   She is going to ask for an explanation.
We can often use *going to* in place of *shall* or *will* in simple statements and questions.
(**KS** 13) We cannot use *going to* in sentences like this one:
You will enjoy yourself if you travel by sea.

Exercises
A. Underline the verbs in the passage which tell us *what will happen, what is going to happen,* and *what will be happening.* (**KS** 37)

B. Give the correct form of the verbs in brackets. Do not refer to the passage until you finish the exercise:
Erna Hart (swim) across the English Channel tomorrow. She (set out) from the French coast at five o'clock in the morning. Erna is only fourteen years old and she hopes to set up a new world record. Erna's father (set out) with her in a small boat. Mr Hart has trained his daughter for years. Tomorrow he (watch) her anxiously as she swims the long distance to England. Erna intends to take short rests every two hours. She (have) something to drink but she (not eat) any solid food. Most of Erna's school friends (wait) for her on the English coast. Among them (be) Erna's mother, who swam the Channel herself when she was a girl.

C. Write these sentences again. Use *going to* in place of the verbs in italics:
1. We *intend to* leave at six o'clock.
2. I *intend to* pay these bills tomorrow.
3. *Do* you *intend to* write to him?
4. She *does not intend to* look for a new job.
5. When *do* you *intend to* buy a new car?

Special Difficulties

Words Often Confused
a Watch, Look at, Follow.
Watch (something happening): Tomorrow he will be watching her anxiously. (ll. 10–11)
Look at : Look at the blackboard. Look at your book. Look at this picture.
Follow (go after): I followed my mother into the kitchen.

b Solid, Firm, Stable.
Solid (not liquid): She will not eat any solid food. (ll. 14–15)
Firm (not loose): I've fixed that hook. It is firm now.
(not doubtful): He gave me a firm refusal.
(not lenient): You must be very firm with that child.
Stable (often describing character): He is a very stable person.

Exercise
Use any of the above words in the following sentences:
1. I came to a . . . decision and I will not change my mind.
2. I stood on the bridge and . . . the boats passing by.
3. May I . . . your photograph album?
4. The ice in the pond is so . . . that you can walk on it.
5. I tried to persuade him but he remained . . .

37 The Olympic Games

The Olympic Games will be held in our country in four years' time. As a great many people will be visiting the country, the government will be building new
5 hotels, an immense stadium, and a fine new swimming pool. They will also be building new roads and a special railway-line. The Games will be held just outside the capital and the whole area will be
10 called 'Olympic City'. Workers will have completed the new roads by the end of this year. By the end of next year, they will have finished work on the new stadium. The fine modern buildings have
15 been designed by Kurt Gunter. Every-body will be watching anxiously as the new buildings go up. We are all very excited and are looking forward to the Olympic Games because they have never been held before in this country.

looking forward to the Olympic Games

Comprehension and Précis

Answer these questions *in not more than 70 words.*
1. When will the Olympic Games be held in our country? Where will the government be putting up new buildings? (*so*)
2. Who has designed the buildings? When will workers have completed the new stadium? (*and*)
3. Will the Games be held in this country for the first time or not? Are we looking forward to them or not? (*and*)

Composition

Rewrite the following sentences using the joining words in brackets:
1. My brother is going to the Olympic Games. I am going to the Olympic Games. (*Both . . . and*)
2. We bought tickets a long time ago. We shall be leaving soon. (*and*)
3. We shall see the Games. We shall visit many parts of the country. (*not only . . . but . . . as well*)

Letter-writing

We must write the date in full under the address. We can write the date in two ways: e.g. 17th April, 19— or April 17th, 19—. Numbers are written as follows: 1st (the first); 2nd (the second); 3rd (the third); 4th (the fourth) etc.

Exercise
Write these dates as they would appear in a letter:
May 6; June 21; July 30; March 3; April 22; July 1.

Key Structures

Workers will have completed the new roads by the end of this year.

a Do you remember these sentences: (**KS 37**)

Now	*Tomorrow*
I am writing letters now.	I shall be writing letters all day tomorrow.
I'll see you tomorrow.	I'll be seeing you tomorrow.

b Compare these two questions and answers:

When will they finish this bridge?

They will finish it next year.

When will they have finished this bridge?

They will have finished this bridge in a year's time.

Study these examples:

I shall have completed this novel by next June.

He will have moved to a new flat in two months' time.

You will have learnt the results of the examination by then.

I shall have received a reply by this time tomorrow.

Exercises

A. Underline the verbs in the passage which tell us *what will happen*, *what will be happening*, and *what will have happened*.

B. Give the correct form of the verbs in brackets. Do not refer to the passage until you finish the exercise:

The Olympic Games (hold) in our country in four years' time. As a great many people (visit) the country, the government (build) new hotels, an immense stadium, and a fine new swimming pool. They also (build) new roads and a special railway-line. The Games (hold) just outside the capital and the whole area (call) 'Olympic City'. Workers (complete) the new roads by the end of this year. By the end of next year they (finish) work on the new stadium. The fine modern buildings have been designed by Kurt Gunter. Everybody (watch) anxiously as the new buildings go up.

Special Difficulties

a Hold. The Olympic Games will be held in our country. (ll. 1–2)

This verb may be used in the sense of 'conduct', 'observe' or 'celebrate'. Study these examples:

A festival is held at Edinburgh every year.

We are going to hold a meeting tomorrow to discuss the subject.

The next conference will be held in Geneva.

b Study these sentences. The verb *look* has a different meaning in each sentence:

Look forward to (expect with pleasure): I am looking forward to the summer holidays.

Look out (be careful): Look out! A bus is coming.

Look up (get information from a reference book): I don't understand this word. I shall
      look it up in a dictionary.

      (visit): Don't forget to look me up when you return.

Exercise

Supply the correct form of *hold* or *look* in these sentences:

1. We shall be . . . a party tomorrow. I am . . . it very much.
2. . . . ! You nearly knocked that jug over!
3. They say he is very famous. I shall . . . him . . . in 'Who's Who'.
4. The students' union . . . an interesting debate on capital punishment yesterday.
5. My friend Ingrid lives in Stockholm. Why don't you . . . her . . . when you're there?
6. Examinations will be . . . next week. I'm not . . . them.

38 Everything Except the Weather

My old friend, Harrison, had lived in the Mediterranean for many years before he returned to England. He had often dreamed of retiring in England and had
5 planned to settle down in the country. He had no sooner returned than he bought a fine house and went to live there. Almost immediately he began to complain about the weather, for even though it was still
10 summer, it rained continually and it was often bitterly cold. After so many years of sunshine, Harrison got a shock. He acted as if he had never lived in England before. In the end, it was more than he could
15 bear. He had hardly had time to settle down when he sold the house and left the country. The dream he had had for so many years ended there. Harrison had thought of everything except the weather.

He dreamed of retiring in England

Comprehension and Précis

Answer these questions in not more than 60 words.

1. Where had the writer's friend, Harrison, spent many years? What did he want to do? What did he buy? (*but . . . so*)
2. Was the summer that year very good, or was it very bad? What did he complain about? (*and*)
3. Did Harrison sell the house in the end or not? Did he leave the country or not? (*Harrison not only . . . but also*)

Composition

Rewrite the following sentences using the joining words in brackets:
1. He bought an old car. It was in a very bad state. (*but*)
2. The engine was worn out. The gear-box was full of sawdust. (*The engine . . . not only . . . but . . . as well*)
3. He could not drive it. He could not sell it. He could not even give it away. (*neither . . . nor . . . nor*)

Letter-writing

The Date: The following months of the year are usually written in full: March, April, May, June and July. The remaining months are often written as follows: 'Jan.', 'Feb.', 'Aug.', 'Sept.', 'Oct.', 'Nov.', and 'Dec.'.

Exercise Write today's date in the way it should appear on a letter.

Key Structures

He acted as if he had never lived in England before.
a Do you remember these sentences? (**KS 39**)
The children ran away *after they had broken* the window.
As soon as the sun had set we returned to our hotel.

When he had finished lunch he asked for a glass of water.
I had not understood the problem until he explained it.

b Now study these sentences. They tell us *what happened some time ago* and *what had happened some time before.*
He *lived* in Scotland fifteen years *ago.*
He *had lived* in Scotland for fifteen years *before* he came to England.
The police *found* Billy Wilkins *last night.* He *had run away* from home five days *before.*
He *had spent* the last two nights near a farmhouse. The police *took* him home at once.
When she *saw* him, his mother *burst* into tears. She *said* he *had never run away before.*

Exercises
A. Underline the verbs in the passage which tell us *what happened some time ago* and *what had happened some time before.*

B. Give the correct form of the verbs in brackets. Do not refer to the passage until you finish your exercise.
My old friend, Harrison, (live) in the Mediterranean for many years before he (return) to England. He often (dream) of retiring in England and (plan) to settle down in the country. He no sooner (return) than he (buy) a fine house and (go) to live there. Almost immediately he (begin) to complain about the weather, for even though it (be) still summer, it (rain) continually and it (be) often bitterly cold. After so many years of sunshine, Harrison (get) a shock. He (act) as if he never (live) in England before. In the end, it (be) more than he could bear. He hardly (have) time to settle down when he (sell) the house and (leave) the country. The dream he (have) for so many years (end) there. Harrison (think) of everything except the weather.

Special Difficulties

Words Often Confused and Misused
a No sooner . . . than; hardly . . . when.
Study these examples:
He had no sooner returned than he bought a fine house. (ll. 6–7)
He had hardly had time to settle down when he sold the house. (ll. 15–16)

b Country and Countryside.
Study these examples:
He had planned to settle down in the country. (ll. 4–5)
He sold the house and left the country. (ll. 16–17)
The countryside around Vienna is very beautiful.

c Continuously and Continually.
Study these examples:
It rained continually. (l. 10) (i.e. At frequent intervals.)
The river flows under this bridge continuously. (i.e. It does not stop at all.)

Exercises
A. Join these sentences using *no sooner . . . than*:
1. I had left the house. It began to rain.
2. We had hung the picture on the wall. It fell down.

B. Choose the correct words in the following sentences:
1. The sea moves (continuously) (continually).
2. He borrows money from people (continuously) (continually).
3. The Robertsons do not live here any more. They now live in the (countryside) (country).

39 Am I All Right?

While John Gilbert was in hospital, he asked his doctor to tell him whether his operation had been successful, but the doctor refused to do so. The following
5 day, the patient asked for a bedside telephone. When he was alone, he telephoned the hospital exchange and asked for Doctor Millington. When the doctor answered the phone, Mr Gilbert said he was in-
10 quiring about a certain patient, a Mr John Gilbert. He asked if Mr Gilbert's operation had been successful and the doctor told him that it had been. He then asked when Mr Gilbert would be allowed
15 to go home and the doctor told him that he would have to stay in hospital for an-

asked for a bedside telephone

other two weeks. Then Dr Millington asked the caller if he was a relative of the patient. 'No,' the patient answered, 'I am Mr John Gilbert.'

Comprehension and Précis

Answer these questions *in not more than 60 words.*
1. What did Dr Millington refuse to tell his patient, John Gilbert?
2. Whom did the patient telephone next day? Whom did he inquire about? (*and*)
3. Did the doctor answer a number of questions about the patient or not? Did he ask whether the caller was a relative or not? (*and then*)
4. Did the caller then tell him who he was or not?

Composition

Rewrite the following sentences using the joining words in brackets:
1. After the telephone call, Dr Millington was angry. He went to Gilbert's room. (*so*)
2. Gilbert was telephoning the nurses. He was asking questions about himself. (*and*)
3. Then the doctor burst out laughing. The patient burst out laughing. (*both . . . and*)

Letter-writing

Write the following dates in the way they might appear on a letter:
3 January; February 28; 20 August; 13 September; October 22.

Key Structures

He said that . . . He told me . . . He asked . . . (KS 41)
'I am very tired,' he said.
What did he say?
He said that he was very tired.
He told me that he was very tired.

'Are you tired?' she asked.
What did she ask?
She asked if (or whether) you were tired.

'Will Jack arrive tomorrow?' Tom asked.
What did Tom ask?
Tom asked if (or whether) Jack would arrive the next day.

'When will Jack arrive?' Tom asked.
What did Tom ask?
Tom asked when Jack would arrive.

'Have you ever been abroad?' Mary asked.
What did Mary ask?
Mary asked if (or whether) you had ever been abroad.

'Why didn't you write to me?' Jane asked.
What did Jane ask?
Jane asked why I hadn't written to her.

Exercise
Here is part of the conversation between Mr Gilbert and Dr Millington:
1. 'I am inquiring about a certain patient,' Mr Gilbert said.
2. 'Was Mr Gilbert's operation successful?' he asked.
3. 'Yes, it was,' the doctor told him.
4. ' When will Mr Gilbert be allowed to go home?' he asked.
5. 'He will have to stay in hospital for another two weeks,' the doctor told him. 'Are you a relative of the patient?' Dr Millington asked the caller.
6. 'No,' the patient answered, 'I am Mr John Gilbert.'
Now answer these questions. Do not refer to the passage until you finish the exercise.
1. What did Mr Gilbert say?
2. What did he ask?
3. What did the doctor tell him?
4. What did he (Mr Gilbert) ask?
5. What did the doctor tell him? What did Dr Millington ask the caller?
6. What did the patient answer?

Special Difficulties

Speech Marks. (SD 74)

Exercise
Write this piece of conversation again using speech marks. Refer to the dialogue in the exercise above when you have finished:
I am inquiring about a certain patient, Mr Gilbert said. Was Mr Gilbert's operation successful? he asked. Yes, it was, the doctor told him. When will Mr Gilbert be allowed to go home? he asked. He will have to stay in hospital for another two weeks, the doctor told him. Are you a relative of the patient? Dr Millington asked the caller. No, the patient answered, I am Mr John Gilbert.

40 Food and Talk

Last week at a dinner-party, the hostess asked me to sit next to Mrs Rumbold. Mrs Rumbold was a large, unsmiling lady in a tight black dress. She did not even
5 look up when I took my seat beside her. Her eyes were fixed on her plate and in a short time, she was busy eating. I tried to make conversation.

'A new play is coming to "The Globe"
10 soon,' I said. 'Will you be seeing it?'

'No,' she answered.

'Will you be spending your holidays abroad this year?' I asked.

'No,' she answered.

15 'Will you be staying in England?' I asked.

'No,' she answered.

In despair, I asked her whether she was enjoying her dinner.

'Young man,' she answered, 'if you ate more and talked less, we would both
20 enjoy our dinner!'

a large, unsmiling lady

Comprehension and Précis
Answer these questions *in not more than 70 words.*
1. Where did the writer sit at the dinner-party?
2. Did he try to make conversation or not? Was she busy eating or not? (*but*)
3. Did he talk about the new play at 'The Globe' or not? Did he talk about the holidays or not? (*and*)
4. Did she answer his questions briefly or not?
5. Did he ask her if she was enjoying her dinner or not? What did she answer? (*Then . . . and*)

Composition
Rewrite the following sentences using the joining words in brackets:
1. She refused to answer any questions. She did not ask any questions (*not only . . . but . . . either*)
2. She was not interested in the theatre. She was not interested in travel. (*neither . . . nor*)
3. She liked eating good food. She did not like talking about it. (*but*)

Letter-writing
Rewrite the following dates in the way they would appear on a letter:
·2/3/65; 21/9/54; 13/8/61; 1/12/67; 22/1/66; 11/11/70.

Key Structures
If you ate more and talked less we would both enjoy our dinner.
a Do you remember these sentences: (**KS 43**)
If he is out, I'll call tomorrow.
You'll miss the train *if you don't hurry*.

If he is working I shall not disturb him.

If I have time, I shall be writing to him tomorrow.

Please don't disturb him *if he is busy*.

b Now study these sentences carefully:

If you went to the exhibition you would enjoy it.

If you saw him now you wouldn't recognize him.

Would he get annoyed *if I told* him about it?

If I were in your position, I would act differently.

He would help you *if he were* here.

If you could make him change his mind, you would save him a lot of trouble.

Exercise

Give the correct form of the verbs in brackets:

1. He would enjoy this if he (be) present.
2. She can do better if she (try).
3. If you play with matches you (burn) your fingers.
4. If you broke this window you (have to) pay for it.
5. If you (lose) your way you would have to ask a policeman.
6. If you (not apologize) he will never speak to you again.
7. If he (be) clever, he would not have any difficulty.
8. What would you do if you (win) a lot of money?
9. If I were you I (not be) so confident.
10. If you (can) help me I would be grateful.

Special Difficulties

Make and Do

Study these phrases:

a Make I tried to make conversation. (ll. 7 8)

When she had *made the beds* she went downstairs.

You mustn't *make so much noise*.

I *made a promise* never to see him again.

He's the sort of person who always *makes trouble*.

Do you think it will *make any difference*?

He is learning English but he hasn't *made much progress*.

He *made a lot of money* in South America.

I was asked to *make a speech*.

I'll never *make the same mistake* again.

I found it difficult to *make up my mind.*

b Do

He always *does his best*.

When did you *do your homework*?

Do me a favour please.

I *did a few jobs* about the house.

I can't *do any more work* today.

I want you to *do exercise* 24 on page 16.

I *did a lot of shopping* yesterday.

That shop *does very good business*.

Exercise

Supply the correct form of *make* or *do* in the following:

1. He . . . a mistake and I told him to . . . the exercise again.
2. He . . . business in Australia and . . . a lot of money.
3. I know you are . . . your best but you are not . . . very much progress.
4. After I had . . . the beds, I went out and . . . some shopping.

41 Do You Call That a Hat?

'Do you call that a hat?' I said to my wife.

'You needn't be so rude about it,' my wife answered as she looked at herself in the mirror.

5 I sat down on one of those modern chairs with holes in it and waited. We had been in the hat shop for half an hour and my wife was still in front of the mirror.

10 'We mustn't buy things we don't need,' I remarked suddenly. I regretted saying it almost at once.

'You needn't have said that,' my wife answered. 'I need not remind you of that

15 terrible tie you bought yesterday.'

'I find it beautiful,' I said. 'A man can never have too many ties.'

a hat like a lighthouse

'And a woman can't have too many hats,' she answered.

Ten minutes later we walked out of the shop together. My wife was wearing
20 a hat that looked like a lighthouse!

Comprehension and Précis

Answer these questions *in not more than 70 words*.
1. Was the writer's wife trying on a hat or not? Did he like it or not? (*but*)
2. Did he sit down or not? Did he wait for her or did he leave the shop? (*and*)
3. Did they begin arguing again or not? (*Then*)
4. What had he bought the day before? Did his wife like it or not? (*but*)
5. Did he say, 'A man can never have too many ties,' or did he say, 'A man can never have too many hats.'?
6. Did his wife use exactly the same argument or not? Did she buy the hat or not? (*and*)
7. What did it look like?

Composition

Rewrite the following sentences using the joining words in brackets:
1. My wife has too many hats. She has too many dresses. (*not only . . . but . . . as well*)
2. We have been invited to a party this evening. She does not want to go. (*but*)
3. She keeps looking at all those dresses. She keeps saying, 'I haven't got anything to wear!' (*and*)

Letter-writing

Rewrite the following dates in the way they would appear on a letter:
7/5/55; 1/10/68; 31/1/67; 18/2/63; 23/6/70; 17/4/27.

Key Structures

Must, Have to and Need

a Do you remember these sentences: (**KS 45**)
I must leave now. I have (got) to leave now.
He must be a fool.

b Now study these sentences:

I need a new hat. I must buy one.
He needs a haircut. He must have one.
I won't buy that. I don't need it.

c Instead of saying: *We can say:*
You needn't wait for me.   You don't have to wait for me.
You needn't have waited for me.   You didn't have to wait for me.

d Now compare *mustn't* and *needn't* in these sentences:
    You mustn't make a noise. The children are asleep.
    You needn't drive so quickly; we have plenty of time.
Or: You don't have to (haven't got to) drive so quickly; we have plenty of time.

    You mustn't smoke in a theatre. It is forbidden.
    You needn't come with us if you don't want to.
Or: You don't have to (haven't got to) come with us if you don't want to.

Exercises

A. Study the use of *need*, *needn't* and *mustn't* in the passage.

B. Supply *need*, *needn't* and *mustn't* in the following. Do not refer to the passage until you finish the exercise:
1. 'You ... be so rude about it,' my wife answered as she looked at herself in the mirror.
2. 'We ... buy things we don't ...,' I remarked suddenly.
3. 'You ... have said that,' my wife answered. 'I ... not remind you of that terrible tie you bought yesterday.

C. Supply *mustn't* or *needn't* in these sentences:
1. You ... leave your car here. Can't you see the 'No Parking' sign?
2. I ... go to bed late tonight. I have to get up early tomorrow.
3. You ... finish your soup if you don't like it.
4. You ... push. There's plenty of room on the bus.
5. You ... read in bed. It's bad for your eyes.

Special Difficulties

Words Often Confused.
Remark, Observe, and Notice.
Study these examples:
'We mustn't buy things we don't need,' I remarked. (ll. 10–11)
'We mustn't buy things we don't need,' I observed.
He observed me carefully. (He looked at me.)
Did you notice how she was dressed?

Exercise

Supply the correct form of *remark* or *notice* in the following:
1. 'That's a fine picture,' he ...
2. No one ... me when I entered the room.
3. He made a lot of rude ... about the hat she was wearing.
4. He failed to ... that I had changed the furniture round.

42 Not Very Musical

As we had had a long walk through one of the markets of Old Delhi, we stopped at a square to have a rest. After a time, we noticed a snake-charmer with two
5 large baskets at the other side of the square, so we went to have a look at him. As soon as he saw us, he picked up a long pipe which was covered with coins and opened one of the baskets. When he be-
10 gan to play a tune, we had our first glimpse of the snake. It rose out of the basket and began to follow the movements of the pipe. We were very much surprised when the snake charmer sud-
15 denly began to play jazz tunes and popular modern songs. The snake, however, continued to 'dance' slowly. It obviously could not tell the difference between Indian music and jazz!

began to play jazz tunes

Comprehension and Précis

Answer these questions *in not more than 70 words.*
1. What did we watch in a square in Old Delhi?
2. Did he have a long pipe and two large baskets or not?
3. Did he play a tune or not? What did the snake in one of the baskets do? (*and*)
4. Did the snake-charmer play modern tunes or not? Did the snake continue to dance slowly, or did it dance quickly? (*Then . . . but*)
5. Did it know the difference between Indian music and jazz or not?

Composition

Rewrite the following sentences using the joining words in brackets:
1. The snake-charmer opened his basket. He started to play a tune. The snake refused to move. (*and . . . but*)
2. The snake-charmer shook the basket. The snake obeyed him. (*Then . . . and*)
3. Everybody was frightened. These snakes are not dangerous. (*but*)

Letter-writing

Arrange the following headings in the correct order. Supply full stops and commas; make any other changes you consider necessary:
1. 84 Wiley Drive/Buxton/England/Derbyshire/8 January 19—
2. May 21 19—/New York/844 West 54th Street/N.Y./U.S.A.

Key Structures

Have
a Do you remember these sentences: (KS 47)

Instead of saying:	*We can say:*
He owns a new house.	He has a new house.
	Or: He has got a new house.
He possesses a lot of money.	He has a lot of money.
	Or: He has got a lot of money.

I took a bath before dinner. I had a bath before dinner.
I enjoyed myself at the party. I had a good time at the party.

b Sometimes we can use *have* in place of an ordinary verb.

Study these examples:
Instead of saying: *We can say:*
I *walked* in the garden. I *had a walk* in the garden.
He wanted to *drink* a glass of water. He wanted to *have a drink* of water.
We *will talk* about the problem to- We *will have a talk* about the problem to-
morrow. morrow.
Look at this. *Have a look* at this.

Exercises

A. Point out four examples in the passage where *have* is used in place of an ordinary verb.

B. Write these sentences again using *have* in place of the verbs in italics:
1. Yesterday I *rode* on a horse for the first time in my life.
2. I *was looking* at those old photographs last night.
3. He *washed* before going out.
4. I *swam* in the sea this morning.
5. Those two sailors *fought* in the bar last night.
6. Mary and John have been *quarrelling*.
7. He *tried* again. (Use 'another' in place of 'again').
8. She is *resting*.
9. I wanted to *smoke*.
10. Did you *sleep well last night*? (Use 'a good' in place of 'well'.)

Special Difficulties

See **SD 24** and **26**

Study these sentences. Each sentence contains the verb *pick*. This verb has a different meaning in each sentence:
He *picked up* a long pipe which was covered with coins. (ll. 7–8)
I shall *pick you up* in the car this evening.
I *picked up* a lot of English while I was in England. (I learnt.)
There are so many beautiful cards on display, I can't *pick out* the ones I like best. (I can't choose.)
Exercise
Use the correct form of the verb *pick* in place of the verbs in italics:
1. That book has fallen on the floor. Please *get* it for me.
2. I shall *collect* the parcel on my way to work.
3. I can't *select* the material I want.
4. Where did you *learn* those tricks?

43   Over the South Pole

In 1929, three years after his flight over
the North Pole, the American explorer,
R. E. Byrd, successfully flew over the
South Pole for the first time. Though, at
5 first, Byrd and his men were able to take
a great many photographs of the mountains that lay below, they soon ran into
serious trouble. At one point, it seemed
certain that their plane would crash. It
10 could only get over the mountains if it
rose to 10,000 feet. Byrd at once ordered
his men to throw out two heavy food
sacks. The plane was then able to rise and
it cleared the mountains by 400 feet.
15 Byrd now knew that he would be able to
reach the South Pole which was 300 miles
away, for there were no more mountains in sight. The aircraft was able to fly
over the endless white plains without difficulty.

flew over the South Pole

Comprehension and Précis

Answer these questions *in not more than 65 words.*
1. When did the American explorer, R. E. Byrd become the first man to fly over the South Pole?
2. Did he take a lot of photographs during the flight or not? Did he run into diffi-culties or not? (*but then*)
3. Could his plane get over the mountains or not? What did he order his men to do? (*so*)
4. Did the plane then fly over the mountains or did it crash? Did it continue without further trouble or not? (*and*)

Composition

Rewrite the following sentences using the joining words (conjunctions) in brackets:
1. Byrd stayed in the Antarctic for a year. He made many more flights. (*and*)
2. He went back to America in 1930. He returned to the Antarctic in 1946. (*but*)
3. This time he had 4000 men with him. He had thirteen ships and seventeen aero-planes. (*not only . . . but . . . as well*)

Letter-writing

1. Write your home address and the date in the way they would appear in a letter to a friend in your own country.
2. Write the address of a person who lives abroad.

Key Structures

Can and Able to
a Do you remember these sentences: (**KS 49a**)
Can I use your telephone?
Could I use your telephone?

b *Can* and *Able to*. Study these examples carefully:

Instead of saying:	*We can say:*
He will come if he *can*.	He will come if he *is able to*.
I *can* see you tomorrow.	I *shall be able to* see you tomorrow.
I *couldn't* understand him.	I *wasn't able to* understand him.
He said he *could* see me next week.	He said he *would be able to* see me next week.

c We must use *was able to* when we want to show that an action has been completed successfully. We cannot use *could* in these sentences:

He *was able to* go to London yesterday and he enjoyed himself very much.

He didn't agree with me at first but I *was able to* persuade him.

He *was able to* leave Europe before the war began.

Exercises

A. Underline the verbs *can* and *able to* in the passage.

B. Give the correct form of *can* and *able to* in this paragraph. Do not refer to the passage until you finish the exercise.

Though, at first, Byrd and his men . . . take a great many photographs of the mountains that lay below, they soon ran into serious trouble. At one point, it seemed certain that their plane would crash. It . . . only get over the mountains if it rose to 10,000 feet. Byrd at once ordered his men to throw out two heavy food sacks. The plane then . . . rise and it cleared the mountains by 400 feet. Byrd now knew that he . . . reach the South Pole which was 300 miles away, for there were no more mountains in sight. The aircraft . . . fly over the endless white plains without difficulty.

Special Difficulties

Phrases with At.

Study these examples:

At first Byrd and his men were able to take photographs. (ll. 4–6)

Byrd *at once* ordered his men to throw out two food sacks. (ll. 11–13)

Billy is not *at home at present*. He's *at school*.

After walking for several hours, we arrived at the village *at last*.

It's a pity you can't come to the concert. *At any rate* you'll be able to hear it on the radio.

I know he's often rude to people, but he's a very pleasant person *at heart*.

I didn't know you wouldn't be coming. *At least* you could have telephoned me.

He behaves very strangely *at times*.

I don't know what I can do about it. I'm completely *at a loss*.

Exercise

Use a phrase with *at* in place of the words in italics. Make any other necessary changes:

1. We found our way home *in the end*.
2. He stayed *in the house* all day yesterday.
3. You must write to him *immediately*.
4. He cannot see you *now* as he is busy.
5. He annoys me *sometimes*.
6. When I saw that the house was on fire I *didn't know what to do*.
7. *When it began* I thought it would be a good film but I was wrong.

44 Through the Forest

Mrs Anne Sterling did not think of the risk she was taking when she ran through a forest after two men. They had rushed up to her while she was having a picnic
5 at the edge of a forest with her children and tried to steal her handbag. In the struggle, the strap broke and, with the bag in their possession, both men started running through the trees. Mrs Sterling
10 got so angry that she ran after them. She was soon out of breath, but she continued to run. When she caught up with them, she saw that they had sat down and were going through the contents of the bag, so
15 she ran straight at them. The men got such a fright that they dropped the bag

The men got a fright

and ran away. 'The strap needs mending,' said Mrs Sterling later, 'but they did not steal anything.'

Comprehension and Précis

Answer these questions *in not more than 70 words.*
1. How many men tried to steal Mrs Sterling's handbag?
2. What was she doing at the time?
3. Did they take the bag after a struggle or not? Where did they run? (*and*)
4. Did she run after them or not? Did she catch up with them or not? (*and*)
5. Had the men sat down or not? What were they doing? (*and*)
6. What did Mrs Sterling do? What did they do? (*so*)

Composition

Rewrite the following sentences using the joining words in brackets:
1. Thieves can be very daring. They can be very timid. (*either . . . or*)
2. A thief once broke into a house. He stole some money. The lady of the house caught him. (*and . . . but*)
3. The thief gave back the money. He paid for the window he had broken. (*not only . . . but*)

Letter-writing

Addressing the envelope
The name and address must appear in the middle of the envelope. Titles are always used with names. Study these examples:
Mr James Thompson, James Thompson Esq., ('Esquire')
Miss H. Thompson, Mrs D. Thompson,
Mr and Mrs J. Thompson,

Exercise
Address an envelope to a friend who lives abroad.

Key Structures

Both men started running through the trees.

a Do you remember these sentences: (**KS 51**)

Eating is always a pleasure.

I am very keen on *cycling*.

He sat there without *saying* anything.

I must apologize for not *letting* you know earlier.

b Now study these examples:

I am looking forward to *seeing* him tomorrow. (**SD 96b**)

I am accustomed to *getting* up early.

I am used to *getting* up early.

(Compare: I used to get up early but I don't any more. **KS 83**)

c Instead of saying:	*We can say:*
The men started *to run* through the trees.	The men started *running* through the trees.
They began *to run.*	They began *running.*
They continued *to run.*	They continued *running.*

d Compare these sentences:

Now	*Always*
I hate *to disturb* you, but can I come in for a moment please?	I hate *disturbing* people when they are busy.
I'd love (or like) *to sit* in the garden.	I love (or like) *sitting* in the garden when it's fine.

e Study these expressions:

My shirt is torn. It needs *mending.*

Those windows are dirty. They want *washing.*

Exercises

A. There are some verbs in the passage which are similar in form to the examples given above. Can you find them?

B. Give the correct form of the verbs in brackets:

1. I'd love (see) that film. Will it be on tomorrow?
2. He's accustomed to (work) very hard.
3. These shirts need (iron).
4. I hate (leave) so early, but I'm afraid I have to.
5. They continued (argue) till after midnight.
6. Would you like (come) with me?
7. I shall be looking forward to (see) you soon.
8. You must never come into this room without (knock) first.
9. I got tired of (wait) so I left.
10. It began (rain) just as I was going out.
11. I don't believe in (work) too hard.
12. He accused me of (take) his umbrella.

Special Difficulties

Study these uses of the verbs *catch* and *run*:

When she *caught up with* them, she saw that they had sat down. (ll. 12–13) (When she reached them . . .)

They dropped the bag and *ran away.* (ll. 16–17)

Exercise

Write two sentences using each of the verbs given above.

45 A Clear Conscience

The whole village soon learnt that a large sum of money had been lost. Sam Benton, the local butcher, had lost his wallet while taking his savings to the post-office. Sam
5 was sure that the wallet must have been found by one of the villagers, but it was not returned to him. Three months passed, and then one morning, Sam found his wallet outside his front door. It had
10 been wrapped up in newspaper and it contained half the money he had lost, together with a note which said: 'A thief, yes, but only 50 per cent a thief!' Two months later, some more money was sent
15 to Sam with another note: 'Only 25 per cent a thief now!' In time, all Sam's

the local butcher lost his wallet

money was paid back in this way. The last note said: 'I am 100 per cent honest now!'

Comprehension and Précis

Answer these questions *in not more than 70 words.*
1. Where was the local butcher, Sam Benton, taking his savings? What did he lose? (*but*)
2. Did Sam receive half his money three months later, or did he receive all his money? Did he receive a note or not? (*not only . . . but . . . as well*)
3. What did the note say?
4. Did the thief include a note every time he sent Sam more money or not?
5. What did the last note say?

Composition

Rewrite the following sentences using the joining words in brackets:
1. Sam told everybody about the wallet. He did not try to find the thief. (*but*)
2. The man was not really a thief. He needed money badly. (*but*)
3. He paid back the money. He bought himself a clear conscience. (*not only . . . but also*)

Letter-writing

Address an envelope to a married lady who lives abroad.

Key Structures

Review **KS 31, 53,** and **89.**
a Do you remember these sentences:
This bridge was built in 1942.
The thief was arrested by the police. (**KS 31**)
I can't find my bag. It must have been stolen.
I must be paid for this. (**KS 53**)
I was told to wait for him.
He never expected the bicycle to be found. (**KS 89**)

b Now study these examples:

Instead of saying:	We can say:
I found out that *someone had sent the parcel* to the wrong address.	I found out that *the parcel had been sent* to the wrong address.
He told me *the police had arrested the thief*.	He told me the *thief had been arrested* (by the police).

Exercises

A. There are some verbs in the passage which are similar in form to the examples given above. Can you find them?

B. Change the form of the expressions in italics. Do not refer to the passage until you finish the exercise:

The whole village soon learnt that *someone had lost a large sum of money*. Sam Benton, the local butcher, had lost his wallet while taking his savings to the post-office. Sam was sure that *one of the villagers must have found the wallet*, but *no one returned it to him*. Three months passed, and then one morning, Sam found his wallet outside his front door. *Someone had wrapped it up* in newspaper and it contained half the money he had lost, together with a note which said: 'A thief, yes, but only 50 per cent a thief!' Two months later, *someone sent more money* to Sam with another note: 'Only 25 per cent a thief now!' In time, *someone paid back all Sam's money* in this way.

C. Change the form of the verbs in italics. Omit the word *someone* from each sentence:
1. Someone *has prepared* a meal for you.
2. Someone *will translate* the book into English.
3. Someone *must send* a telegram to him.
4. Someone *had put out* the fire before the fire-brigade arrived.
5. Someone *gave* the cat some milk to drink.

Special Difficulties

a Words Often Confused: Steal and Rob.
Steal (something from someone or somewhere): A thief broke into the building last night and stole some money from the safe.
Rob (someone of something): Two thieves attacked him last night and robbed him of all his money.
(a building, a bank, a house etc.) The police have caught the men who robbed the bank.

b Pay back. Study these examples:
All Sam's money was paid back. (ll. 16–17) (It was repaid).
I'll pay you back for what you did to me. (I'll get my revenge on you for what you did to me.)

Exercise
Supply *steal*, *rob* or *back* in the following sentences:
1. Please lend me £5. I'll pay you . . . next week.
2. His house was . . . last night. Thieves broke in and . . . several valuable pictures.
3. He threatened that he would pay me . . . but he hasn't done so yet.
4. The bank clerk . . . some money from the safe.
5. A stranger attacked an old man in the train and . . . him of all his money.

46 Expensive and Uncomfortable

When a plane from London arrived at Sydney airport, workers began to unload a number of wooden boxes which contained clothing. No one could account for
5 the fact that one of the boxes was extremely heavy. It suddenly occurred to one of the workers to open up the box. He was astonished at what he found. A man was lying in the box on top of a pile
10 of woollen goods. He was so surprised at being discovered that he did not even try to run away. After he was arrested, the man admitted hiding in the box before the plane left London. He had had a long
15 and uncomfortable trip, for he had been confined to the wooden box for over ten hours. The man was ordered to pay £345 for the cost of the trip. The normal price of a ticket is £230!

he did not try to run away

Comprehension and Précis

Answer these questions *in not more than 70 words.*
1. Where did the plane from London arrive? What did workers unload from it? (*and*)
2. What did they contain?
3. Was one of the boxes extremely heavy or not? What did a worker do? (*so*)
4. What did he find on top of a pile of woollen goods?
5. Was the man arrested or not?
6. Had he travelled in the box from London or from Sydney?
7. How much did he have to pay?
8. How much does an ordinary ticket cost?

Composition

Rewrite the following sentences using the joining words in brackets:
1. The man had had an uncomfortable trip. He was very hungry. (*not only . . . but . . . as well*)
2. He had not eaten anything for thirteen hours. He had not drunk anything for thirteen hours. (*neither . . . nor*)
3. Woollen goods cannot be eaten. At least they are soft. The man had had a few hours' sleep. (*but . . . so*)

Letter-writing

1. Write your home address and the date in the way they would appear in a letter to a friend who lives abroad.
2. Write the address of a friend who lives abroad in the way it would appear in a letter to you.

Key Structures

Verbs followed by: To, At, For and With. (Compare **KS 55**)
We can put *to*, *at*, *for* and *with* after certain verbs.
Compare: I saw Tom yesterday.
            I shall see *to* the dinner tonight. (I shall prepare it.)
Use this list for reference:

a TO: accustom(ed), amount, appeal, apply (or for), attach(ed), attend, belong, chal-
lenge, compare (or with), condemn(ed), confess, confine, consent, convert, entitle(d),
listen, mention, object, occur, prefer, react (or against), reply, respond, see, submit,
surrender, turn, yield.

b AT: amuse(d) (or by), arrive (or in), astonish(ed) (or by), exclaim, glance, guess,
knock (**SD 24**), look (**SD 96b**), point (or to), shock(ed) (or by), stare, surprise(d) (or
by), wonder (or about), work (or on).

c FOR: account, ask (or of), act (or on), apologize, blame, beg, call (**SD 90**), charge,
exchange, hope, look, mistake, mourn, pay (**SD 112b**), prepare, provide, search, thank,
vote (or on) (**KS 55d**), wait (or on).

d WITH: agree, begin, communicate, compare (or to), compete (or against), comply,
confuse, contrast (or to), cope, correspond, disgust(ed), finish, help (or in), interfere
(or in) mix, occupi(ed), part, please(d), quarrel (or about), reason, satis(fied) (or by),
threaten(ed).

Exercises

A. Point out verbs in the passage which are followed by *to*, *at*, or *for*.

B. Supply the missing words (*to*, *at*, *for* and *with*) without referring to the above
lists as far as possible:

1. I don't agree . . . you. 2. She preferred . . . wait . . . him. 3. We have been corre-
sponding . . . each other for years. 4. How do you account . . . this? 5. Do you object
. . . my smoking? 6. I'm surprised . . . you! 7. You must reply . . . his letter. 8. He has
some important business to attend . . . 9. Do you mean to say you exchanged that
lovely car . . . this? 10. Has it occurred . . . you that she must have arrived . . . London
Airport by now? 11. I was shocked . . . his indifference! 12. You must comply . . . the
rules of the game. 13. Poor Mary! She has so much to cope . . .! 14. Please don't mention it . . . my husband, but I paid £10 . . . this hat. 15. She was quite unprepared . . .
the news. 16. Don't blame me . . . the accident! 17. I'm disgusted . . . your behaviour!
18. You forgot to thank Aunt Jane . . . her present. 19. It is rude to stare . . . people.
20. I'm not satisfied . . . your work. 21. His debt now amounts . . . £100. 22. Mix
the contents of this packet . . . a little water. 23. I knocked . . . the door. 24. Whom
does this book belong . . .? 25. I reasoned . . . him, but he would not listen . . . me.
26. She's accustomed . . . living in comfort. She'll never part . . . her precious pos-
sessions. 27. At what time will you call . . . me? 28. The spy surrendered himself . . .
the enemy and was condemned . . . death. 29. I've looked . . . it everywhere, but I can't
find it. 30. I'll see . . . the cooking tonight. 31. I must apologize . . . keeping you waiting. 32. The class failed to respond . . . the teacher's new methods. 33. He turned . . .
me for help, even after I had quarrelled . . . him. 34. Like Micawber, I hope . . . something better. 35. Please apply . . . the secretary for information. 36. There was a note
attached . . . the parcel. 37. Just guess . . . the price of this carpet. 38. How long have
you been working . . . this exercise? 39. The concert began . . . a piece by an un-
known composer. 40. How much did they charge you . . . that?

47 A Thirsty Ghost

A public house which was recently bought by Mr Ian Thompson is up for sale. Mr Thompson is going to sell it because it is haunted. He told me that he could not go
5 to sleep one night because he heard a strange noise coming from the bar. The next morning, he found that the doors had been blocked by chairs and the furniture had been moved. Though Mr
10 Thompson had turned the lights off before he went to bed, they were on in the morning. He also said that he had found five empty whisky bottles which the ghost must have drunk the night before.
15 When I suggested that some villagers must have come in for a free drink, Mr

five empty bottles which the ghost must have drunk

Thompson shook his head. The villagers have told him that they will not accept the inn even if he gives it away.

Comprehension and Précis

Answer these questions *in not more than 70 words.*
1. What did Mr Ian Thompson buy recently? Is it haunted or not? What is he going to do with it? (*but . . . so*)
2. Was there a strange noise in the bar one night or not? Was the room in disorder next morning or not? (*and*)
3. What else did Mr Thompson find?
4. Does he believe that some villagers broke into the bar and had a drink or not?
5. Does anybody in the village want to buy the inn?

Composition

Rewrite the following sentences using the joining words in brackets:
1. One night Mr Thompson heard a noise. He went downstairs. (*and*)
2. In the bar, five men were drinking whisky. They did not see him. (*but*)
3. Mr Thompson put a sheet over his head. He went into the bar. (*and*)
4. The villagers ran away in fear. They never came back again. (*and*)

Letter-writing

Write your name and home address in the way they would appear on an envelope.

Key Structures

Review **KS 93–111**
She is going to swim across the Channel tomorrow. (**KS 93**)
Workers will have completed the new roads by the end of this year. (**KS 96**)
He acted as if he had never lived in England before. (**KS 97**)
He said that . . . He told me . . . He asked . . . (**KS 99**)
If you ate more and talked less we would both enjoy our dinner. (**KS 101**)
Must, Have to and Need. (**KS 104**)

Have. (**KS 105**)
Can and Able to. (**KS 107**)
A large sum of money had been lost. (**KS 111**)

Exercises
A. Underline all the verbs in the passage. Revise any Key Structures you have forgotten.

B. Give the correct form of the verbs in brackets. Do not refer to the passage until you finish the exercise:
A public house which recently (buy) by Mr Ian Thompson is up for sale. Mr Thompson (sell) it because it (haunt). He told me that he (can) not go to sleep one night because he (hear) a strange noise coming from the bar. The next morning he (find) that the doors (block) by chairs and the furniture (move). Though Mr Thompson (turn) the lights off before he (go) to bed, they (be) on in the morning. He also (say) that he (find) five empty whisky bottles which the ghost (must drink) the night before. When I (suggest) that some villagers (must come) in for a free drink, Mr Thompson (shake) his head. The villagers (tell) him that they (not accept) the inn even if he (give) it away.

C. Give the correct form of the verbs in brackets:
1. By the end of next year they (finish) work on the new stadium.
2. If you (break) this window, you would have to pay for it.
3. He would enjoy the concert if he (be) present.
4. If you (can) help me I would be grateful.

D. Supply *mustn't* or *needn't* in these sentences:
1. I . . . go to bed late tonight. I have to get up early tomorrow.
2. You . . . finish your soup if you don't like it.

E. Read this paragraph, then answer the questions below:
1. 'What are these people looking at?' I asked George.
2. 'I don't know,' George answered. 'I think a new road is being built. It will be finished soon.'
3. George and I joined the crowd. 'All these people are very silly,' I whispered to George. 'They are looking into an empty hole.'
4. 'Some people enjoy watching others work,' George said.
5. Half an hour passed. Suddenly George said to me, 'Hurry up! We've been here for half an hour.' Then he added, 'There is nothing to see in an empty hole.'
6. 'I don't want to go yet,' I answered. 'It's very interesting.'

Questions
1. What did I ask George?
2. What did George answer? What did he think?
3. Why did I tell George that all those people were very silly?
4. What did George say?
5. How much time passed? What did George tell me to do? How long had we been there? What did he add?
6. What did I answer?

48 Did You Want to Tell Me Something?

Dentists always ask questions when it is impossible for you to answer. My dentist had just pulled out one of my teeth and had told me to rest for a while. I tried to
5 say something, but my mouth was full of cotton-wool. He knew I collected birds' eggs and asked me whether my collection was growing. He then asked me how my brother was and whether I
10 liked my new job in London. In answer to these questions I either nodded or made strange noises. Meanwhile, my tongue was busy searching out the hole where the tooth had been. I suddenly felt
15 very worried, but could not say anything. When the dentist at last removed the

I suddenly felt very worried

cotton-wool from my mouth, I was able to tell him that he had pulled out the wrong tooth.

Comprehension and Précis
Answer these questions *in not more than 75 words.*
1. Had the dentist in the story pulled out one of the writer's teeth or not? What had he told him to do? (*and*)
2. Did he ask several questions or not? Could the writer answer them or not? (*but*)
3. What was his mouth full of?
4. Did he suddenly discover something wrong or not? Could he say anything or not? (*but*)
5. What did the dentist eventually remove from his mouth? What did the writer tell him? (*and*)

Composition
Rewrite the following sentences using the joining words in brackets:
1. The dentist smiled. He showed me the tooth. (*and*)
2. He had pulled out the right one. I had not realized it. (*but*)
3. I had made a mistake. I had criticized his work. (*not only . . . but . . . as well*)

Letter-writing
Arrange the following heading in the correct order. Supply full stops and commas; make any other changes you consider necessary.
England/Seaview Hotel/Princes' Avenue/23 September 19—/Brighton.

Special Difficulties
Review: **SD 74–112**

Exercises
A. Words Often Confused.
Choose the correct words in the following sentences:
1. The new school, (which) (who) has just been completed, is a fine building. (**SD 78**)

2. He (denied) (refused) that he had taken it. (**SD 80a**)
3. The waiter (took) (fetched) me a clean glass. (**SD 80b**)
4. He is (too) (very) ill to do any work. (**SD 80c**)
5. I had a few (works) (jobs) to do in town this morning. (**SD 84c**)
6. (A) (One) day I spoke to (one) (a) man (who) (whom) had won the Nobel Prize. (**SD 78, 86**)
7. A bird flew (past) (passed) my window. (**SD 88a**)
8. We spent the first day of our holidays in Geneva. The (next) (other) day we went to Basle. (**SD 88b**)
9. I spent the afternoon (watching) (following) the match. (**SD 94a**)
10. Ships (continuously) (continually) cross the sea. (**SD 98c**)
11. 'Did you take that book from the shelf?' he (remarked) (noticed) suddenly. (**SD 104**)
12. The bank has been (stolen) (robbed). (**SD 112a**)

B. Write sentences using *so*, *such*, or *such a* with the following words: trouble, beautiful, nice day, tired. (**SD 92**)

C. Join these sentences using *no sooner . . . than*. (**SD 98a**)
1. He had come home. They rang him up from the office.
2. The plane had taken off. It returned to the airport.

D. Supply the correct form of *make* or *do* in the following sentences: (**SD 102**)
1. He has . . . good progress.
2. You never . . . a job properly.
3. Why can't you . . . up your mind?
4. I have to go out now. I must . . . some shopping.
5. . . . me a favour, will you?
6. Don't . . . such a noise.
7. You have just . . . a mistake.
8. He always . . . his best.

E. *Put* (**SD 76**); *call* (**SD 90**); *look* (**SD 96b**); *pick* (**SD 106**); *catch* (**SD 110**); *pay* (**SD 112b**).
Complete these sentences by adding any of the following words: up with, up, off, out, away.
1. Have they put . . . that forest fire?
2. Haven't you learnt how to look . . . a word in the dictionary?
3. I tried to call her . . . but her phone was out of order.
4. Pick . . . all those toys and put them . . .
5. If you can't find a room at the hotel, I can put you . . .
6. Look . . .! That bus nearly hit you!
7. I'll pay . . . the money I borrowed as soon as I can.
8. I can't put . . . . . . those children any longer.
9. He's so far ahead of you, you'll never catch . . . . . . him.

F. Phrases with *at*. (**SD 108**)
Use each of the following phrases in sentences:
at once, at a loss, at last, at present, at home.

IF YOU CAN DO THIS TEST GO ON TO UNIT 3

Key Structures

A. Word Order in Compound Statements.
Join these pairs of sentences. Use the joining words in brackets:
1. He read the book. He returned it to the library. (*and*)
2. The boy climbed the tree. He picked some apples. (*and*)
3. I opened the door. He came into the hall. (*and*)
4. He looked for his pen. He could not find it. (*but*)
5. She called to him. He did not answer her. (*but*)
6. Everyone was out. I left a message. (*so*)
7. He plays soccer. He plays rugby. (*both . . . and*)
8. Children enjoy holidays. Adults enjoy holidays. (*both . . . and*)
9. He must be very clever. He must be very foolish. (*either . . . or*)
10. George does not play football. John does not play football. (*neither . . . nor*)
11. George does not play soccer. He does not play rugby. (*neither . . . nor*)
12. He does not know. He does not care. (*neither . . . nor*)
13. He forgot to take his umbrella. He forgot to take his briefcase. (*not only . . . but . . . as well*)

B. Verbs.
a These things always happen.
What is happening? What always happens?
Give the correct form of the verbs in brackets:
'Some people still (believe) the world is flat,' he said.
'You (joke),' I replied. 'I (not know) anyone who does.'
'Well, you (know) me,' he replied. 'I (believe) that the earth is flat. I met a man the other day. I (forget) his name now. He said that the earth (look) like a flat dish.'
'. . . you (try) to tell me that you (believe) him?' I asked.
'I certainly do,' he answered. 'I (think) that he is right.'
'And which side of the dish . . . you (live) on?
'Oh, I (not know). He didn't tell me that!'

b What happened?
The verbs in brackets tell us *what happened*. Give the correct form of each verb:
Late in the afternoon, the boys (put) up their tent in the middle of a field. Then they (cook) a meal over an open fire. They were all hungry and the food (smell) good. After a wonderful meal, they (tell) stories and (sing) songs by the camp fire. But some time later it (begin) to rain. The boys (feel) tired so they (put) out the fire and (creep) into their tent.

c What happened? What has happened?
The verbs in brackets tell us *what happened* and *what has happened*. Give the correct form of each verb:
Captain Ben Fawcett has bought an unusual taxi and (begin) a new service. The 'taxi' is a small Swiss aeroplane called a 'Pilatus Porter'. This wonderful plane can carry seven passengers. Captain Fawcett's first passenger (be) a doctor who (fly) from Birmingham to a lonely village in the Welsh mountains. Since then, Captain Fawcett (fly) passengers to many unusual places. Once he (land) on the roof of a block of flats

and on another occasion, he (land) in a deserted car park. Captain Fawcett just (refuse) a strange request from a business-man. The man (want) to fly to Rockall, but Captain Fawcett (not take) him because the trip (be) too dangerous.

d What was happening? What happened? What used to happen?
The verbs in brackets tell us *what was happening, what happened*, and *what used to happen*. Give the correct form of each verb:
Yesterday afternoon Frank Hawkins (tell) me about his experiences as a young man. Frank is now the head of a very large business company, but as a boy he (work) in a small shop. It (be) his job to repair bicycles and at that time he (work) fourteen hours a day. He (save) money for years and in 1938 he (buy) a small workshop of his own. During the war Frank (make) spare parts for aeroplanes. At that time he (have) two helpers. By the end of the war, the small work-shop had become a large factory which (employ) seven hundred and twenty-eight people. Frank (smile) when he (remember) his hard early years. He still (smile) when the door (open) and his wife (come) in. She (want) him to repair their son's bicycle!

e Going to.
Write these sentences again. Use *going to* in place of the verbs in italics:
1. We *intend to* leave at six o'clock.
2. I *intend to* pay these bills tomorrow.
3. *Do you intend to* write to him?
4. She *does not intend to* look for a new job.
5. When *do you intend to* buy a new car?

f What will happen? What will be happening? What will have happened?
The verbs in brackets tell us *what will happen, what will be happening*, and *what will have happened*. Give the correct form of each verb:
The Olympic Games (hold) in our country in four years' time. As a great many people (visit) the country, the government (build) new hotels, an immense stadium, and a fine new swimming pool. They also (build) new roads and a special railway-line. The Games (hold) just outside the capital and the whole area (call) 'Olympic City'. Workers (complete) the new roads by the end of this year. By the end of next year they (finish) work on the new stadium.

g What happened some time ago? What had happened some time before?
The verbs in brackets tell us *what happened some time ago* and *what had happened some time before*. Give the correct form of each verb:
The police (find) Billy Wilkins last night. He (run) away from home five days before. He (spend) the last two nights near a farmhouse. The police (take) him home at once. When she (see) him, his mother (burst) into tears. She (say) he never (run) away before.

h He was asked to call at the station.
Supply the correct form of the verbs in brackets:
Last Tuesday Ted received a letter from the local police. He (ask) to call at the station. Ted wondered why he (want) by the police, but he went to the station. There he (tell) by a smiling policeman that his bicycle (pick) up in a small village four hundred miles away. It now (send) to his home by train. Ted never expected his bicycle to (find). It (steal) twenty years ago when Ted was a boy of fifteen.

i Answer the questions after each statement and question:
1. 'I am very tired,' he said.
   What did he say? (He said that . . .)
2. 'Are you tired?' she asked.
   What did she ask? (She asked if . . .)
3. 'Will Jack arrive tomorrow?' Tom asked.
   What did Tom ask?

4. 'When will Jack arrive?' Tom asked.
   What did Tom ask?
5. 'Have you ever been abroad?' Mary asked.
   What did Mary ask?
6. 'Why didn't you write to me?' Jane asked.
   What did Jane ask?

j If.

Give the correct form of the verbs in brackets:
1. If he (be) out, I'll call tomorrow.
2. You'll miss the train if you (not hurry).
3. If you went to the exhibition, you (enjoy) it.
4. If I (be) in your position, I would act differently.

k Give the correct form of the verbs in brackets:
1. I'd love (see) that film. Will it be on tomorrow?
2. These shirts need (iron).
3. I hate (leave) so early, but I'm afraid I have to.
4. They continued (argue) till after midnight.
5. I shall be looking forward to (see) you tomorrow.
6. I got tired of (wait) so I left.
7. I don't believe in (work) too hard.
8. I did some shopping before (go) home.

C. Must, Need, Have, Can and Able to.

a Supply *mustn't* or *needn't* in these sentences:
1. You . . . make a noise. The children are asleep.
2. You . . . drive so quickly; we have plenty of time.
3. You . . . come with us if you don't want to.
4. You . . . smoke in a theatre. It is forbidden.

b Write these sentences again using constructions with *have* in place of the verbs in italics:
1. *Look* at this.
2. He *washed* before going out.
3. I *swam* in the sea this morning.
4. She is *resting*.

c Supply *could* or *was able to* in the following sentences:
1. . . . I use your telephone please?
2. He . . . leave Europe before the war began.
3. He said he . . . see me tomorrow.
4. He didn't agree with me at first but I . . . persuade him.

D. A, The, Some and Any.

Put in *a*, *the*, *some* or *any* where necessary:
. . . Wayle is . . . small river that cuts across . . . park near my home. I like sitting by . . . Wayle on fine afternoons. It was warm last Sunday, so I went and sat on . . . river bank as usual. . . . children were playing . . . games on . . . bank and there were . . . people rowing on . . . river. Suddenly, one of . . . children kicked . . . ball very hard and it went towards . . . passing boat. . . . people on . . . bank called out to . . . man in . . . boat, but he did not hear them. . . . ball struck him so hard that he nearly fell into . . . water. I turned to look at . . . children, but there weren't . . . in sight.

E. Little and Few.

Write these sentences again using *little*, *less*, *few*, *fewer*, *a little*, and *a few* in place of the words in italics. Make any other necessary changes:
1. There *isn't much* I can do to help him.
2. There aren't many apples on the tree, but you can pick *some* if you want to.

3. He *hasn't got as much* work to do *as* I have.
4. There isn't much whisky in this bottle, but you can have *some* if you want it.
5. He *hasn't as* many books *as* I have.
6. There *weren't many* people in the shop.

F. Where did he go? He went to the cinema.
Supply the missing words in the following:
1. Tell him to come . . . my office. I want to speak to him.
2. The ship sailed . . . the harbour and disappeared from sight.
3. We climbed . . . the top of the mountain.
4. He aimed . . . the bird, fired, and missed.
5. Please bring the tea things . . . the kitchen for me.

G. Verbs Followed by *to*, *at*, *for* and *with*.
Supply the missing words in the following sentences:
1. I agree . . . you. He never listens . . . anybody.
2. Don't blame me . . . that!
3. We must prepare . . . the coming year.
4. He has quarrelled . . . nearly all his old friends.
5. He came into the room without knocking . . . the door.

Special Difficulties

a Words Often Confused.
Choose the correct words in the following sentences:
1. I can't drink this coffee. It is (too) (very) hot.
2. He (denied) (refused) the accusation.
3. He often does (jobs) (works) about the house.
4. The train (passed) (past) at a terrific speed.
5. Have you seen Frank lately? I met him by accident the (next) (other) day.
6. He (looked at) (watched) the newspaper for a few minutes before going out.
7. I feel (such) (so) sleepy, I shall go to bed at once.
8. He is (so) (such a) difficult child. He objects to everything.
9. This water has been boiling (continuously) (continually) for over an hour.
10. He knocked me down and (stole) (robbed) me of all my money.
11. In the end, I bought (one) (a) tie instead of two.
12. I'm surprised you didn't (remark) (notice) my new hat.

b Speech Marks.
Write this piece of conversation again using speech marks:
Haven't you finished this book yet? he asked. I haven't even started it, I answered. Why not? he asked. It's an exciting story. Perhaps it is, I answered, but it's too difficult for me. I spend more time looking up the dictionary than reading the book.

c Complete these sentences by adding any of the following words: back, out, with, up.
1. The firemen found it difficult to put . . . the fire.
2. I'll have to look that . . . in the encyclopaedia.
3. He ran so fast I couldn't catch up . . . him.
4. All his friends are Americans. He has picked . . . an American accent.
5. I haven't any money now. Can I pay you . . . next week?

d Make and Do.
Supply the correct form of *make* and *do* in the following:
1. I . . . a promise never to see him again.
2. I was asked to . . . a speech.
3. That shop . . . very good business.
4. Do you think it will . . . any difference?
5. When did you . . . your homework?
6. He's the sort of person who always . . . trouble.

Unit 3

INSTRUCTIONS TO THE STUDENT

In Unit 2 you learned how to join simple statements with words like 'and', 'but' and 'so' to make compound statements. In this Unit you will learn how to join simple statements with words like 'when', 'as' and 'while' to make complex statements. You will learn how to write sentences which contain several ideas.

Before you begin each exercise, read these instructions carefully. Read them *each time* you begin a new piece. They are very important.

How to work—Comprehension and Précis

Unit 3 contains twenty-four short passages. There are questions under each piece. Your answers to these questions will often take the form of complex statements. Put your answers together to make a short paragraph.

1. Read the passage carefully two or three times. Make sure you understand it.
2. Write a full answer to each question. When several questions are given together, join your answers with the joining words or phrases given in brackets. Each answer you write must be *a complete sentence*.
3. Your answers to the questions must follow each other so that all your sentences will form a complete paragraph.
4. Read through your work and correct your mistakes.
5. Count the number of words in your paragraph. Do not go over the word limit. Words like 'the', 'a' etc. count as single words. Words which are joined by a hyphen (e.g. 'living-room') also count as single words. At the end of your paragraph write the number of words that you have used.

Example

Work through this example carefully and then try to do the exercises in Unit 3 in the same way.

The Last and Longest Journey

Even ships grow old and have to be destroyed. The last journey of a ship, which people have worked in and grown to love, is always a sad occasion. The *F.S. 949* had not been a great liner, or even a remarkable merchant ship. She was a U-boat and had sunk more ships during the war than any other submarine. In one
5 famous battle, she had sunk six ships in twenty-four hours. Alone, she had gone out to meet a convoy of merchant ships. Though these ships were protected by destroyers, the *F.S. 949* had sunk four of them before she was located. During the long battle that followed, two of the destroyers were sunk and the little submarine was only slightly damaged. Now, under a cold, grey sky, people were
10 watching silently as she came into the harbour. She would soon make her last journey out to sea before resting for ever in the depths she knew so well.

Comprehension and Précis

Answer these questions *in not more than 75 words*.

1. Was the *F.S. 949* an old U-boat or a new one? Would she soon be destroyed or not? (*which*)
2. What had she done during the war?
3. How many ships had she sunk in twenty-four hours in one famous battle?
4. How many merchant ships and destroyers had she sunk on that occasion? Was she slightly damaged or not? (*Though*)

5. What were people doing as the *F.S. 949* now came into the harbour? Would she make her last journey out to sea or not? (*before*)

Answer

The *F.S. 949* was an old U-boat *which* would soon be destroyed. During the war, she had sunk more ships than any other submarine. In one famous battle, she had sunk six ships in twenty-four hours. *Though* on that occasion she had sunk four merchant ships and two destroyers, she was only slightly damaged. People were watching silently as the *F.S. 949* now came into the harbour *before* she made her last journey out to sea.

(74 words)

Composition

Unit 3 contains two types of composition exercise based on ideas suggested by each passage:
1. Writing two or three sentences of your own using the information which has been given in note form.
2. Joining sentences together to make complex statements.

Examples

Work through these examples carefully and then try to do the composition exercises in the same way.

1. Composition

Write two or three sentences using the ideas given below:
Nuclear submarines—may replace ordinary submarines—can travel long distances—*Nautilus*—North Pole—under ice—four days.

A Possible Answer

Nuclear submarines may one day replace ordinary submarines, for they can travel under water over long distances. The American nuclear submarine, *Nautilus*, which sailed across the North Pole, remained under ice for four days.

2. Composition

Rewrite the following sentences using the joining words in brackets:
1. The *F.S. 949* failed to return home after a long sea battle. It was feared that she had been sunk. (*Because*)
2. Everyone was surprised. The submarine suddenly arrived three weeks later. (*when*)
3. She had not been badly damaged. Her radio had been put out of action. (*Although*)

Answer

Because the *F.S. 949* failed to return home after a long sea battle, it was feared that she had been sunk. Everyone was surprised *when* the submarine arrived three weeks later. *Although* she had not been badly damaged, her radio had been put out of action.

Letter-writing

Follow the instructions given under each passage.

Key Structures and Special Difficulties

When you finish the letter-writing exercise, go on to the language exercises that follow. The **Key Structures** deal with exactly the same problems that were considered in Units 1 and 2. You may refer back if you have forgotten anything. A little more new information about the Key Structures is added here. **Special Difficulties** are dealt with after the Key Structures. The work you do in grammar is based on material contained in the passages. Refer to the passages frequently. They will help you to understand the grammar and to do the exercises.

49　The End of a Dream

Tired of sleeping on the floor, a young man in Teheran saved up for years to buy a real bed. For the first time in his life, he became the proud owner of a bed
5　which had springs and a mattress. Because the weather was very hot, he carried the bed on to the roof of his house. He slept very well for the first two nights, but on the third night, a storm
10　blew up. A gust of wind swept the bed off the roof and sent it crashing into the courtyard below. The young man did not wake up until the bed had struck the ground. Although the bed was smashed
15　to pieces, the man was miraculously unhurt. When he woke up, he was still on

miraculously unhurt

the mattress. Glancing at the bits of wood and metal that lay around him, the man sadly picked up the mattress and carried it into his house. After he had put it on the floor, he promptly went to sleep again.

Comprehension and Précis

Answer these questions *in not more than 80 words*.
1. What did a young man in Teheran buy for the first time in his life?
2. Was the weather hot or cold? Did he sleep on the roof of his house or not? (*Because*)
3. Was the bed swept off the roof during a storm three nights later or not?
4. Was the man unhurt, or was he seriously injured? Was he still on his mattress or not? (*not only . . . but*)
5. Was the bed in pieces or not? Did he carry the mattress indoors or not? Where did he put it? Did he go back to sleep or did he stay awake? (*As . . . and*)

Letter-writing

Most letters begin with the word 'Dear' followed by a name. The word 'Dear' should be placed against the left-hand margin:

24 Clayton Ave.,
St. Albans,
Herts.,
England.
17th June, 19—

Dear Tom,

Exercise
Write your address, the date and the beginning of a letter to a friend in the way shown above.

Key Structures

Word Order in Complex Statements (Compare **KS 13, 71**)
We can join simple statements together to make *complex statements*. Here are some of the joining words we use: when, until, after, as soon as, while, before, because, as, since, to, in order to, although, who, which and that.

127

Study these simple statements carefully. Pay close attention to the way they have been joined:

He missed the train. He did not hurry.
He missed the train *because* he did not hurry.
He ran fast. He failed to win the race.
Although he ran fast, he failed to win the race.
I was tired. I went to sleep immediately.
I was *so* tired *that* I went to sleep immediately.
My neighbour went to Tokyo for a holiday. He could not return home. He did not have enough money.
My neighbour, *who* went to Tokyo for a holiday, could not return home *because* he did not have enough money.
I went into the garden. I wanted to pick some flowers.
I went into the garden *to* pick some flowers.
I found the door unlocked. I went into the kitchen.
Finding the door unlocked, I went into the kitchen.

The city was destroyed during the war. It has now been completely rebuilt.
Destroyed during the war, the city has now been completely rebuilt.

Exercises

A. How many joining words can you find in the passage? Underline as many as you can.

B. Rewrite these simple statements using the joining words in brackets. Do not refer to the passage until you finish the exercise.
1. A young man in Teheran was tired of sleeping on the floor. He saved up for years to buy a real bed. (*Tired of sleeping*)
2. He became the proud owner of a bed. It had springs and a mattress. (*which*)
3. The weather was very hot. He carried the bed on to the roof of his house. (*Because*)
4. The young man did not wake up. The bed had struck the ground. (*until*)
5. The bed was smashed to pieces. The man was unhurt. (*Although*)
6. He woke up. He was still on the mattress. (*When*)
7. He glanced at the bits of wood and metal. They lay around him. He sadly picked up the mattress. He carried it into his house. (*Glancing . . . that . . . and*)
8. He put it on the floor. He went to sleep again. (*After*)

Composition

Write two or three sentences using the ideas given below:
The man gathered the pieces next morning—repaired the bed—put it on the roof—tied it down—enjoyed many comfortable nights' sleep.

50   Taken for a Ride

I love travelling in the country, but I
don't like losing my way. I went on an
excursion recently, but my trip took me
longer than I expected.

5   'I'm going to Woodford Green,' I said
to the conductor as I got on the bus, 'but
I don't know where it is.'

'I'll tell you where to get off,' answered
the conductor.

10   I sat in the front of the bus to get a good
view of the countryside. After some time,
the bus stopped. Looking round, I realized
with a shock that I was the only passenger
left on the bus.

15   'You'll have to get off here,' the conductor said. 'This is as far as we go.'

'This is as far as we go'

'Is this Woodford Green?' I asked.

'Oh dear,' said the conductor suddenly. 'I forgot to put you off.'

'It doesn't matter,' I said. 'I'll get off here.'

20   'We are going back now,' said the conductor.

'Well, in that case, I prefer to stay on the bus,' I answered.

Comprehension and Précis

Answer these questions *in not more than 65 words*.
1. Where did the writer want to go? Did he know the way or not? What did the conductor promise to do? (*but as*)
2. Did they arrive at the bus terminus or not? What did the writer ask? (*When*)
3. What did the conductor realize then? (. . . *that*)
4. Why did the writer stay on the bus? (*because*)

Composition

Rewrite the following sentences using the joining words in brackets:
1. I went into the kitchen. I turned on the light. It was dark. (*On going . . . because*)
2. My brother shouted angrily. The lights went on. (*when*)
3. I spoilt a film. He was developing it. (*which*)

Letter-writing

How to begin a letter
a Friends should be addressed by their first names: e.g. 'Dear Fred'. Never begin a
letter with the words 'Dear Friend'.

b When writing to relations you may begin: Dear Mother, Dear Father, Dear Uncle
Fred, Dear Aunt Alice, but never 'Dear Cousin', or 'Dear Cousin Fred'.

Exercise
How would you begin letters to: your grandmother; your cousin Elizabeth, your friend
Jack, your uncle Tom.

Key Structures

These things always happen. (KS 74)
Here are some more verbs that tell us what always happens:
belong to, consist of, contain, desire, detest, dislike, hate, hope, love, matter, mean, mind, need, want, wish:
This box *contains* 48 matches.
He *needs* a new pair of shoes.
Those papers *belong to* me.
I *hate* writing letters.

Exercises

A. How many verbs in the passage tell us what always happens?

B. What is happening? What always happens?
Give the correct form of the verbs in brackets. Supply speech marks and commas where necessary and arrange the passage into paragraphs: (See **SD 74**)
Let's eat here I said to my wife. I (prefer) to have a drink first she answered. That's a good idea I said. I picked up the menu. I (not understand) a thing I said. It's all in Spanish. It (not matter) said my wife. What . . . that word (mean) I asked. I (not know) she answered. We called the waiter and pointed to the word on the menu. Two I said, holding up two fingers. After some time, my wife said suddenly Look! He (bring) us two boiled eggs!

Special Difficulties

Words Often Confused.
a Lose, Loose, Miss.
Study these examples:
I don't like losing my way. (ll. 1–2)
Take care not to lose your passport.
Several screws have come loose. I'll have to tighten them.
We haven't seen you for a long time. We have missed you.
We must hurry or we'll miss the train.

b Expect and Wait for.
Study these examples:
My trip took me longer than I expected. (ll. 3–4)
I am expecting Jack to arrive at 6 o'clock, but I shall not wait for him if he is not here by 6.15.

Exercise

Choose the correct words in these sentences:
1. Hurry up! You'll (lose) (miss) the bus.
2. That door-knob has come (lose) (loose). It will fall off soon.
3. Do you (expect) (wait for) him to change his mind?
4. If you bet on that horse you will (loose) (lose) your money.
5. He (waited) (expected) at the street corner for over half an hour before his girl friend arrived.

c My trip took me longer than I expected. (ll. 3–4)
Study these examples:
I did the trip in two hours.
The trip took me two hours.

Exercise

Rewrite these sentences so that they begin with *It takes* or *It took*.
1. I get to the office in an hour.
2. I reached Tokyo in fifteen hours.
3. He wrote the book in six months.

51   Reward for Virtue

My friend, Herbert, has always been fat,
but things got so bad recently that he decided to go on a diet. He began his diet
a week ago. First of all, he wrote out a
5 long list of all the foods which were forbidden. The list included most of the
things Herbert loves: butter, potatoes,
rice, beer, milk, chocolate, and sweets.
Yesterday I paid him a visit. I rang the
10 bell and was not surprised to see that
Herbert was still as fat as ever. He led me
into his room and hurriedly hid a large
parcel under his desk. It was obvious that
he was very embarrassed. When I asked
15 him what he was doing, he smiled guiltily
and then put the parcel on the desk. He
explained that his diet was so strict that he had to reward himself occasionally.
Then he showed me the contents of the parcel. It contained five large bars of
chocolate and three bags of sweets!

*The list included the things
Herbert loves*

Comprehension and Précis

Answer these questions *in not more than 65 words.*
1. Is Herbert fat or not? Has he gone on a diet or not? (*so . . . that*)
2. Has he forbidden himself all the foods he likes, or has he forbidden himself all the
   foods he does not like? Has he lost weight or not? (*but*)
3. What did he hide under his desk when the writer visited him yesterday?
4. Did the parcel contain chocolates and sweets, or did it contain biscuits?
5. Why did Herbert say that he had to reward himself occasionally? (*because*)

Composition

Write two or three sentences using the ideas given below:
I invited a friend to dinner—expensive restaurant—good meal—asked for the bill—
not enough money—borrowed some from my guest.

Letter-writing

How to begin a letter
If you are writing to a person you do not know very well, you should begin as follows:
Dear Mr Brown, Dear Miss Williams, Dear Mrs Smith. Always put a comma after
the name.

Exercise
How would you begin a letter to: your sister, your friend Bill, your employer, your
old headmaster.

Key Structures

What happened? (KS 76)
Study these sentences carefully. The verbs in italics tell us what happened:
I *got on* the bus and *sat* down.
The magazine I *ordered* *was sent* to the wrong address.
A fire *broke out* in our town recently and a large factory *was burnt* to the ground.

Exercises
A. Underline the verbs in the passage that tell us *what happened*.

B. Give the correct form of the verbs in brackets. Do not refer to the passage until you finish the exercise:
My friend, Herbert, has always been fat, but things (get) so bad recently that he (decide) to go on a diet. He (begin) his diet a week ago. First of all, he (write) out a long list of all the foods which were forbidden. The list (include) most of the things Herbert loves. Yesterday I (pay) him a visit. I (ring) the bell and (not surprise) to see that Herbert was still as fat as ever. He (lead) me into his room and hurriedly (hide) a large parcel under his desk. It was obvious that he (embarrass). When I (ask) him what he was doing, he (smile) guiltily and then (put) the parcel on the desk. He (explain) that his diet (be) so strict that he (have to) reward himself occasionally. Then he (show) me the contents of the parcel. It (contain) five large bars of chocolate and three bags of sweets!

Special Difficulties

Verbs Often Confused.
a Raise and Rise.
Study these examples:
That boy always raises his hand when I ask a question.
That shelf was too low so we raised it a few inches.
Heavy rains have raised the level of the river this year.

I always rise at six o'clock.
After the concert, everybody rose and clapped.
The sun has just risen.

b Lay and Lie.
Study these examples:
Lay those parcels on the floor please.
Where's my book? I laid it on that shelf a moment ago.
Haven't you laid the table yet?

It's nice to get up in the morning, but it's nicer to lie in bed.
I lay in bed till 10 o'clock last Sunday morning.
The children are playing a game. They've all just lain on the grass.

c Beat and Win.
Study these examples:
Arsenal beat Manchester United last Saturday.
Arsenal won the game.

Exercise
Choose the correct verbs in the following sentences:
1. Everybody (raised) (rose) when he entered the room.
2. I have been (laying) (lying) here for half an hour.
3. Mrs Jones (laid) (lay) the table before breakfast.
4. The aeroplane (raised) (rose) into the air.
5. I'm not very good at chess. He always (wins) (beats) me.
6. 'Did you (win) (beat) or lose?' I asked.

52 A Pretty Carpet

We have just moved into a new house and I have been working hard all morning. I have been trying to get my new room in order. This has not been easy because I
5 own over a thousand books. To make matters worse, the room is rather small, so I have temporarily put my books on the floor. At the moment, they cover every inch of floor space and I actually have
10 to walk on them to get in or out of the room. A short while ago, my sister helped me to carry one of my old bookcases up the stairs. She went into my room and got a big surprise when she saw all those
15 books on the floor. 'This is the prettiest carpet I have ever seen,' she said. She gazed at it for some time then added, 'You don't need bookcases at all. You can sit here in your spare time and read the carpet!'

You can sit here and read the carpet

Comprehension and Précis

Answer these questions *in not more than 75 words.*

1. Has the writer been trying to get his new room in order all morning or not?
2. Why has this proved difficult? Do they cover every inch of floor space at the moment or not? (*because . . . which*)
3. What did his sister help him to do a short while ago?
4. Did she get a surprise when she saw his room or not? Did she think that the books made a pretty carpet, or did she find the room untidy? (*but*)

Composition

Rewrite the following sentences using the joining words in brackets:

1. I moved into a new room. Three workmen brought my things upstairs. (*When*)
2. There were several cases of clothes. There were hundreds of books. (*not only . . . but . . . as well*)
3. The pile was as high as the ceiling. I could not get into my room. (*Since*)

Letter-writing

How would you begin letters to: your cousin Ted, your bank manager, your friend Mary, your grandfather.

Key Structures

What has happened? What has been happening? (**KS 77**)
Compare these pairs of sentences:

It *hasn't rained* for six weeks.
It *has been raining* hard since yesterday and it is still raining.
He *has rung* me up five times since 12 o'clock.
He *has been ringing* me up all morning.

He *has never stayed* at this hotel before.
He *has been staying* at this hotel for the last three weeks.
I *have read* 'Oliver Twist' five times.
I *have been reading* all afternoon.

Exercises

A. Underline the verbs in the passage that tell us *what has happened* and *what has been happening*.

B. Give the correct form of the verbs in brackets. Do not refer to the passage until you finish the exercise:

We just (move) into a new house and I (work) hard all morning. I (try) to get my new room in order. This (not be) easy because I own over a thousand books. The room is rather small, so I temporarily (put) my books on the floor. My sister got a big surprise when she saw all those books on the floor. 'This is the prettiest carpet I ever (see),' she said.

C. What has happened? What has been happening? Give the correct form of the verbs in brackets:

'I (explain) this to you several times already,' said the teacher. 'I hope you (understand) it now.' Then he looked at a little boy at the back of the class. '. . . you (listen), Jones?' he asked. 'Here is a simple problem: "Sally (work) in an office for thirty-four weeks. In that time, she (earn) £10 a week. How much . . . she (earn) so far?" '

'Please, sir,' Jones answered. 'I can only answer your first question. I (not listen).'

Special Difficulties

I have been working hard all morning. (l. 2)
Compare these pairs of sentences:
She has a beautiful voice. She sings beautifully.
He is a slow worker. He works slowly.
He is a hard worker. He works hard.
He is a fast driver. He drives fast.

Now compare these pairs of sentences:
The train arrived very late.
Have you travelled by train lately?
He worked very hard.
He hardly ever does any work.
The plane flew very high.
He thinks very highly of me.
He made sure it was safe before he went near.
He was nearly run over by a car.

Exercise
Choose the correct words in the following sentences:
1. She dusted the furniture very (careful) (carefully).
2. I hit him very (hardly) (hard).
3. This exercise is not (hard) (hardly).
4. I got home from work very (lately) (late) last night.
5. I (near) (nearly) missed the bus this morning.
6. He ran so (fastly) (fast) no one could keep up with him.
7. I can't jump so (highly) (high).

53 Hot Snake

At last firemen have put out a big forest fire in California. Since then, they have been trying to find out how the fire began. Forest fires are often caused by broken glass or by cigarette ends which people carelessly throw away. Yesterday the firemen examined the ground carefully, but were not able to find any broken glass. They were also quite sure that a cigarette end did not start the fire. This morning, however, a fireman accidentally discovered the cause. He noticed the remains of a snake which was wound round the electric wires of a 16,000-volt power line. In this way, he was able to solve the mystery. The explanation was simple but

The explanation was very unusual . . .

very unusual. A bird had snatched up the snake from the ground and then dropped it on to the wires. The snake then wound itself round the wires. When it did so, it sent sparks down to the ground and these immediately started a fire.

Comprehension and Précis

Answer these questions *in not more than 85 words.*
1. Have firemen put out a big forest fire in California or not? Have they been trying to discover its cause? (*Now that . . .*)
2. Was there any evidence that it was started by broken glass or by a cigarette end or not?
3. Who has just solved the mystery? (*However*)
4. What did he notice? Had it been dropped by a bird on to the electric wires or not? (*which*)
5. Where did the snake wind itself? What had it sent to the ground? Did this cause the fire or not? (*In winding . . . and*)

Composition

Write two or three sentences using the ideas given below:
I was smoking in bed—went to sleep—suddenly woke up—the sheet was burning—I jumped up—put the fire out—a big hole in the sheet.

Letter-writing

Write your home address, the date and the beginning of a letter to a married woman you do not know well.

Key Structures

What happened? What has happened? (**KS 80**). What has been happening? (**KS 133**)
Study these examples:
I stayed at this hotel five years ago.
Have you ever stayed at this hotel?
I have been staying at this hotel for three weeks.

A. Underline the verbs in the passage which tell us *what happened*, *what has happened*, and *what has been happening*.

B. Give the correct form of the verbs in brackets. Do not refer to the passage until you finish the exercise:
At last firemen (put) out a big forest fire in California. Since then, they (try) to find out how the fire (begin). Yesterday the firemen (examine) the ground carefully, but (not be) able to find any broken glass. They (be) also quite sure that a cigarette end (not start) the fire.

C. What happened? What has happened? What has been happening? Give the correct form of the verbs in brackets. Supply speech marks and commas where necessary and arrange the passage into paragraphs. (**SD 74**)
Jack (look) at his watch for the twentieth time. Suddenly Jill (arrive). I (wait) for over an hour he said angrily. You never come on time. Oh, is that so? Jill (answer). (Be) you here at 2.30? Jack (go) red. Well he (say) I (get) here five minutes late myself, but you (not be) here. I (come) here at exactly 2.30 Jill (say) and I (wait) for five minutes, but you (not come). What you (do) since then? Jack (ask). I just (be) to the hairdresser's Jill (answer) brightly.

Special Difficulties

Words Often Confused.

a Throw to, Throw at, and Throw away.
Study these examples:
Fires are often caused by cigarette ends which people carelessly throw away. (ll. 4–6)
He threw the ball to me and I caught it.
The boy threw a stone at the window and broke it.

b Quite and Quiet.
Study these examples:
They were quite sure that a cigarette end did not start the fire. (ll. 9–10)
The class kept very quiet during the lesson.

c Cause and Reason.
Study these examples:
A fireman discovered the cause of the fire. (ll. 11–12)
What caused the fire?
That is the reason why he left.
I reasoned with him for hours, but I couldn't persuade him to change his mind.

d Drop and Fall.
Study these examples:
A bird had dropped the snake on to the wires. (ll. 17–18)
He fell down the stairs and broke his leg.

Exercise
Use each of the words given above in sentences of your own.

54 Sticky Fingers

After breakfast, I sent the children to school and then I went to market. It was still early when I returned home. The children were at school, my husband was
5 at work and the house was quiet. So I decided to make some tarts for tea. In a short time I was busy mixing butter and flour and my hands were soon covered with sticky pastry. At exactly that mo-
10 ment, the telephone rang. Nothing could have been more annoying. I picked up the receiver between two sticky fingers and was dismayed when I recognized the voice of Mrs Bates. It took me ten minutes
15 to persuade her to ring back later. At last I hung up the receiver. What a mess!

What a mess!

There was pastry on my fingers, on the telephone, and on the door-knobs. I had no sooner got back to the kitchen than the door-bell rang loud enough to wake the dead. This time it was the postman and he wanted me to sign for a registered
20 letter!

Comprehension and Précis

Answer these questions *in not more than 75 words.*
1. Did the writer return home from market or not? What did she begin to make? (*As soon as*)
2. Did the telephone ring soon afterwards or not? Were her fingers very sticky or not? (*When*)
3. How long did she spend talking to Mrs Bates on the telephone?
4. Did she look at the mess she had made or not? (*After that*)
5. What was covered with pastry?
6. Who rang the door-bell? (*Just then*)
7. What did he want her to do?

Composition

Rewrite the following sentences using the joining words in brackets:
1. I put the cake in the oven. I forgot all about it. (*After putting*)
2. Two hours had passed. I smelt something burning. (*When*)
3. I went into the kitchen. I found it full of smoke. (*On going*)

Letter-writing

In the first paragraph of your letter you should refer either to a letter you have received or to an event which has prompted you to write. Look at the example below. Note where the first paragraph begins:
Dear Fred,
    I was very pleased to learn that you are well.

Exercise

Write your address, the date and the first sentence of a letter to a friend beginning: 'Thank you for . . .'

Key Structures

A, The, Some and Any. (**KS 81**)

a Some and Any. See **KS 81a** and **SD 30**

Study the use of *some* and *any* in these sentences:

Did you get any information? I want some information.

Is there any news in the paper? There is some interesting news in the paper.

Did the storm do any damage? The storm did some damage to the crops.

Did you do any work yesterday? I did some work before breakfast.

Did you bring any luggage? I have some luggage in the car.

b Compare these pairs of sentences:

He was very poor years ago, but now he is a rich man.

The rich should help *the* poor.

She was born deaf and blind.

There are many organizations to help *the* deaf and *the* blind.

c Compare these pairs of sentences:

The school in our village was built last year.

The children went *to school* early this morning.

There is a market for these goods abroad.

The farmer goes *to market* on Saturdays (i.e. to buy and sell).

But: I'm going to *the market*. I want to buy some fruit.

We need a new cinema and a new theatre.

I often go to *the cinema* and *the theatre*.

d Compare these sentences:

It is *the* most interesting exhibition I have ever seen.

Most people enjoyed it.

It is *the* biggest shop in London.

Most shops are closed on Saturday afternoon.

Exercises

A. Underline the words *a*, *the* and *some* in the passage.

B. Put in the words *a*, *the* and *some* where necessary. Do not refer to the passage until you finish the exercise:

After . . . breakfast, I sent . . . children to . . . school and then I went to . . . market. It was still early when I returned home. . . . children were at . . . school, my husband was at . . . work, and . . . house was quiet. So I decided to make . . . tarts for . . . tea. In . . . short time I was busy mixing . . . butter and . . . flour and my hands were soon covered with . . . sticky pastry. At exactly that moment, . . . telephone rang. Nothing could have been more annoying. I picked up . . . receiver between . . . two sticky fingers and was dismayed when I recognized . . . voice of Mrs Bates. It took me ten minutes to persuade her to ring back later. At last I hung up . . . receiver. What . . . mess! There was . . . pastry on my fingers, on . . . telephone, and on . . . door-knobs. I had no sooner got back to . . . kitchen than . . . door-bell rang loud enough to wake . . . dead. This time it was . . . postman and he wanted me to sign for . . . registered letter!

55 Not a Gold Mine

Dreams of finding lost treasure almost came true recently. A new machine called 'The Revealer' has been invented and it has been used to detect gold which has
5 been buried in the ground. The machine was used in a cave near the sea-shore where—it is said—pirates used to hide gold. The pirates would often bury gold in the cave and then fail to collect it.
10 Armed with the new machine, a search party went into the cave hoping to find buried treasure. The leader of the party was examining the soil near the entrance to the cave when the machine showed
15 that there was gold under the ground. Very excited, the party dug a hole two

almost worthless

feet deep. They finally found a small gold coin which was almost worthless. The party then searched the whole cave thoroughly but did not find anything except an empty tin trunk. In spite of this, many people are confident that 'The
20 Revealer' may reveal something of value fairly soon.

Comprehension and Précis

Answer these questions *in not more than 65 words.*

1. Is 'The Revealer' a new machine or an old machine? Is it used for detecting buried gold or not? (*which*)
2. Did a search party use this machine or not? Where did they try to find gold recently? (*Using this machine . . .*)
3. Did they examine the cave thoroughly or not? Did they only find a small gold coin? Was it valuable or was it practically worthless? (*Although . . . which*)
4. Do many people believe that the machine may reveal something of value soon or not? (*However*)

Composition

Write two or three sentences using the ideas given below:
I was digging in the garden—lost a gold ring—searched everywhere—dug up the garden—did not find it—found a valuable old coin instead.

Letter-writing

Arrange this heading in the correct order: Sevenoaks, 17 Bunyan St., England, Kent, 27th March, 19—. Now write the first sentence of a letter to a friend beginning: 'I was very pleased to . . .'

Key Structures

Pirates would often bury gold in the cave and then fail to collect it.

a Study these sentences carefully:
I dropped my briefcase as I was getting off the bus. (**KS 25**)
I used to go to work by bus. Now I go by car. (**KS 83**)
I have given up smoking. I used to smoke very heavily.

b When we refer to a definite time in the past, we can sometimes use *would* in place of *used to*. We cannot, for instance, use *would* in this sentence:
This sort of novel used to be very popular.

But note the use of *would* in these sentences:
When I was young I used to have a lot more free time than I do now. I used to live near my work and *would* always get home early. Sometimes I *would* do a bit of gardening or go for a long walk. Now I never have time for anything like that.

Exercises
A. Underline the verbs in the passage which tell us *what happened, what was happening* and *what used to/would happen.*

B. Give the correct form of the verbs in brackets. Do not refer to the passage until you finish the exercise:
The machine (use) in a cave near the sea-shore where—it is said—pirates (hide) gold. The pirates often (bury) gold in the cave and then (fail) to collect it. Armed with the new machine, a search party (go) into the cave hoping to find buried treasure. The leader of the party (examine) the soil near the entrance to the cave when the machine (show) that there (be) gold under the ground. Very excited, the party (dig) a hole two feet deep. They finally (find) a small gold coin which was almost worthless.

Special Difficulties

Words Often Confused.
a I use, I am used to, I used to.
Study these examples:
The machine has been used to detect gold which has been buried in the ground. The machine was used in a cave near the sea-shore where—it is said—pirates used to hide gold. (ll. 4–8)
I am used to staying up late. (**KS 110b**)
I am used to looking after myself.
She didn't like this district at first, but she is used to it now.

Exercise
Choose the correct form of the verbs given in brackets:
1. He (is used to) (used to) work sixteen hours a day.
2. I (use to) (used to) see him often.
3. He always (uses) (used to) scented soap.
4. He (used to) (is used to) buy twenty cigarettes a day.
5. I couldn't stand the noise at first but I (am used to) (used to) it now.
6. I (am used to) (used to) swimming in cold water.

b Gold and Golden.
Study these examples:
It has been used to detect gold. (ll. 3–4)
He has a gold watch.
He missed a golden opportunity.

Exercise
Supply *gold* or *golden*:
1. All that glitters is not . . .
2. Silence is . . .

56 Faster than Sound!

Once a year a race is held for old cars. A lot of cars entered for this race last year and there was a great deal of excitement just before it began. One of the most
5 handsome cars was a Rolls-Royce Silver Ghost. The most unusual car was a Benz which had only three wheels. Built in 1885, it was the oldest car taking part. After a great many loud explosions, the
10 race began. Many of the cars broke down on the course and some drivers spent more time *under* their cars than *in* them! A few cars, however, completed the race. The winning car reached a speed of forty
15 miles an hour—much faster than any of its rivals. It sped downhill at the end of

It was different from modern car races

the race and its driver had a lot of trouble trying to stop it. The race gave everyone a great deal of pleasure. It was very different from modern car races but no less exciting.

Comprehension and Précis

Answer these questions *in not more than 70 words.*
1. Did a lot of old cars enter for the race or not? How often is it held? (*which*)
2. What could be heard when they set off? Did many cars break down during the race or not? Did a few manage to complete the course or not? (*and though*)
3. Did the winning car go downhill quickly or slowly? When did its driver have a lot of difficulty trying to stop it? (*so quickly . . . that*)

Composition

Rewrite the following sentences using the joining words in brackets. Where necessary omit the words in italics.
1. There was a loud explosion. My old car stopped. (*and*)
2. I got out. *I wanted to* have a look at the engine. (*to*)
3. Then a man passed me. *He* was driving a large modern car. (*a man who*)
4. I waved to him. He did not stop. (*but*)
5. I passed the large car later. Its driver was changing a wheel. (*When*)

Letter-writing

Learn the following opening phrases by heart:
I am sorry it has taken me so long to write, but . . .
I was glad to hear from you at last and to learn that . . .

Exercise
Write two short paragraphs (of not more than two sentences each) completing the above phrases.

Key Structures

A lot of cars entered for this race.
a Do you remember these sentences: (**KS 86**)
He is as old as I am.
She is not as intelligent as we think.

There is little I can do to help him.
There were few people in the shop.
There isn't much whisky, but you can have a little.
There aren't many apples, but you can pick a few.

b Now study these sentences:

Instead of saying:	*We can say:*
There isn't *much* I can do to help him.	There isn't *a lot* I can do to help him.
	Or: There isn't *a great deal* I can do to help him.
Many of our products are sold overseas.	*A lot of* our products are sold overseas.
	Or: *A great many of* our products are sold overseas.
	Or: *A great number of* our products are sold overseas.

c Study these sentences:

Instead of saying:	*We can say:*
My jacket is *like* yours.	My jacket is *the same as* yours.
My jacket *isn't like* yours.	My jacket is *different from* yours.

Exercises

A. How many comparisons can you find in the passage? Underline them. Note the use in the passage of the following: a lot of, a great deal of, a great many, a few, and different from.

B. Supply the missing words in the following. Do not refer to the passage until you finish the exercise:

Once a year a race is held for old cars. A . . . . . . cars entered for this race last year and there was a great . . . of excitement just before it began. One of the . . . handsome cars was a Rolls-Royce Silver Ghost. The . . . unusual car was a Benz which had only three wheels. Built in 1885 it was the . . . (old) car taking part. After a great . . . loud explosions, the race began. . . . of the cars broke down on the course and some drivers spent . . . time *under* their cars than *in* them! A . . . cars, however, completed the race. The winning car reached a speed of forty miles an hour—much faster . . . any of its rivals. It sped down-hill at the end of the race and its driver had a . . . . . . trouble trying to stop it. The race gave everyone a great . . . of pleasure. It was very different . . . modern car races but no . . . exciting.

Special Difficulties

Words Often Confused and Misused.
Study the examples given under each heading:

a Handsome (l. 5), Beautiful, Pretty, Good-looking.
He is a very handsome young man.
She used to be very pretty as a child. She is now a beautiful woman.
She's a very good-looking girl, and her boy friend's good-looking too.

b Reach and Arrive in / at.
The winning car reached a speed of forty miles an hour. (ll. 14–15)
Will you pass me that book please. I can't reach it.
We arrived in New York yesterday. We arrived at the station in good time.

c Take part and Take place.
It was the oldest car taking part. (l. 8)
The next race will take place in a year's time.

Exercise

Write eight sentences using each of the above words.

57   Can I Help You Madam?

A woman in blue jeans stood at the window of an expensive shop. Though she hesitated for a moment, she finally went in and asked to see a dress that was in the
5 window. The assistant who served her did not like the way she was dressed. Glancing at her scornfully, he told her that the dress was sold. The woman walked out of the shop angrily and de-
10 cided to punish the assistant next day. She returned to the shop the following morning dressed in a fur coat, with a handbag in one hand and a long umbrella in the other. After seeking out the rude
15 assistant she asked for the same dress. Not realizing who she was, the assistant

The assistant did not like the way she was dressed

was eager to serve her this time. With great difficulty, he climbed into the shop window to get the dress. As soon as she saw it, the woman said she did not like it. She enjoyed herself making the assistant bring almost everything in the window
20 before finally buying the dress she had first asked for.

Comprehension and Précis
Answer these questions *in not more than 80 words*.
1. Did the woman in blue jeans hesitate for a moment or not? Did she enter an expensive shop or not? What did she ask to see? (*Though . . . and*)
2. What did an assistant tell her? When did the woman return? Was she dressed in a fur coat or not? (*On being told by*)
3. What was the assistant eager to do this time?
4. What did she make him bring her? What did the woman finally buy? (*After making*)

Composition
Write two or three sentences using the ideas given below:
A shop-owner wanted to see how polite his assistants were—dressed as a tramp—went into his shop—asked to see a suit—was thrown out.

Letter-writing
Learn the following opening phrases by heart:
What a surprise it was to . . .
Forgive me for not writing earlier, but . . .

Exercise
Write two short paragraphs (of not more than two sentences each) completing the above phrases.

Key Structures
At, In, Off and With. Compare **KS 29** and **87**.
a Study these sentences carefully. Pay close attention to the words in italics.
Phrases with *at*:
He lives *at 27 West Street*.
A large crowd was waiting *at the bus-stop*.

I'll see you *at the station.*
On the way home, we stopped *at a small village called Puddleton.*
Someone is *at the door.*

Phrases with *in*:
There were a lot of people *in the street.*
I would like to live *in a warm country.*
He lives *in Berlin.*
Let's go for a walk *in the park.*
Where's Tom? He's *in his room.*

Phrases with *off*:
The lid came *off* easily.
Take your coat *off.*
The pencil rolled *off* the table.

b Now study these phrases with *in* and *with*:
Can you see that woman *in the blue coat*?
He was dressed *in a black suit.*
That man *with long hair* is supposed to be a poet.
The police are looking for a man *with a scar* on his face.
The woman *with the brown handbag* and long umbrella is a famous novelist.

Exercises

A. Study the use in the passage of the following words: *in, at, out of, to, with* and *into.*

B. Supply the missing words in the following sentences. Do not refer to the passage until you finish the exercise.
1. A woman . . . blue jeans stood . . . the window of an expensive shop. Though she hesitated for a moment, she finally went . . . and asked to see a dress that was . . . the window.
2. Glancing . . . her scornfully, he told her that the dress was sold. The woman walked . . . . . . the shop angrily.
3. She returned . . . the shop the following morning dressed . . . a fur coat, . . . a handbag . . . one hand and a long umbrella . . . the other.
4. . . . great difficulty, he climbed . . . the shop window.
5. She enjoyed herself making the assistant bring almost everything . . . the window.

Special Difficulties

Make and Let
Study these examples:
She enjoyed herself making the assistant *bring* almost everything in the window. (l. 19)
I can't make him *change* his mind.
The teacher made the boy *write* the exercise again.
Don't let him *persuade* you.
Let me *try.*
Don't let the children *touch* anything in this room please.

Exercise
Complete these sentences:
1. Don't let him . . .
2. Why don't you make him . . .
3. No one can make me . . .
4. Will your parents let you . . .
5. Let's . . .

58 A Blessing in Disguise?

The tiny village of Frinley is said to possess a 'cursed tree'. Because the tree was mentioned in a newspaper, the number of visitors to Frinley has now in-
5 creased. The tree was planted near a church fifty years ago, but it is only in recent years that it has gained an evil reputation. It is said that if anyone touches the tree, he will have bad luck; if he picks
10 a leaf, he will die. Many villagers believe that the tree has already claimed a number of victims. The vicar has been asked to have the tree cut down, but so far he has refused. He has pointed out that the
15 tree is a useful source of income as tour- ists have been coming from all parts of the country to see it. In spite of all that has been said, the tourists have been picking leaves and cutting their names on the tree-trunk. So far, not one of them has been struck down by sudden death!

not one has been struck down

Comprehension and Précis

Answer these questions *in not more than 80 words.*
1. Has the number of visitors to the village of Frinley increased or not? Is there said to be a 'cursed tree' near a church or not? (*because*)
2. Do the villagers believe that if anyone picks a leaf he will die. What have they asked the vicar to do? (*Since*)
3. Is the tree a useful source of income or not? Has the vicar agreed to have the tree cut down, or has he refused to do so? (*As*)
4. Have tourists been picking leaves or not? Have any of them come to harm or not? (*Meanwhile, though . . .*)

Composition

Rewrite the following sentences using the joining words in brackets:
1. A village well was said to be cursed. It was bought by a man. (*which*)
2. Tourists came to see it. There was not even any water in it. (*though*)
3. The tourists could look into the well. They had to throw a coin in first. (*Before*)

Letter-writing

Learn the following opening phrases by heart:
You will be glad to hear that . . .
Thank you for letting me know that . . .

Exercise
Write two short paragraphs (of not more than two sentences each) completing the above phrases.

Key Structures

Frinley is said to possess a 'cursed tree'.

a Do you remember these sentences: (**KS 89**)

He is being sent abroad.

I was told to wait for him.

Your wallet has been found.

b Now study these sentences:

Instead of saying:	*We can say:*
People say he is a genius.	*He is said to be* a genius.
	Or: *It is said that* he is a genius.
People say that there is oil under the North Sea.	*There is said to be* oil under the North Sea.
	Or: *It is said that* there is oil under the North Sea.
She gave me a pen.	*I was given* a pen.
	A pen was given to me.
The manager offered the vacant post to him.	*He was offered* the vacant post.
	Or: *The vacant post was offered* to him.

Exercises

A. There are some verbs in the passage which are similar in form to the examples given above. Can you find them?

B. Give the correct form of the verbs in brackets. Do not refer to the passage until you finish the exercise.

1. The tiny village of Frinley (say) to possess a 'cursed tree'. Because the tree (mention) in a newspaper, the number of visitors to Frinley has now increased. The tree (plant) near a church fifty years ago, but it is only in recent years that it has gained an evil reputation. It (say) that if anyone touches the tree he will have bad luck.
2. The vicar (ask) to have the tree cut down, but so far he has refused.
3. In spite of all that (say), the tourists have been picking leaves and cutting their names on the tree-trunk. So far, not one of them (strike) down by sudden death!

Special Difficulties

Verbs Often Confused.

a Increase and Grow. Compare **SD 46c**. Study these examples:

The number of visitors to Frinley has now increased. (ll. 3–5)

She has grown so much she is nearly as tall as I am.

b Gain and Earn. Study these examples:

It has gained an evil reputation. (ll. 7–8)

He has gone abroad and I hear he is earning a lot of money.

c Pick and Cut. Study these examples:

The tourists have been picking the leaves and cutting their names on the tree trunk. (ll. 17–18)

She has picked a lot of flowers.

She cut the apple into two.

Exercise

Choose the correct words in these sentences:

1. This fruit is fresh. I have just (cut) (picked) it.
2. If you travel by air, you will (earn) (gain) time.
3. He (earns) (gains) £20 a week.
4. Judy has (increased) (grown) so much I can hardly recognize her.

59 In or Out?

Our dog, Rex, used to sit outside our front gate and bark. Every time he wanted to come into the garden he would bark until someone opened the gate. As the
5 neighbours complained of the noise, my husband spent weeks training him to press his paw on the latch to let himself in. Rex soon became an expert at opening the gate. However, when I was going out
10 shopping last week, I noticed him in the garden near the gate. This time he was barking so that someone would let him out! Since then, he has developed another bad habit. As soon as he opens the gate
15 from the outside, he comes into the garden and waits until the gate shuts. Then

My husband spent weeks training him

he sits and barks until someone lets him out. After this he immediately lets himself in and begins barking again. Yesterday my husband removed the gate and Rex got so annoyed we have not seen him since.

Comprehension and Précis

Answer these questions *in not more than 80 words*.
1. Why did our dog, Rex, use to sit outside the front gate and bark? (*so that*)
2. Did my husband train him to open the gate himself or not? Has Rex developed another bad habit or not? (*Ever since*)
3. Why does he bark when he is in the garden? (*so that*)
4. Does he let himself in after this or not? Does he bark until someone opens the gate again or not? (*and*)
5. Has my husband removed the gate or not? Has Rex disappeared or not? (*Now that*)

Composition

Write two or three sentences using the ideas given below:
My husband put the gate back—kept it locked—Rex returned—delighted at first—could not open the gate—dissatisfied—disappeared.

Letter-writing

How would the following appear in a letter:
August the first; the third of December; July the second; Avenue; Place; Street; London, East Central 4.

Key Structures

Review **KS 130–146**
These things always happen. (**KS 130**)
What happened? (**KS 132**)
What has happened? What has been happening? (**KS 133**)
Pirates would often bury gold in the cave . . . (**KS 139**)
Frinley is said to possess a 'cursed tree'. (**KS 146**)

Exercises

A. Which verbs in the passage tell us *a* what is happening now; *b* what always happens; *c* what happened; *d* what has happened; *e* what was happening.

B. Give the correct form of the verbs in brackets. Do not refer to the passage until you finish the exercise:

Our dog, Rex (sit) outside our front gate and bark. Every time he (want) to come into the garden he (bark) until someone opened the gate. As the neighbours (complain) of the noise, my husband (spend) weeks training him to press his paw on the latch to let himself in. Rex soon (become) an expert at opening the gate. However, when I (go) out shopping last week, I (notice) him in the garden near the gate. This time he (bark) so that someone would let him out! Since then, he (develop) another bad habit. As soon as he opens the gate from the outside, he (come) into the garden and (wait) until the gate shuts. Then he (sit) and (bark) until someone lets him out. After this he immediately lets himself in and (begin) barking again. Yesterday my husband (remove) the gate and Rex (get) so annoyed we (not see) him since.

C. Write these sentences again changing the form of the words in italics. Omit any words that are not necessary.
1. *People say* that he is very rich.
2. *People say that there is* a hold-up on the roads.
3. She *gave me* a pen.
4. They *gave her a prize*.
5. They *promised us a new office*.

Special Difficulties

To, in order to, so as to, so that, in order that.

Note the way these pairs of sentences have been joined:
He ran to the station. He wanted to catch the train.
He ran to the station *to* catch the train.

I told him about it. I wanted to help you.
I told him about it *in order to* help you.

I opened the door quietly. I did not want to disturb him.
I opened the door quietly *so as not to* disturb him.

He works hard. He wants to pass his exams.
He works hard *in order that he may* pass his exams.

He left the letter on the table. He wanted me to see it.
He left the letter on the table *in order that I might(should)* see it.

He was barking. He wanted someone to let him out.
He was barking *so that someone would* let him out. (ll. 11–13)
He was barking *for someone to* let him out.

He sent a telegram. He wanted his mother to learn the good news.
He sent a telegram *in order that his mother might(should)* learn the good news.
He sent a telegram *for his mother to* learn the good news.

Exercise

Join the following sentences leaving out the verb *to want*.
1. He left early. He did not want to see me. (*so as to*)
2. The secretary asked me into the office. The manager wanted to speak to me. (*so that*)
3. I ran to the station. I did not want to be late. (*so as to*)
4. He worked hard. He wanted to learn English. (*in order to*)
5. He has not sent me his address. He does not want me to write to him. (*so that*)
6. I went to see him. I wanted to find out what had happened. (*to*)

60 The Future

At a village fair, I decided to visit a fortune-teller called Madam Bellinsky. I went into her tent and she told me to sit down. After I had given her some money, she looked into a crystal ball and said: 'A relation of yours is coming to see you. She will be arriving this evening and intends to stay for a few days. The moment you leave this tent, you will get a big surprise. A woman you know well will rush towards you. She will speak to you and then she will lead you away from this place. That is all.'

As soon as I went outside, I forgot all about Madam Bellinsky because my wife hurried towards me. 'Where have you been hiding?' she asked impatiently. 'Your sister will be here in less than an hour and we must be at the station to meet her. We are late already.' As she walked away, I followed her out of the fair.

A woman will rush towards you

Comprehension and Précis

Answer these questions *in not more than 80 words.*
1. Whom did the writer visit at a village fair? Did she tell him that a relation was coming to see him or not? (*who*)
2. Who would speak to him when he left the tent? Would he follow her out of the fair or not? (*She added that . . . and*)
3. Did this come true or not? Did his wife speak to him when he went outside, or did a strange woman speak to him? (*because*)
4. Whom did she tell him they had to meet at the station? Did she lead him out of the fair or not? (*and*)

Composition

Rewrite the following sentences using the joining words in brackets:
1. Fortune-tellers always tell the truth. They speak in general terms. (*because*)
2. They say you will go on a journey. You will meet a friend. They are right. We often do these things. (*If . . . or . . . because*)

Letter-writing

Address an envelope to a married couple who live abroad.

Key Structures

The moment you leave this tent, you will get a big surprise.
a Do you remember these sentences: (**KS 93**)
I am going to travel by air.
You will enjoy yourself if you travel by sea.

b Now study these sentences carefully:

Instead of saying:	We can say:
He will arrive tomorrow.	He is arriving tomorrow.
He will come at 4 o'clock.	He is coming at 4 o'clock.
She will leave in two days' time.	She is leaving in two days' time.

c Study these sentences. Pay close attention to the words in italics:
If it rains tomorrow we shall stay at home. (KS 43)
The moment he arrives, I shall let you know.
I shall wait here *until he comes.*
As soon as the rain stops, we shall go out.
You must finish your dinner *before you leave the table.*
We'll go into the living-room *after we finish dinner.*
I'll give him the message *when he returns.*

Exercises
A. Underline all the verbs in the passage which tell us what will happen in the future.

B. This is what Madam Bellinsky told the writer. Give the correct form of the verbs in brackets. Note that more than one form can be used for some of these verbs. Do not refer to the passage until you finish the exercise:
A relation of yours (come) to see you. She (arrive) this evening and intends to stay for a few days. The moment you (leave) this tent, you (get) a big surprise. A woman you know well (rush) towards you. She (speak) to you and then she (lead) you away from this place.

C. What will happen tonight? Give the correct form of the verbs in brackets:
A life-boat (set) out tonight to search for the ship-wreck. The crew (send) radio messages to the wreck until they (receive) a signal from the men on board. As soon as they (receive) a signal, they (try) and find the wreck with powerful searchlights. The moment the crew (locate) the wreck, they (fire) a special gun which (carry) a rope from the life-boat to the sinking ship. If the sea is rough, they (pour) oil on the water. They are sure to succeed, but if they fail, a helicopter (send) out tomorrow morning. Helicopters are very useful for rescue work, but they cannot be used at night.

Special Difficulties

At a village fair, I decided to visit a fortune-teller. (Compare SD 38)

Instead of saying:	It is better to say:
We went to the fair in the village.	We went to the *village fair*.

Exercise
Write these sentences again. Express the phrases in italics in a different way:
1. *The dining-room in our school* is very large.
2. He told us a *story about ghosts*.
3. She gave me a *present for my birthday*.
4. We stopped at *an inn in the village*.
5. *The leader of the party* made a speech.
6. I have lost the *key to the front door*.
7. He sent me a *card for Christmas*.
8. We are painting the *gate in our garden*.

61 Dangerous Descent

In future, astronauts will be required to descend from a spaceship while it is still in space and to return to it. The ability to do this will be necessary in future 5 flights to distant planets. Scientists are now trying to discover if this is possible. The spaceship *Astra* which left the earth a short time ago, will be travelling three hundred miles into space. At a certain 10 point, the *Astra* will stop for a short time and an astronaut will attempt to leave the stationary spaceship and then return to it. We shall not know whether the experiment has been successful until we have 15 received a radio message. The first message is expected to arrive at 7

. . . discover if this is possible

o'clock this evening. By that time, the *Astra* will have been flying through space for seventeen hours and will have circled the earth a great many times. When the first radio messages have been received, the results of the trip will be 20 announced immediately.

Comprehension and Précis

Answer these questions *in not more than 75 words.*
1. What will it be necessary for astronauts to do in future flights to distant planets?
2. When shall we know whether the astronaut in the spaceship *Astra* has succeeded in his attempt to do this?
3. When is a message expected? When will the results of the trip be announced? (*and*)

Composition

Write three or four sentences using the ideas given below:
A message was received at 7 o'clock—the *Astra* had stopped successfully—the astronaut descended—returned—the spaceship came back to earth—the astronaut received a hero's welcome.

Letter-writing

Learn the following opening phrases by heart:
I have not heard from you for some time, so . . .
It was very kind of you to . . .

Exercise
Write two short paragraphs (of not more than two sentences each) completing the above phrases.

Key Structures

By that time, the *Astra* will have been flying through space for seventeen hours.
a Do you remember these sentences: (KS 96)
I shall be writing letters all day tomorrow.
They will have finished this bridge in a year's time.

b Compare these pairs of sentences:

They will have finished this bridge in a year's time.

By next June they will have been working on it for ten months.

I shall have completed this novel by December.

By then I shall have been working on it for three years.

c Compare these pairs of sentences. Pay close attention to the words in italics. (See **KS 49c**)

He will have arrived by this time tomorrow.
The moment he has arrived, I shall let you know.

You can go home at 5 o'clock. You will have finished work by then.
Now that you have finished work, you can go home.

We shall go out this afternoon. It will have stopped raining by then.
As soon as it has stopped raining, we shall go out.

Exercises

A. Underline all the verbs in the passage which tell us what will happen in the future.

B. Give the correct form of the verbs in brackets. Do not refer to the passage until you finish the exercise:

The spaceship *Astra* which left the earth a short time ago, (travel) three hundred miles into space. At a certain point, the *Astra* (stop) for a short time and an astronaut (attempt) to leave the stationary spaceship and then return to it. We (not know) whether the experiment has been successful until we (receive) a radio message. The first message is expected to arrive at 7 o'clock this evening. By that time, the *Astra* (fly) through space for seventeen hours and (circle) the earth a great many times. When the first radio messages (receive), the results of the trip (announce) immediately.

Special Difficulties

Words Often Confused.

a Discover and Invent. Study these examples:
Scientists are trying to discover if this is possible. (ll. 5–6)
Whittle invented the jet engine.

b Leave, Live, and Let. Study these examples:
The *Astra* left the earth a short time ago. (ll. 7–8)
He lives in West Street. He leaves home early every morning.
Will he let you try again? (SD 144)

c Travel, Trip, Journey, and Voyage. Study these examples:
We travelled for over fifteen hours.
He wrote a book about his travels.
How long does the trip last?
We had a terrible journey.
He is going on a voyage round the world.

d Stationary and Stationery. Study these examples:
An astronaut will attempt to leave the stationary spaceship. (ll. 11–12)
That bookseller also sells stationery. (He sells writing materials.)

Exercise

Choose the correct words in the following sentences:

1. Some people never (leave) (live) home; others (travel) (trip) all the time.
2. She would not (let) (leave) the boy get on the bus even though it was (stationery) (stationary).
3. During the (journey) (travel) I shall write to you on ship's (stationery) (stationary).
4. Who (discovered) (invented) the camera?

62   After the Fire

Firemen had been fighting the forest fire for nearly three weeks before they could get it under control. A short time before, great trees had covered the countryside
5 for miles around. Now, smoke still rose up from the warm ground over the desolate hills. Winter was coming on and the hills threatened the surrounding villages with destruction, for heavy rain would
10 not only wash away the soil but would cause serious floods as well. When the fire had at last been put out, the forest authorities ordered several tons of a special type of grass-seed which would grow
15 quickly. The seed was sprayed over the ground in huge quantities by aeroplanes.

*The seed was sprayed
by aeroplanes*

The planes had been planting seed for nearly a month when it began to rain. By then, however, in many places the grass had already taken root. In place of the great trees which had been growing there for centuries, patches of green had
20 begun to appear in the blackened soil.

Comprehension and Précis

Answer these questions *in not more than 75 words*.
1. How long did it take the firemen to get the forest fire under control?
2. Had all the great trees been burnt or not? Was there danger that heavy rain would cause serious floods or not? Would the floods destroy the surrounding villages or not? (*Now that . . . which*)
3. Did the forest authorities order grass-seed to prevent this or not? For how long was it sprayed over the ground by planes? (*To prevent this . . . which . . .*)
4. Did it begin to rain or not? Where had the grass taken root? (*By the time that . . .*)

Composition

Rewrite the following sentences using the joining words in brackets:
1. The firemen cut down trees. They prevented the fire from spreading. (*in order to*)
2. The fire raged for two weeks. It caused millions of pounds worth of damage. (*which*)
3. Forest workers planted young trees quickly. The whole area would become a desert. (*so that . . . not*)

Letter-writing

Write six sentences beginning with each of the following phrases:
I am sorry . . .; Forgive me for . . .; I was so glad . . .; I have not heard . . .; What a surprise . . .; It was very kind . . .

Key Structures

The planes had been planting seed for nearly a month when it began to rain.
a Do you remember these sentences: (**KS 97b**)
He *lived* in Scotland fifteen years *ago*.
He *had lived* in Scotland for fifteen years *before* he came to England.

Now compare these pairs of sentences:

b He had already finished work before I arrived.
He had been working in a factory for years before he got this job.

I asked him what he had lost.
I asked him what he had been doing all afternoon.

Exercises

A. Underline the verbs in the passage which tell us *what had happened* and *what had been happening*.

B. Give the correct form of the verbs in brackets. Do not refer to the passage until you finish the exercise:
1. Firemen (fight) the forest fire for nearly three weeks before they could get it under control. A short time before, great trees (cover) the countryside for miles around.
2. The planes (plant) seed for nearly a month when it began to rain. By then, however, in many places the grass already (take) root. In place of the great trees which (grow) there for centuries, patches of green (begin) to appear in the blackened soil.

C. What happened? What had happened? What had been happening? Give the correct form of the verbs in brackets:
After Howard Carter (discover) Tutankhamen's tomb, strange reports (appear) in the newspapers. Three of the people who (take) part in the discovery (die) soon afterwards. Though nothing (happen) to Carter himself, newspapers (claim) that these people (die) because of the 'curse of the Pharaohs'. These absurd stories have been forgotten, but Carter's great discovery remains. Archaeologists (search) the Valley of Kings for years, but until 1922 nothing (find).

Special Difficulties

Words Often Confused.
a Control (l. 3) and Check. Study these examples:
He controls a large business company.
A mechanic checked my car engine.

b Great (l. 4) and Big. Study these examples:
The Parthenon is a great building. (An important building.)
Skyscrapers are big buildings.

c Soil (l. 10) and Ground (l. 6).
Olive trees can grow in poor soil.
The ball fell to the ground.

Exercise
Choose the correct words in the following sentences:
1. The inspector (checked) (controlled) my ticket.
2. Nothing can grow in this poor (soil) (ground).
3. Have you (checked) (controlled) those figures?
4. Beethoven was a (big) (great) composer.

63 She was not Amused

Geoffrey Hampden has a large circle of friends and is very popular at parties. Everybody admires him for his fine sense of humour—everybody, that is, except his 5 six-year-old daughter, Jenny. Recently, one of Geoffrey's closest friends asked him to make a speech at a wedding reception. This is the sort of thing that Geoffrey loves. He prepared the speech carefully 10 and went to the wedding with Jenny. He had included a large number of funny stories in the speech and, of course, it was a great success. As soon as he had finished, Jenny told him she wanted to go home. 15 Geoffrey was a little disappointed by this but he did as his daughter asked. On the

his fine sense of humour

way home, he asked Jenny if she had enjoyed the speech. To his surprise, she said she hadn't. Geoffrey asked her why this was so and she told him that she did not like to see so many people laughing at him!

Comprehension and Précis

Answer these questions *in not more than 80 words.*
  1. Is Geoffrey Hampden greatly admired for his fine sense of humour or not? What was he invited to do? Did he immediately agree to do so or not? (*When Geoffrey . . . who is . . .*)
  2. Did the speech contain a lot of funny stories or not? Was it a great success or not? (*Since*)
  3. What did his six-year-old daughter, Jenny, want to do after his speech? Was Geoffrey disappointed or not? (*When*)
  4. Why had she not enjoyed it? (*because*)

Composition

Write two or three sentences using the ideas given below:
Geoffrey was amused by Jenny's answer—he explained why everybody laughed—there was another reception some time later—Geoffrey made a speech—not very funny—Jenny asked why no one laughed.

Letter-writing

Learn the following opening phrases by heart:
You must be very annoyed with me for . . .
I have just heard that . . .

Exercise
Write two short paragraphs (of not more than two sentences each) completing the above phrases.

Key Structures

He said that . . . He told me . . . He asked . . . (KS 41, 99)
Study these sentences carefully:
'Open the door for me please,' she said to me.
What did she ask me to do?
She asked me to open the door for her.

'Don't make so much noise,' she said to the children.
What did she tell the children?
She told them not to make so much noise.

'Stay to lunch,' he insisted.
What did he do?
He insisted that I should stay to lunch.

'Come with me,' he suggested.
What did he suggest?
He suggested that I should go with him.

Exercises

A. This is the conversation which took place between Jenny and her father. Supply speech marks, commas and question marks where necessary: (**SD 74**)
1. I want to go home Jenny told him.
2. Did you enjoy the speech Jenny? Geoffrey asked.
3. No she said.
4. Why didn't you enjoy it Geoffrey asked.
5. I do not like to see so many people laughing at you she told him.

B. Now answer these questions. Do not refer to the passage until you finish the exercise:
1. What did Jenny tell him?
2. What did Geoffrey ask Jenny?
3. What did she answer?
4. What did Geoffrey ask her?
5. What did she tell him?

C. Answer these questions:
1. 'Keep quiet!' he said.
   What did he tell me to do?
2. 'Send him a telegram,' he suggested.
   What did he suggest?
3. 'Don't worry about it,' he told me.
   What did he tell me?
4. 'Ask him about it,' he insisted.
   What did he do?

D. Study these examples:
Will it rain tomorrow?
I wonder if it will rain tomorrow.

Why didn't he mention this to me?
I wonder why he didn't mention this to me.

Write the following sentences again beginning each one with 'I wonder'.
1. Can he wait a few minutes longer? I wonder if . . .
2. When will be arrive? I wonder when . . .
3. Has he passed his examination?
4. Where is he?
5. Why didn't she telephone?
6. When shall we see him again?
7. Did she catch the wrong bus?
8. Could you spare me a moment?

156

64 The Channel Tunnel

In 1858, a French engineer, Aimé Thomé de Gamond, arrived in England with a plan for a twenty-one mile tunnel across the English Channel. He said that it would be possible to build a platform in the centre of the Channel. This platform would serve as a port and a railway station. The tunnel would be well-ventilated if tall chimneys were built above sea-level. In 1860, a better plan was put forward by an Englishman, William Low. He suggested that a double railway tunnel should be built. This would solve the problem of ventilation, for if a train entered this tunnel, it would draw in fresh air behind it. Forty-two years later a tunnel was actually begun. If, at the time, the British had not feared invasion, it would have been completed. Recently, there has again been great interest in the idea of a Channel Tunnel. If it is built, it will connect Britain to Europe for the first time in history.

. . . connect Britain to Europe

Comprehension and Précis

Answer these questions *in not more than 85 words*.
1. Who planned to build a tunnel across the English Channel in 1858? How would it be ventilated? (*The tunnel, which . . .*)
2. Who suggested a better plan two years later?
3. How would passing trains solve the problem of ventilation in his proposed double railway tunnel? (*because they would*)
4. Did work begin forty-two years later or not? Why was it stopped? (*Though . . . because*)
5. Has there been renewed interest in the idea lately or not? (*However*)

Composition

Rewrite the following sentences using the joining words in brackets:
1. The English Channel separates Britain from Europe. The country has not been invaded since 1066. (*Thanks to . . . which*)
2. Modern warfare is far more complex. Such fears no longer exist. (*However, now that . . .*)
3. Britain would benefit enormously from a Channel Tunnel. Europe would benefit enormously from a Channel Tunnel. (*Both . . . and*)

Letter-writing

Write opening sentences which would be suitable for letters to the following:
1. A former school mistress who has just got engaged.
2. A friend who has sent you a telegram on your birthday.
3. A librarian who has sent you information you wanted.
4. An aunt you failed to meet for an appointment.

Key Structures

If the British had not feared invasion, it would have been completed.

a Do you remember these sentences:

If he is out, I'll call tomorrow. (**KS 43a**)

You'll miss the train *if you don't hurry*.

If you went to the exhibition you would enjoy it. (**KS 101b**)

If I were in your position, I would act differently.

b Now study these sentences carefully:

You would have missed the train *if you had not hurried*.

If you had gone to the exhibition, you would have enjoyed it.

If I had been in your position, I would have acted differently.

If you could have made him change his mind, you would have saved him a lot of trouble.

Exercises

A. How many sentences in the passage contain the word *if*? Study the form of the verbs in these sentences.

B. Give the correct form of the verbs in brackets. Do not refer to the passage until you finish the exercise:

1. The tunnel would be well-ventilated if tall chimneys (be) built above sea-level.
2. If a train entered this tunnel, it (draw) in fresh air behind it.
3. If, at the time, the British had not feared invasion, it (complete).
4. If it (be) built, it will connect Britain to Europe for the first time in history.

C. Give the correct form of the verbs in brackets:

1. If you had told me about it earlier I (be able) to help you.
2. If you (can/come) with us, we would have been pleased.
3. You (not make) such a mistake if you had been more careful.
4. If father (be) alive he would be horrified.
5. If it (be) fine tomorrow we shall go for a swim.

Special Difficulties

The verb *draw* has a different meaning in each of these sentences. Study them carefully:

If a train entered this tunnel, it would *draw in* fresh air behind it. (ll. 14–16)

The dog *drew back* in terror when it saw the snake.

A taxi *drew up* outside the bank. (It stopped.) Two men got out and then the taxi *drew off*. (It went away.)

A new trading agreement was *drawn up* between Holland and Denmark. (A new agreement was made.)

Exercise

Choose the correct words in the following sentences:

1. We shall have to draw (in) (up) a new plan.
2. When I recognized who he was I drew (back) (up) in horror.
3. The car drew (back) (up) outside the cinema.

65   Jumbo versus the Police

Last Christmas, the circus owner, Jimmy
Gates, decided to take some presents to a
children's hospital. Dressed up as Father
Christmas and accompanied by a 'guard
5 of honour' of six pretty girls, he set off
down the main street of the city riding a
baby elephant called Jumbo. He should
have known that the police would never
allow this sort of thing. A policeman
10 approached Jimmy and told him he ought
to have gone along a side-street as Jumbo
was holding up the traffic. Though Jimmy
agreed to go at once, Jumbo refused to
move. Fifteen policemen had to push
15 very hard to get him off the main street.
The police had a difficult time, but they

The police had a difficult time

were most amused. 'Jumbo must weigh a few tons,' said a policeman afterwards,
'so it was fortunate that we didn't have to carry him. Of course, we should arrest
him, but as he has a good record, we shall let him off this time.'

Comprehension and Précis

Answer these questions *in not more than 80 words.*
1. What did he decide to take to a children's hospital? How did the circus owner,
   Jimmy Gates, dress up? Did he set off down the main street of the city, or did he go
   down a side-street? Was he riding an elephant called Jumbo or not? (*After having
   . . . and . . . riding*)
2. Was he told that he was holding up the traffic or not? Did Jimmy agree to go at
   once, or not? Did Jumbo agree to go, or did he refuse to move? How many policemen had to push him off the main street? (*On being . . . but . . . so . . .*)
3. Did he have a good record or not? Was Jumbo arrested or not? (*As . . . however, . . .*)

Composition

Write three or four sentences using the ideas given below:
The children were waiting at the hospital—Jimmy and the guard of honour arrived—a
great welcome—Jimmy gave presents to the children—they rode on Jumbo—time to
leave—Jumbo refused to move.

Letter-writing

Learn the following opening phrases by heart:
I really hate to complain, but . . .
Some time ago, I . . .

Exercise
Write two short paragraphs (of not more than two sentences each) completing the
above phrases.

Key Structures

Must, Have to, Should and Ought to.
a Do you remember these sentences:
I must leave now. I have got to leave now. (**KS 45a**)
She had to go shopping yesterday.

b Now compare these pairs of sentences:
I can't go to the cinema tonight; I must (or have to) write some letters.
I should (or ought to) do some work tonight, but I think I shall go to the cinema instead.
I missed the train, so I had to take a taxi.
I'm sorry I'm late. I should have taken (or ought to have taken) a taxi.

Exercises
A. Study the use in the passage of *have to*, *should* and *ought*.

B. Give the correct form of the verbs in brackets. Do not refer to the passage until you finish the exercise:
1. He (should/know) that the police would never allow this sort of thing. A policeman approached Jimmy and told him he (ought/go) along a side-street as Jumbo was holding up the traffic.
2. Fifteen policemen (have to) push very hard.
3. It was fortunate that we (not have to) carry him. Of course, we (should/arrest) him, but we shall let him off this time.

C. Supply the correct form of *should*, *ought to*, or *have to* in these sentences:
1. He (. . . come) at 4 o'clock if the plane arrives on time.
2. I didn't go shopping this morning as I (. . . do) the housework.
3. She (. . . come) to see me yesterday, but she forgot.
4. You (. . . ask) for permission before you left the table.
5. As they didn't understand, I (. . . explain) everything again.

Special Difficulties

a The verb *let* has a different meaning in each of these sentences. Study them carefully:
As he has a good record, we shall *let him off* this time. (l. 19) (We shall not punish him.)
I expected him to help me, but he *let me down*. (He failed to do what I expected him to do.)
If anyone knocks at the door when I am out, don't *let him in*.
Who *let the dog out*?
b Words Often Confused.
Agree and Accept. Study these examples:
Though Jimmy agreed to go at once, Jumbo refused to move. (ll. 12–14)
We are not allowed to accept presents from customers.

c Dress up and Dress.
Dressed up as Father Christmas . . . (ll. 3–4) (Wearing fancy dress.)
I got up at 6 o'clock, washed, shaved, dressed and had breakfast.

Exercise
Choose the correct words in the following sentences:
1. The teacher (agreed) (accepted) the boy's apology and let him (off) (down).
2. He was going to lend me a policeman's uniform so that I could (dress) (dress up) for the party, but he let me (in) (down).

66 Cycling through the Air

The Hatfield Puffin is a modern aeroplane, but its designer, Mr John Wimpenny, is finding it difficult to get it off the ground. The reason for this is that
5 this plane is also a bicycle. Its pilot has to pedal hard to get it into the air. After Mr Wimpenny had the plane built, it was tested thoroughly. In 1961, it was the first man-powered aircraft to fly half a
10 mile. While being flown by a champion amateur cyclist in 1963, the plane crashed on an airfield. Since then, Mr Wimpenny has had it rebuilt. He has had the length of the wings increased so that they now
15 measure 93 feet—almost as long as those of a Dakota. Many people have shown interest in this new and unusual sport. But though air cyclists may learn how to fly over short distances, and may, eventually, even get across the English Channel, it is doubtful whether they will ever cycle across the Atlantic.

. . . difficult to get it off the ground

Comprehension and Précis
Answer these questions *in not more than 80 words*.
1. Why is the Hatfield Puffin different from other aeroplanes? (*because*)
2. When did it become the first man-powered aeroplane to cover half a mile?
3. Where did it crash when flown by an amateur champion cyclist two years later?
4. Has its designer, Mr Wimpenny, had it rebuilt or not? Has he had the length of the wings increased to 93 feet or not? Is it likely that planes of this sort will be able to fly great distances or not? (*Though . . . and*)

Composition
Rewrite the sentences below using the joining words in brackets:
1. Few champion cyclists know how to fly. Few pilots are champion cyclists. It is difficult to get a man-powered aircraft off the ground. (*Because . . . and*)
2. The first man-powered aircraft has now been built. It can carry two men. (*which*)
3. It will carry a cyclist. It will carry a pilot. (*not only . . . but . . . as well*)

Letter-writing
Write a short opening paragraph of a letter to a friend who has invited you to go to the theatre with him.

Key Structures
Have. (**KS 47 and 105**)
Study these sentences carefully:
I washed my car. (I washed it myself.)
I had my car washed. (Someone else washed it for me.)
I shall clean this suit. (I shall clean it myself.)
I shall have this suit cleaned. (Someone else will clean it for me.)

Note this use of *have*:
He had his hair cut yesterday.
I shall have to have my watch repaired.
Did you have your watch repaired?
I didn't have my watch repaired.

Exercises
A. Study this use of *have* in the passage.

B. Write these sentences again using *have* with the verbs in italics. Do not refer to the passage until you finish the exercise.
1. After Mr Wimpenny *built* the plane, it was tested thoroughly.
2. While being flown by a champion amateur cyclist in 1963, the plane crashed on an airfield. Since then, Mr Wimpenny *has rebuilt* it.
3. He *has increased* the length of the wings so that they now measure 93 feet.

C. Rewrite these sentences using *have* with the verbs in italics:
1. He *is building* a new house.
2. She *will make* a new dress.
3. I *did not decorate* the house.
4. They *repaired* the washing machine.
5. We *must cut* this tree down.
6. We have *to install* this new television set.
7. Mr Smith wants *to mend* this clock.

Special Difficulties

He is finding it difficult to get it off the ground. (ll. 3–4)
Study these sentences:
I can't *make him change* his mind. (**SD 144**) (I can't compel him to change his mind.)
I can't *get him to change* his mind. (I can't persuade him to change his mind.)

Exercise
Rewrite the following sentences using *get* in place of *make*.
1. I made him tell me the truth.
2. He made me answer his questions.
3. She made the boy take the examination.
4. He made me translate the article into English.
5. I shall make the driver stop the bus.
6. You will never make him do it.
7. I can't make him realize how dangerous this is.
8. I couldn't make him do so much work.

67   Volcanoes

Haroun Tazieff, the Polish scientist, has spent his life-time studying active volcanoes and deep caves in all parts of the world. In 1948, he went to lake Kivu in
5 the Congo to observe a new volcano which he later named Kituro. Tazieff was able to set up his camp very close to the volcano while it was erupting violently. Though he managed to take a number of
10 brilliant photographs, he could not stay near the volcano for very long. He noticed that a river of liquid rock was coming towards him. It threatened to surround him completely, but Tazieff man-
15 aged to escape just in time. He waited until the volcano became quiet and he was able to return two days later. This time, he managed to climb into the mouth of Kituro so that he could take photographs and measure temperatures. Tazieff has often risked his life in this way. He has been able to tell us more about active
20 volcanoes than any man alive.

he could not stay for very long

Comprehension and Précis

Answer these questions *in not more than 80 words.*
  1. Where did Tazieff, the Polish scientist, go in 1948? Why did he go there? What did he call it? (*to . . . which*)
  2. Did he take photographs or not? Did he have to leave almost at once or not? Did a river of liquid rock threaten to surround him or not? (*After taking . . . because*)
  3. Did he escape just in time or not? When did he return? Had the volcano become quiet, or was it still active? (*but . . . when*)
  4. Where did he climb this time? Why did he do so? (*in order to*)

Composition

Write three or four sentences using the ideas given below:
Tazieff went into mouth of Kituro—saw the boiling red centre—ash—lumps of rock shooting up—in great danger—took photographs—returned to camp.

Letter-writing

Write six sentences beginning with each of the following:
Thank you . . .; What a . . .; Forgive . . .; I have not . . .; I am sorry . . .; It was very . . .

Key Structures

Can, Able to and Manage to
a Do you remember these sentences: (**KS 107b and c**)
I couldn't understand him.
I wasn't able to understand him.
He was able to leave Europe before the war began.

b Managed to can be used like *was able to* to show that an action has been completed successfully. (**KS 107c**)

Instead of saying :	*We can say :*
He didn't agree with me at first but I *was able to* persuade him.	He didn't agree with me at first but I *managed to* persuade him.
He *was able to* leave Europe before the war began.	He *managed to* leave Europe before the war began.

Exercises

A. Underline the verbs *could*, *was able to* and *managed to* in the passage. Note how they have been used.

B. Supply *could*, *was able to* or *managed to* in this paragraph. Do not refer to the passage until you finish the exercise.
Tazieff . . . set up his camp very close to the volcano while it was erupting violently. Though he . . . take a number of brilliant photographs, he . . . not stay near the volcano for very long. He noticed that a river of liquid rock was coming towards him. It threatened to surround him completely, but Tazieff . . . escape just in time. He waited until the volcano became quiet and he . . . return two days later. This time, he . . . climb into the mouth of Kituro so that he . . . take photographs and measure temperatures.

C. Rewrite these sentences using *managed to* in place of *could not*.
1. I could not get into town this morning.
2. They could not find the boy who had run away.
3. He could not find a new job.
4. I could not translate the passage into English.
5. They could not swim to the other side of the river.

Special Difficulties

Phrases with Say and Tell. (**KS 41**) Study these phrases:
a Say
Did he *say anything* to you about it? No, he *said nothing*.
He knelt down and *said his prayers*.
If you want some more cake, please *say so*.
I'm sure it would help if you could *say a good word* for him.
He *said goodbye* and left.
Please *say no more* about it.

b Tell
He has been able to tell us more about volcanoes . . . (ll. 19–20)
Can you *tell me* anything *about* it?
Please *tell us a story*.
Can you *tell the time* in English?
I want you to *tell me the truth*.
He often *tells lies*.
If you promise not to tell anyone, I'll *tell you a secret*.
Can't you *tell the difference* between an Austin and a Morris?

Exercise
Supply the correct form of *say* or *tell* in the following sentences:
1. He is only five, but he can already . . . the time.
2. They asked the prisoner several questions, but he . . . nothing.
3. If you . . . so, I suppose it's true. I don't think you would . . . me a lie.
4. They are so alike, I can't . . . the difference between them.
5. He . . . me about his experiences in the Navy.
6. If you could . . . a good word for him, he might get the job.

68 Persistent

I crossed the street to avoid meeting him,
but he saw me and came running towards
me. It was no use pretending that I had
not seen him, so I waved to him. I never
5 enjoy meeting Bert Dykes. He never has
anything to do. No matter how busy you
are, he always insists on coming with you.
I had to think of a way of preventing him
from following me around all morning.
10   'Hullo, Bert,' I said. 'Fancy meeting
you here!'
   'Hullo, Elizabeth,' Bert answered. 'I
was just wondering how to spend the
morning—until I saw you. You're not
15 busy doing anything, are you?'

There's always plenty to read

   'No, not at all,' I answered. 'I'm going
to . . .'
   'Would you mind my coming with you?' he asked, before I had finished
speaking.
20   'Not at all,' I lied, 'but I'm going to the dentist.'
   'Then I'll come with you,' he answered. 'There's always plenty to read in the
waiting room!'

Comprehension and Précis

Answer these questions *in not more than 70 words.*
1. Did Elizabeth try to avoid meeting Bert Dykes or not? Was she able to do so or not?
   (*Even though*)
2. Did he always insist on accompanying her or not? What did she have to do? (*As*)
3. Where did she tell him she was going? Why did he say he would come with her?
   (*When*)

Composition

Rewrite the sentences below using the joining words in brackets:
1. There was a dentist nearby. She knew him well. Elizabeth decided to go there. She
   would explain what had happened. (*As . . . whom . . . in order to*)
2. Bert was in the waiting room. Elizabeth spoke to the dentist. He told her to leave at
   once through another door. (*While . . . and*)
3. Elizabeth left. The dentist went into the waiting room. 'Do you want to have your
   teeth examined?' he asked Bert. (*After . . . and asked Bert if . . .*)

Letter-writing

Write four sentences beginning with each of the following:
You must be very annoyed with me for . . .
I have just heard that . . .
I really hate to complain, but . . .
Some time ago, I . . .

Key Structures

I crossed the street to avoid meeting him.
Compare **KS 51** and **110**.

a Study these sentences carefully. Pay close attention to the words in italics:
I always *avoid travelling* during rush-hour.
He *enjoys playing* football.
He completely *denies taking* it.
Fancy meeting you here!
It's no use crying about it.
It's not worth worrying about.
I can't stand people *shouting* and *pushing*.
Can't you see *I'm busy writing?*
Would you mind opening the window?
I don't mind waiting.

b Compare these sentences:
Would you mind opening the window?
Would you mind my opening the window?

Fancy writing a letter like that!
Fancy her writing a letter like that!

c See, Hear and Smell. Study these sentences:
I *saw him coming*.
He *heard me opening* the door.
I can *smell something burning*.

d Go and Come. Study these sentences:
Let's *go dancing*.
I *went shopping* this morning.
Come swimming with me tomorrow.

Exercises
A. Underline all the verbs in the passage that end in *-ing*.

B. Give the correct form of the verbs in brackets. Do not refer to the passage until you finish the exercise:
I crossed the street to avoid (meet) him, but he saw me and came (run) towards me. It was no use (pretend) that I had not seen him, so I waved to him. I never enjoy (meet) Bert Dykes. No matter how busy you are, he always insists on (come) with you. I had to think of a way of (prevent) him from (follow) me around all morning.
    'Hullo, Bert,' I said. 'Fancy (meet) you here!'
    'Hullo, Elizabeth,' Bert answered. 'I was just wondering how to spend the morning —until I saw you. You're not busy (do) anything, are you?'
    'No, not at all,' I answered. 'I'm going to . . .'
    'Would you mind my (come) with you?' he asked, before I had finished (speak).

C. Write sentences beginning with each of the following:
1. It's no use . . .
2. Let's go . . .
3. Forgive my . . .
4. Do you deny . . .
5. He came . . .
6. I'm busy . . .
7. I always enjoy . . .
8. Would you mind . . .

166

69 But Not Murder!

I was being tested for a driving licence for the third time. I had been asked to drive in heavy traffic and had done so successfully. After having been instructed to drive out of town, I began to acquire confidence. Sure that I had passed, I was almost beginning to enjoy my test. The examiner must have been pleased with my performance, for he smiled and said, 'Just one more thing, Mr Eames. Let us suppose that a child suddenly crosses the road in front of you. As soon as I tap on the window, I want the car to be stopped immediately.' I continued driving and after some time, the examiner tapped loudly. Though the sound could be heard clearly, it took me a long time to react. I suddenly pressed the brake pedal hard and we were both thrown forward. The examiner looked at me sadly. 'Mr Eames,' he said, in a mournful voice, 'you have just killed that child!'

The examiner must have been pleased

Comprehension and Précis

Answer these questions *in not more than 80 words.*

1. Had Mr Eames driven successfully in heavy traffic during his third driving test or not? What did the examiner instruct him to do? (*when*)
2. What did he tell him to suppose? (*that ... would*)
3. What would Mr Eames have to do when the examiner tapped on the window?
4. Did he tap loudly or not? Did Mr Eames react quickly enough or not? What was he told? (*Though ... and*)

Composition

Write two or three sentences using the ideas given below:
Three months later Eames appeared for his fourth test—again told to stop—the examiner was thrown forward, but the child's life was saved—Eames passed his test, but the examiner said, 'You nearly killed me this time!'

Letter-writing

Write five opening phrases which could be used in letters to friends or relations.

Key Structures

After having been instructed to drive out of town, I began to acquire confidence.
a You have learnt to write sentences like these:
It was made in Germany in 1681. (**KS 31**)
I told you it could be done. (**KS 53**)
I can't find my bag. It must have been stolen.
The man was being questioned by the police. (**KS 89**)
He never expected the bicycle to be found.
I found the parcel had been sent to the wrong address. (**KS 111**)

b Now study these sentences:

Instead of saying:	*We can say:*
After he was arrested, the man confessed that he had stolen the money.	*After being arrested*, the man confessed that he had stolen the money.
After he had been instructed to drive out of town, he began to acquire confidence.	*After having been instructed* to drive out of town, he began to acquire confidence.

Exercises

A. Underline the verbs in the passage which are similar in form to the examples given above.

B. Give the correct form of the verbs in brackets. Do not refer to the passage until you finish the exercise.

I (test) for a driving licence for the third time. I (ask) to drive in heavy traffic and had done so successfully. After (have/instruct) to drive out of town, I began to acquire confidence. Sure that I had passed, I was almost beginning to enjoy my test. The examiner (must/please) with my performance, for he smiled and said, 'Just one more thing, Mr Eames. Let us suppose that a child suddenly crosses the road in front of you. As soon as I tap on the window, I want the car to (stop) immediately.'

I continued driving and after some time, the examiner tapped loudly. Though the sound (could/hear) clearly, it took me a long time to react. I suddenly pressed the brake pedal hard and we both (throw) forward.

Special Difficulties

Words Often Confused.
a Licence, Practice, Advice.
Study these pairs of sentences:
I was being tested for a driving licence. (l. 1)
We are licensed to sell beer and spirits.

He still needs a lot of practice.
He practises the piano every day.

I want to give you some advice.
What do you advise me to do?

b Enjoy, Entertain, and Amuse. Study these examples:
I was almost beginning to enjoy my test. (ll. 6–7)
We enjoyed ourselves at the party.

He entertained me to dinner.
He entertained everybody with his clever tricks.

The children were amused by the circus clown. (They laughed.)
His funny stories amused us all. (They made us laugh.)
That child can amuse himself for hours playing in the sand. (He can pass his time happily.)

Exercise

Choose the correct words in the following sentences:
1. I never (amuse) (enjoy) (practicing) (practising) the piano.
2. We were all (amused) (enjoyed) by the jokes he told us.
3. He (advised) (adviced) me to get a (license) (licence).
4. We rarely (entertain) (amuse) these days.
5. We (entertained) (enjoyed) some friends to dinner last night.
6. The magician (amused) (enjoyed) the audience very much.

70 Red for Danger

During a bullfight, a drunk suddenly wandered into the middle of the ring. The crowd began to shout, but the drunk was unaware of the danger. The bull was busy
5 with the matador at the time, but it suddenly caught sight of the drunk who was shouting rude remarks and waving a red cap. Apparently sensitive to criticism, the bull forgot all about the matador and
10 charged at the drunk. The crowd suddenly grew quiet. The drunk, however, seemed quite sure of himself. When the bull got close to him, he clumsily stepped aside to let it pass. The crowd broke into
15 cheers and the drunk bowed. By this time, however, three men had come into the
ring and they quickly dragged the drunk to safety. Even the bull seemed to feel sorry for him, for it looked on sympathetically until the drunk was out of the way before once more turning its attention to the matador.

Apparently sensitive to criticism

Comprehension and Précis

Answer these questions *in not more than 75 words*.
1. Did a drunk suddenly wander into the middle of the ring during a bullfight or not? What did he do? (*and*)
2. Did the bull ignore the matador or not? What did it do? Why did he step aside? (*Ignoring . . . but*)
3. Did the crowd cheer or not? What did the drunk do? (*and*)
4. Did three men drag the drunk to safety just after this or not? Did the bull look on sympathetically or not? Did it once more turn its attention to the matador or not? (*Just after this . . . while . . . before it . . .*)

Composition

Rewrite the following sentences using the joining words in brackets:
1. The man became sober. It was possible to discover his identity. (*When*)
2. He was Domingo Cordova. He had been a great matador in his youth. He had failed in the ring. He had taken to drinking. (*. . . a man who . . . but having . . .*)
3. He had changed. No one recognized him. (*so much that*)

Letter-writing

Learn the following opening phrases by heart:
I have not forgotten that . . .
You will find it hard to believe, but . . .
I am afraid I . . .

Exercise
Write sentences completing each of the above phrases.

Key Structures

Words Followed by: For, With, Of, To, At, From, In, On, and About. (Compare KS 55 and 114)
Use this list for reference:

a FOR: eager, enough, famous, fit, grateful (or to), qualified (or in), ready (or to), responsible, sorry, sufficient, thankful (or to), valid.

b WITH: angry (with someone; at something), busy (or at), consistent, content, familiar (or to), identical, patient, popular.

c OF: afraid, ahead, aware, capable, careful (or with), certain, conscious, envious, fond, guilty, ignorant, independent, jealous, kind (or to), north/south/east/west, short, shy, sure, worthy.

d TO: close, contrary, cruel, dear, equal, faithful, fatal, harmful, indifferent, inferior, liable, new, obedient, obvious, polite, previous, rude, sensitive, similar, useful.

e AT: bad, clever, efficient, expert (or in), good, indignant, quick, sad (or about), slow, skilful (or in).

f FROM: away, different, far, safe.

g IN: deficient, fortunate, honest, weak.

h ON: dependent, intent, keen.

i ABOUT: curious, doubtful (or of), enthusiastic, reluctant (or to), right (or in), uneasy.

Exercises

A. There are some words in the passage which are included in the above list. These words are followed by *for*, *with*, *of*, and *to*. Can you find them?

B. Supply the missing words (*for*, *with*, *of*, *to*, *at*, *from*, *in*, *on* or *about*) without referring to the above list as far as possible.

1. George is jealous . . . his younger sister. 2. She is well-qualified . . . typing and very efficient . . . her work. 3. We are fortunate . . . having sufficient supplies of fuel . . . the winter. 4. Contrary . . . my expectations, there was no need to be uneasy . . . the results of the match. 5. I am not familiar . . . his novels and not very keen . . . reading them. 6. I know he is slow . . . understanding, but you have to be patient . . . him. 7. It is obvious . . . everyone that he is not responsible . . . this mistake. 8. I think he's quite honest . . . his intentions. 9. He is not only indifferent . . . other people; he is often extremely rude . . . them as well. 10. I'm not very fond . . . dancing. 11. Children remain dependent . . . their parents for a long time. 12. I should be grateful . . . any advice you can give. 13. He is not different . . . anyone else. 14. He may be quick . . . understanding, but he's not capable . . . remembering anything. 15. He is intent . . . passing the examination, but I'm doubtful . . . his chances. 16. He says he's sorry . . . what he did, so you need not get angry . . . him. 17. I've never been good . . . arithmetic. 18. That boy is far ahead . . . everyone else in the class. 19. Even though he was often cruel . . . his dog, it remained faithful . . . him. 20. Your conclusions are not consistent . . . the facts. 21. This diary will prove useful . . . you. 22. I'm not sure . . . the exact date, but I think he arrived here in 1959. 23. He was found guilty . . . a great many crimes. 24. You should not be so sensitive . . . criticism. 25. This passport is valid . . . all countries except China.

71 A Famous Clock

When you visit London, one of the first things you will see is Big Ben, the famous clock which can be heard all over the world on the B.B.C. If the Houses of Parliament had not been burned down in 1834, the great clock would never have been erected. Big Ben takes its name from Sir Benjamin Hall who was responsible for the making of the clock when the new Houses of Parliament were being built. It is not only of immense size, but is extremely accurate as well. Officials from Greenwich Observatory have the clock checked twice a day. On the B.B.C. you can hear the clock when it is actually striking because microphones are con-

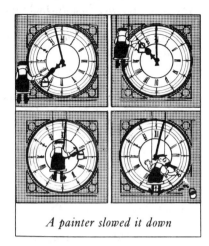

A painter slowed it down

nected to the clock tower. Big Ben has rarely gone wrong. Once, however, it failed to give the correct time. A painter who had been working on the tower hung a pot of paint on one of the hands and slowed it down!

Comprehension and Précis

Answer these questions *in not more than 75 words.*
1. When were the Houses of Parliament burnt down? Who was made responsible for the construction of a huge clock? Did it become known as Big Ben or not? (*After ... which ...*)
2. Why is it very accurate despite its immense size? (*for*)
3. Has this clock often gone wrong, or has it rarely gone wrong? Why can it be heard on the B.B.C. when it is striking? (*This clock which ... because ...*)

Composition

Write two or three sentences using the ideas given below:
Big Ben tells correct time—it also tells us when Parliament is in session—there is a light in the clock tower—it is kept on until the House closes—sometimes it is on all night.

Letter-writing

Learn the following phrases by heart:

I wonder how you learnt that ...
You will never guess who/what ...

Exercise
Write two short paragraphs (of not more than two sentences each) completing the above phrases.

Key Structures

Review KS 149–167
The moment you leave this tent, you will get a big surprise. (KS 149)
By that time, the *Astra* will have been flying through space for seventeen hours. (KS 151)

The planes had been planting seed for nearly a month when it began to rain. (**KS 153**)
If the British had not feared invasion, it would have been completed. (**KS 158**)
Must, Have to, Should and Ought to. (**KS 160**)
Have. (**KS 161**)
After having been instructed to drive out of town, I began to acquire confidence. (**KS 167**)

Exercises

A. Underline the verbs in the passage. Revise any Key Structures you have forgotten.

B. Give the correct form of the verbs in brackets. Do not refer to the passage until you finish the exercise.

1. When you (visit) London, one of the first things you will see is Big Ben, the famous clock which (can/hear) all over the world on the B.B.C. If the Houses of Parliament (not burn) down in 1834, the great clock would never have been erected.
2. Officials from Greenwich Observatory have the clock (check) twice a day. On the B.B.C. you can hear the clock when it actually (strike) because microphones (connect) to the clock tower.
3. Once it failed to give the correct time. A painter who (work) on the tower hung a pot of paint on one of the hands.

C. Give the correct form of the verbs in brackets:

1. I shall have completed this novel by December. By then I (work) on it for ten months.
2. Now that you (finish) work you can go home.

D. Supply the correct form of *should*, *ought to* or *have to* in these sentences:

1. I couldn't go shopping yesterday afternoon. I (. . . go) to the dentist.
2. I really (. . . buy) a new car but I can't afford to.
3. I didn't know you would be late. You (. . . telephone).

Special Difficulties

Words Often Confused.
a Official, Clerk, Employee, Shop-assistant.
Study these examples:
Officials from Greenwich Observatory have the clock checked twice a day. (ll. 12–14)
The Customs official asked me several questions.
He works as a clerk for an insurance firm.
Over a thousand factory employees went on strike.
She works as a shop-assistant in a clothing store.

b Hang/Hung and Hang/Hanged.
Study these examples:
A painter hung a pot of paint on one of the hands. (ll. 18–19)
When the sun came out, she hung the washing on the line.
The murderer was hanged.

Exercise
Choose the correct words in the following sentences:

1. The (clerk) (shop-assistant) who served me was very helpful.
2. I (hanged) (hung) my coat in the hall.
3. Capital punishment has been abolished. Murderers will not be (hung) (hanged) in future.
4. He used to work as a (clerk) (shop-assistant) in a government department before he joined the army.

72 A Car called 'Bluebird'

The great racing driver, Sir Malcolm
Campbell, was the first man to drive at
over 300 miles per hour. He set up a new
world record in September 1935 at Bonne-
5 ville Salt Flats, Utah. *Bluebird*, the car he
was driving, had been specially built for
him. It was over 30 feet in length and had
a 2500 horse-power engine. Although
Campbell reached a speed of over 304
10 miles per hour, he had great difficulty in
controlling the car because a tyre burst
during the first run. After his attempt,
Campbell was disappointed to learn that
his average speed had been 299 miles per
15 hour. However, a few days later, he was
told that a mistake had been made. His

301 miles per hour

average speed had been 301 miles per hour. Since that time, racing drivers have
reached speeds of over 400 miles an hour. Following his father's footsteps many
years later, Sir Malcolm's son, Donald, also set up a world record. Like his
20 father, he was driving a car called *Bluebird*.

Comprehension and Précis

Answer these questions *in not more than 75 words.*
1. Who set up a land-speed record in 1935? What was his car called? Had it been
   specially built for him or not? (*driving a car . . . which*)
2. Was his average speed incorrectly declared to be 299 miles per hour or 289 miles
   per hour? Was this mistake corrected later or not? (*but*)
3. How many miles an hour had he averaged?
4. Have racing drivers exceeded 400 miles an hour since that time or not?
5. Is Sir Malcolm's son, Donald, among them? What was his car called? (*Among them
   is . . . whose*)

Composition

Write two or three sentences using the ideas given below:
During a car race—leading car skidded—overturned—the driver was not hurt—got
his car back on to the course—won the race.

Letter-writing

Write sentences completing each of the following phrases:
I have not forgotten that . . .
You will find it hard to believe, but . . .
I am afraid I . . .
I wonder how you learnt that . . .
You will never guess who/what . . .

Special Difficulties

Review SD 130–172

Exercises

A. Words Often Confused.

Choose the correct words in the following sentences:

1. Hurry up or you will (lose) (miss) (loose) the train. (**SD 130a**)
2. I'm (expecting) (waiting) to receive a letter soon. (**SD 130b**)
3. You should (raise) (rise) that picture a few inches. (**SD 132a**)
4. I love (lying) (laying) in bed. (**SD 132b**)
5. He always (beats) (wins) me at chess. (**SD 132c**)
6. Are you (quiet) (quite) ready? (**SD 136b**)
7. I dislike getting up early, but I (am used to) (used to) it now. (**SD 140a**)
8. People often come into our garden and (pick) (cut) flowers. (**SD 146c**)
9. No one knows who (invented) (discovered) the wheel. (**SD 152a**)
10. I can't (leave) (let) you do that. (**SD 152b**)
11. His (travel) (journey) lasted four days. (**SD 152c**)
12. The oil level in the engine must be (checked) (controlled). (**SD 154a**)
13. I could not (accept) (agree) his offer. (**SD 160b**)
14. Who is going to (dress) (dress up) as Father Christmas? (**SD 160c**)
15. How many hours a day do you (practise) (practice)? (**SD 168a**)
16. We were (enjoyed) (amused) by his stories. (**SD 168b**)
17. She (hung) (hanged) the clothes on the line. (**SD 172b**)
18. The train arrived (late) (lately) as usual. (**SD 134**)
19. He has been working too (hardly) (hard). (**SD 134**)
20. He was (near) (nearly) run over by a car. (**SD 134**)

B. Join the following sentences leaving out the verb *want to*. (**SD 148**)

1. I told him about it. I wanted to help you. (*in order to*)
2. I opened the door quietly. I did not want to disturb him. (*so as to*)
3. He left the letter on the table. He wanted me to see it. (*in order that*)

C. Draw (**SD 158**); Let (**SD 160a**)

Complete these sentences by adding any of the following words:
out, down, up, off.

1. A big car drew . . . outside our house.
2. You can't rely on him. He is sure to let you . . .
3. Don't let the children . . . of the garden.
4. We shall have to draw . . . a new agreement.
5. He was going to punish the boy, but he let him . . .

D. Supply the correct form of *say* or *tell* (**SD 164**) in the following sentences:

1. I can . . . no more. He . . . me a secret and I have to keep it.
2. Why don't you . . . him the truth?
3. If you didn't want it, why didn't you . . . so?
4. He knelt down and . . . a prayer.
5. I can't prevent him from . . . lies.

174

IF YOU CAN DO THIS TEST GO ON TO UNIT 4

Key Structures

A. Word Order in Complex Statements.
Rewrite these sentences using the joining words in brackets:
1. He missed the train. He did not hurry. (*because*)
2. He ran fast. He failed to win the race. (*Although*)
3. I was tired. I went to sleep immediately. (*so . . . that*)
4. My neighbour went to Tokyo for a holiday. He could not return home. He did not have enough money. (*who . . . because*)
5. I found the door unlocked. I went into the kitchen. (*Finding*)
6. I bought a picture. It was very valuable. (*which*)
7. He walked quietly down the corridor. He did not want anyone to hear him. (*so that*)
8. They cleared the ground. They wanted to build a house. (*to*)

B. Composition.
Write two or three sentences using the ideas given below:
A workman was digging in a field—struck a 6000 volt electricity cable with his spade—was thrown twenty feet—unhurt—town was in darkness—no one knew what had happened.

C. Verbs.
a These things always happen.
What is happening? What always happens?
Give the correct form of the verbs in brackets:
'Let's eat here,' I said to my wife.
'I (prefer) to have a drink first,' she answered.
'That's a good idea,' I said. I picked up the menu. 'I (not understand) a thing,' I said. 'It's all in Spanish.'
'It (not matter),' said my wife.
'What . . . that word (mean)?' I asked.
'I (not know),' she answered.
We called the waiter and pointed to the word on the menu.
'Two,' I said, holding up two fingers.
After some time, my wife said suddenly, 'Look! He (bring) us two boiled eggs!'

b What happened?
The verbs in brackets tell us *what happened*. Give the correct form of each verb:
My friend, Herbert, has always been fat, but things (get) so bad recently that he (decide) to go on a diet. He (begin) his diet a week ago. First of all, he (write) out a long list of all the foods which were forbidden. The list (include) most of the things Herbert loves. Yesterday I (pay) him a visit. I (ring) the bell and (not surprise) to see that Herbert was still as fat as ever. He (lead) me into his room and hurriedly (hide) a large parcel under his desk. It was obvious that he (embarrass).

c What happened? What has happened? What has been happening?
Give the correct form of the verbs in brackets:
Jack (look) at his watch for the twentieth time. Suddenly Jill (arrive). 'I (wait) for over an hour,' he (say) angrily. 'You never come on time.'
'Oh, is that so?' Jill (answer). '(Be) you here at 2.30? Jack (go) red. 'Well,' he (say),

'I (get) here five minutes late myself, but you (not be) here.'

'I (come) here at exactly 2.30,' Jill (say) and I (wait) for five minutes, but you (not come).'

'What you (do) since then?' Jack (ask).

'I just (be) to the hairdresser's,' Jill (answer) brightly.

d What was happening? What happened? What used to happen?
Give the correct form of the verbs in brackets. Use *would* in place of *used to* where possible:
Dreams of finding lost treasure almost (come) true recently. A new machine called 'The Revealer' has been invented and it has been used to detect gold which has been buried in the ground. The machine (use) in a cave near the sea-shore where—it is said—pirates (hide) gold. The pirates often (bury) gold in the cave and then (fail) to collect it. Armed with the new machine, a search party (go) into the cave hoping to find buried treasure. The leader of the party (examine) the soil near the entrance to the cave when the machine (show) that there (be) gold under the ground. Very excited, the party (dig) a hole two feet deep. They finally (find) a small gold coin which was almost worthless.

e What will happen tonight? Give the correct form of the verbs in brackets:
A life-boat (set) out tonight to search for the ship-wreck. The crew (send) radio messages to the wreck until they (receive) a signal from the men on board. As soon as they (receive) a signal, they (try) and find the wreck with powerful searchlights. The moment the crew (locate) the wreck, they (fire) a special gun which (carry) a rope from the life-boat to the sinking ship. If the sea is rough, they (pour) oil on the water. They are sure to succeed, but if they fail, a helicopter (send) out tomorrow morning. Helicopters are very useful for rescue work, but they cannot be used at night.

f What will happen? What will be happening? What will have happened? What will have been happening?
Give the correct form of the verbs in brackets:
The spaceship, *Astra*, which left the earth a short time ago, (travel) three hundred miles into space. At a certain point, the *Astra* (stop) for a short time and an astronaut (attempt) to leave the stationary spaceship and then return to it. We (not know) whether the experiment has been successful until we (receive) a radio message. The first message is expected to arrive at 7 o'clock this evening. By that time, the *Astra* (fly) through space for seventeen hours and (circle) the earth a great many times. When the first radio messages (receive), the results of the trip (announce) immediately.

g What happened? What had happened? What had been happening?
Give the correct form of the verbs in brackets:
After Howard Carter (discover) Tutankhamen's tomb, strange reports (appear) in the newspapers. Three of the people who (take) part in the discovery (die) soon afterwards. Though nothing (happen) to Carter himself, newspapers (claim) that these people (die) because of the 'curse of the Pharaohs'. These absurd stories have been forgotten, but Carter's great discovery remains. Archaeologists (search) the Valley of Kings for years, but until 1922 nothing (find).

h Give the correct form of the verbs in brackets:
I (test) for a driving licence for the third time. I (ask) to drive in heavy traffic and had done so successfully. After (have/instruct) to drive out of town, I began to acquire confidence. Sure that I had passed, I was almost beginning to enjoy my test. The examiner (must/please) with my performance, for he smiled and said, 'Just one more thing, Mr Eames. Let us suppose that a child suddenly crosses the road in front of you. As soon as I tap on the window, I want the car to (stop) immediately.' I continued driving and after some time, the examiner tapped loudly. Though the sound (could/

hear) clearly, it took me a long time to react. I suddenly pressed the brake pedal hard and we both (throw) forward.

i Answer the questions after each statement:
1. 'Keep quiet!' he said.
   What did he tell me to do?
2. 'Send him a telegram,' he suggested.
   What did he suggest?
3. 'Ask him about it,' he insisted.
   What did he do?
4. 'Don't worry about it,' he told me.
   What did he tell me?

j Write the following sentences again beginning each one with ' I wonder '.
1. Can he wait a few minutes longer?
2. When will he arrive?
3. Has he passed his examination?
4. Where is he?

k If.
Give the correct form of the verbs in brackets:
1. If you (listen) to me you would not have lost all that money.
2. I could have saved you a lot of trouble if you (write) to me.
3. If you had applied earlier, you (have) your passport by now.

l Give the correct form of the verbs in brackets:
I crossed the street to avoid (meet) him, but he saw me and came (run) towards me. It was no use (pretend) that I had not seen him, so I waved to him. I never enjoy (meet) Bert Dykes. No matter how busy you are, he always insists on (come) with you. I had to think of a way of (prevent) him from (follow) me around all morning.

   'Hullo, Bert,' I said. 'Fancy (meet) you here!'
   'Hullo, Elizabeth,' Bert answered. 'I was just wondering how to spend the morning —until I saw you. You're not busy (do) anything, are you?'
   'No, not at all,' I answered. 'I'm going to . . .'
   'Would you mind my (come) with you?' he asked, before I had finish (speak).

D. Other Verbs.
a Supply the correct form of *should*, *ought to*, or *have to* in these sentences:
1. He (. . . come) at 4 o'clock if the plane arrives on time.
2. I didn't go shopping this morning as I (. . . do) the housework.
3. She (. . . come) to see me yesterday, but she forgot.
4. You (. . . ask) for permission before you left the table.

b Rewrite these sentences using *have* with the verbs in italics:
1. He *is building* a new house.
2. She *will make* a new dress.
3. I *cut* my hair yesterday.
4. We *must cut* this tree down.

c Rewrite these sentences using *managed to* in place of *could not*.
1. I could not get into town this morning.
2. They could not find the boy who had run away.
3. He could not find a new job.
4. I could not translate the passage into English.

E. A, The and Some.
Put in *a*, *the* and *some* where necessary:
After . . . breakfast, I sent . . . children to . . . school and then I went to . . . market. It was still early when I returned home. . . . children were at . . . school, my husband

was at ... work, and ... house was quiet. So I decided to make ... tarts for ... tea. In ... short time I was busy mixing ... butter and ... flour and my hands were soon covered with ... sticky pastry. At exactly that moment, ... telephone rang. Nothing could have been more annoying. I picked up ... receiver between ... two sticky fingers and was dismayed when I recognized ... voice of Mrs Bates. It took me ten minutes to persuade her to ring back later. At last I hung up ... receiver. What ... mess! There was ... pastry on my fingers, on ... telephone, and on ... door-knobs. I had no sooner got back to ... kitchen than ... door-bell rang loud enough to wake ... dead. This time it was ... postman and he wanted me to sign for ... registered letter!

F. A lot of cars entered for the race.
Supply the missing words in the following:
Once a year a race is held for old cars. A lot ... cars entered for this race last year and there was a great ... of excitement just before it began. One of the ... handsome cars was a Rolls Royce Silver Ghost. The ... unusual car was a Benz which had only three wheels. Built in 1885, it was the ... (old) car taking part. After a great ... loud explosions, the race began. ... of the cars broke down on the course and some drivers spent ... time *under* their cars than *in* them! A ... cars, however, completed the race. The winning car reached a speed of forty miles an hour—much faster ... any of its rivals. It sped downhill at the end of the race and its driver had a ...... trouble trying to stop it. The race gave everyone a great ... of pleasure. It was very different ... modern car races but no ... exciting.

G. Supply the missing words in the following sentences:
1. A woman ... blue jeans stood ... the window of an expensive shop. Though she hesitated for a moment, she finally went ... and asked to see a dress that was ... the window.
2. Glancing ... her scornfully, the assistant told her that the dress was sold. The woman walked ...... the shop angrily.
3. She returned ... the shop the following morning dressed ... a fur coat, ... a handbag ... one hand and a long umbrella ... the other.

H. Words followed by *for, with, of, to* and *at.*
Supply the missing words in the following sentences:
1. You shouldn't get so angry ... him.
2. He is very good ... finding excuses.
3. I'm not very fond ... ice-cream.
4. I would be thankful ... any advice you can give me.
5. He remained faithful ... the firm even after he had been dismissed.
6. I cannot be held responsible ... other people's mistakes.
7. Don't be so sure ... yourself.
8. His excellent progress should be obvious ... everyone.

Special Difficulties

a Words Often Confused.
Choose the correct words in the following sentences:
1. This screw is (loose) (lose).
2. I always (rise) (raise) at six o'clock.
3. He (laid) (lay) the book on the table.
4. He works very (hard) (hardly).
5. Who (won) (beat) the match?
6. Please keep (quiet) (quite).
7. I (used to) (am used to) smoke a lot once.

8. The waitress (fell) (dropped) her tray.
9. The teacher got angry and threw a book (to) (at) the boy.
10. We went into the orchard to help him (pick) (cut) some apples.
11. Your son has (increased) (grown) since I last saw him.
12. Sir Frank Whittle (discovered) (invented) the jet engine.
13. Please (leave) (let) him come with me.
14. Would you like to take (part) (place) in the contest?
15. No one knows the (reason) (cause) for his disappearance.
16. We were (amused) (enjoyed) by the circus clown.
17. They are now (controlling) (checking) our passports.
18. What do you (advice) (advise) me to do?

b Say and Tell.
Write sentences using either *say* or *tell* with the following: a secret, your prayers, a lie, nothing, a story, so.

c Write these sentences again. Express the phrases in italics in a different way:
1. *The dining-room in our school* is very large.
2. He told us a *story about ghosts*.
3. She gave me a *present for my birthday*.
4. We stopped at *an inn in the village*.
5. *The leader of the party* made a speech.

Unit 4

INSTRUCTIONS TO THE STUDENT

In Unit 4 you will be expected to write simple, compound and complex statements. You will have less help than you had in the previous Units.

Before you begin each exercise, read these instructions carefully. Read them each time you begin a new piece. They are very important.

How to work—Précis

Unit 4 contains twenty-four short passages. There are no Comprehension questions under these passages. Instead, you will find the answers to imaginary questions. These 'answers' have been written in note form and are, in fact, the main points of a précis.

1. Read the passage carefully two or three times. Make sure you understand it.
2. Read the general instructions immediately below each passage. They will tell you what you have to do.
3. Under the titles CONNECTIONS, you will find two sets of joining words which have been given with each list of POINTS.
4. Using the first set of connections, join up the points to make sentences. The number of points which each sentence will contain is given in brackets. All your sentences together should form *a complete paragraph*. When joining up the points, you may refer to the passage as much as you like.
5. Read through your work and correct your mistakes.
6. Count the number of words in your paragraph. Do not go over the word limit. Words like 'the', 'a' etc. count as single words. Words which are joined by a hyphen (e.g. 'living-room') also count as single words. At the end of your paragraph, write the number of words that you have used.
7. Now, using the second set of connections, write *another* précis of the passage in exactly the same way.

Example

Work through this example carefully and then try to do the exercises in Unit 4 in the same way.

The Sacred Tree

In the nineteenth century, Mugo Kibiru, a famous prophet of the Kikuyu tribe, foretold that a fig tree at Thika, twenty-six miles north of Nairobi, would wither and die on the day that Kenya gained independence. Kibiru also prophesied that Kenya would become a white man's colony, but that one day the white man
5 would return the land to the Africans. He foresaw the coming of the railway which he described as 'an iron snake with many legs, like an earthworm.' Kibiru's prophecies proved to be so accurate that for many years the tree at Thika was regarded as sacred. Even the white men took the prophecy seriously, for they built the tree up with earth and put a concrete wall around it so that it would not
10 fall. These measures were doomed to fail. Shortly before Kenya gained independence, the tree was struck by lightning and it began to wither rapidly. By the day Kenya officially became independent, it had decayed completely, fulfilling the prophecy made over seventy years before by Kibiru.

Précis

In not more than 80 words write an account of the tree at Thika. Write two different paragraphs using the points and connections given below.

CONNECTIONS	POINTS	CONNECTIONS
that	1. 19th century—Kibiru foretold.	*According to*
when	2. Fig tree—wither—Kenya independent.	*on the day that*
As	3. Other prophecies accurate.	
	4. Tree sacred.	*so*
Though	5. White men—wall.	
	6. Prevent it falling.	*to*
	7. Prophecy true.	*but*
for	8. Tree—lightning—before independence.	*After having been*
and	9. Decayed.	

1. A Possible Answer (First set of Connections)

In the nineteenth century, Kibiru, a famous prophet of the Kikuyu tribe, foretold *that* a fig tree at Thika would wither *when* Kenya became independent. *As* many of Kibiru's prophecies proved to be accurate, the tree was considered sacred. *Though* white men built a wall round the tree, they could not prevent it from falling. Kibiru's prophecy came true, *for* the tree was struck by lightning just before Kenya gained her independence *and* it decayed completely.   (76 words)

2. A Possible Answer (Second set of Connections)

According to a prophecy made in the nineteenth century by the Kikuyu prophet, Kibiru, a fig tree at Thika would wither *on the day that* Kenya gained independence. Other prophecies made by Kibiru proved to be accurate *so* the tree was regarded as sacred. The white men even built a wall round it *to* prevent it from falling, *but* the prophecy came true. *After having been* struck by lightning just before Kenya became independent, the tree decayed completely.   (78 words)

Composition

In Unit 4 Composition exercises are based on ideas suggested by each passage. You will be asked to write *two* paragraphs of about 150 words using ideas which have been given in note form. You may, of course, add to these ideas if you wish or change them to make them suit your purposes.

Example

Work through this example carefully and then try to do the Composition exercises in the same way.

Composition

Write an imaginary account of what happened to the tree from the time it was struck by lightning to when Kenya gained her independence. Write two paragraphs of about 150 words using the ideas given below.

1. Shortly before independence—storm—tree struck—news to Nairobi—whole of Kenya—Kibiru's prophecy true.
2. Visitors from all parts of Kenya—excitement—tree decayed—completely by independence day—high wall remained—life to a new country.

A Possible Answer

Shortly before Kenya gained her independence, there was a terrible storm. The next morning, the inhabitants of Thika were astonished to find that the sacred tree had been struck by lightning. Its trunk was split in the middle and blackened branches lay everywhere. The news travelled quickly to Nairobi. Soon everybody in Kenya heard that the sacred tree had begun to wither. It now seemed certain that Kibiru's prophecy would come true.

During the next few weeks, people came from all parts of Kenya to see the sacred tree. The tree decayed before their eyes. Everybody was excited and a little frightened by what was happening. Day by day, branches fell, until only part of the trunk remained. By independence day, the trunk had decayed completely. Only the high wall which had been built by the white men was still standing. The dead tree had given its life to a new country.   (About 150 words)

Letter-writing

Follow the instructions given under each passage.

Key Structures and Special Difficulties

When you finish the Letter-writing exercise, go on to the language exercises that follow. The **Key Structures** deal with exactly the same problems that were considered in Units 1, 2 and 3. In this Unit you will revise what you have learnt so far. You may refer back if you have forgotten anything. **Special Difficulties** are dealt with after the Key Structures. The work you do in grammar is based on material contained in the passages. Refer to the passages frequently. They will help you to understand the grammar and to do the exercises.

73 The Record-Holder

Little boys who play truant from school are unimaginative. A quiet day's fishing, or eight hours in a cinema seeing the same film over and over again, is usually as far
5 as they get. They have all been put to shame by a boy who, while playing truant, travelled 1600 miles. He hitch-hiked to Dover and, towards evening, went into a boat to find somewhere to
10 sleep. When he woke up next morning, he discovered that the boat had, in the meantime, travelled to Calais. No one noticed the boy as he crept off. From there, he hitch-hiked to Paris in a lorry.
15 The driver gave him a few biscuits and a cup of coffee and left him just outside the

He was picked up by a policeman

city. The next car the boy stopped did not take him into the centre of Paris as he hoped it would, but to Perpignan on the French-Spanish border. There he was picked up by a policeman and sent back to England by the local authorities. He
20 has surely set up a record for the thousands of boys who dream of evading school.

Précis

In not more than 80 words, describe the boy's experiences. Write two different paragraphs using the points and connections given below.

CONNECTIONS	POINTS	CONNECTIONS
who	⌈ 1. Boy played truant.	
	⌊ 2. Travelled 1600 miles.	and
	⌈ 3. Hitch-hiked—Dover.	After
where	4. Slept—boat.	
only to find	⌊ 5. Found himself—Calais—morning.	
	⌈ 6. Lorry-driver: lift and something to eat.	where
and	⌊ 7. Boy got off near Paris.	On getting off
but, instead	⌈ 8. Stopped another car.	which . . . not to . . .
of being	⌊ 9. Not taken Paris—Perpignan.	but to . . .
After	⌈10. Picked up—policeman.	There
	⌊11. Sent home—authorities.	and

Composition

Write two paragraphs in about 150 words using the ideas given below:
1. The boy returned—sick, cold and hungry—his parents were worried—met him at the harbour—their reactions.
2. The boy returned to school—he was afraid he would be punished—the boys gave him a hero's welcome—asked questions—the headmaster punished him by making him give a talk to the whole school about his experiences abroad.

Letter-writing

A letter contains three main parts: the Introduction, the Purpose and the Conclusion. The most important part is the Purpose. Here you must explain why you are writing.

Exercise

Write a short Introduction of a letter to a friend beginning:
'You will never guess what . . .'

Key Structures

Simple, Compound and Complex Statements. Review:
KS 13, 71, 127.

Exercises

A. How many joining words can you find in the passage? Underline as many as you can.

B. Rewrite these simple statements using the joining words in brackets. Do not refer to the passage until you finish the exercise.
1. Little boys play truant from school. They are unimaginative. (*who*)
2. They have all been put to shame by a boy. He played truant. He travelled 1600 miles. (*a boy who, while . . .*)
3. He hitch-hiked to Dover. Towards evening, he went into a boat. He wanted to find somewhere to sleep. (*and . . . to*)
4. He woke up next morning. He discovered that the boat had, in the meantime, travelled to Calais. (*When*)
5. No one noticed the boy. He crept off. (*as*)
6. The driver gave him a few biscuits. He gave him a cup of coffee. He left him outside the city. (*and . . . and*)

C. Rewrite the following sentences using the joining words in brackets:
1. The climbers reached the top of the mountain. They spent the night there. (*not only . . . but . . . as well*)
2. A fire broke out in a cinema. Several hundred people tried to leave the building. A number of them were injured. (*When . . . and*)
3. James Sullivan will give a lecture at the local library next week. His book on the Antarctic was published recently. (*whose*)
4. The police searched everywhere. The missing boy could not be found. His dog could not be found. (*Although . . . neither . . . nor*)
5. Fares have increased. The railway company is still losing money. The employees have demanded higher wages. (*In spite of the fact that . . . because*)
6. He gave me a fright. I knocked the teapot over. (*such . . . that*)
7. I made sure. The alarm-clock worked. I set it. It would ring at six o'clock. (*After making . . . that . . . so that*)
8. I hid the Christmas presents under the desk quickly. My young daughter would not see them. She entered the room. (*so that . . . when*)
9. I refused the offer. I explained. I had already been offered a job by another company. (*Refusing . . . that . . .*)
10. He fought the wolves off for three hours. Help arrived. (*before*)

74 Out of the Lime-Light

An ancient bus stopped by a dry river
bed and a party of famous actors and
actresses got off. Dressed in dark glasses
and old clothes, they had taken special
5 precautions so that no one should recognize them. But as they soon discovered,
disguises can sometimes be too perfect.

'*I'm sheriff here*'

'This is a wonderful place for a picnic,'
said Gloria Gleam.

10 'It couldn't be better, Gloria,' Brinksley
Meers agreed. 'No newspaper men, no
film fans! Why don't we come more
often?'

Meanwhile, two other actors, Rockwall
15 Slinger and Merlin Greeves, had carried
two large food baskets to a shady spot
under some trees. When they had all made themselves comfortable, a stranger
appeared. He looked very angry. 'Now you get out of here, all of you!' he
shouted. 'I'm sheriff here. Do you see that notice? It says "No Camping"—in
20 case you can't read!'

'Look, sheriff,' said Rockwall, 'don't be too hard on us. I'm Rockwall Slinger
and this is Merlin Greeves.'

'Oh, is it?' said the sheriff with a sneer. 'Well, I'm Brinksley Meers, and my
other name is Gloria Gleam. Now you get out of here fast!'

Précis

In not more than 80 words describe what happened. Write two different paragraphs
using the points and connections given below.

CONNECTIONS	POINTS	CONNECTIONS
After	⎡ 1. Bus stopped—river bed. ⎤	
	⎣ 2. Film stars descended. ⎦	*A party of*
	⎡ 3. Dressed—glasses, clothes. ⎤	
so as not to	⎣ 4. Recognize. ⎦	*in order that*
	⎡ 5. Picnic things, shady spot. ⎤	
and	⎣ 6. Sat down. ⎦	*Everyone had*
Just then	⎡ 7. Sheriff, rudely—must leave. ⎤	*when*
because	⎣ 8. Camping not allowed. ⎦	*as*
Even when	⎡ 9. Told him who they were. ⎤	
	⎣ 10. Did not believe them. ⎦	*but*

Composition

Write two paragraphs in about 150 words using the ideas given below:
1. A fine day—we prepared for a picnic—drove into the country—found a quiet
   spot—unpacked our hampers.
2. There were a few wasps—then a great many—our efforts to drive them away—
   saw a wasp nest in a tree nearby—seized our things—returned to car pursued by
   wasps—drove away.

Letter-writing

Write a short Introduction of a letter to a friend beginning:
'I have just heard that . . .'

Key Structures

What is happening? What always happens? Review: **KS 15, 74, 130.**

Exercises

A. Give the correct form of the verbs in brackets. Do not refer to the passage until you finish the exercise:

1. 'It couldn't be better, Gloria,' Brinksley Meers agreed. 'No newspaper men, no film fans! Why . . . we (not come) more often?'
2. 'I'm sheriff here. . . . you (see) that notice? It (say) "No Camping"—in case you can't read!'

B. What happens? What is happening?
Give the correct form of the verbs in brackets:

1. The police now (investigate) the matter.
2. Light (travel) at a speed of 186,000 miles a second.
3. He (resemble) his father.
4. The postman who (deliver) my letters is on holiday.
5. It (look) as if it will rain.
6. Mary still (love) him even though he has behaved so badly.
7. Hurry up! The bus (come).
8. Which . . . you (prefer)? The red one or the white one?

C. Write sentences using the following verbs:
contain, mean, believe, understand, want, matter.

Special Difficulties

a The verb *get* has a different meaning in each of these sentences. Study them carefully:

Now you *get out* of here, all of you! (l. 18)
The door is locked. I can't *get out*.
I've lost my key. I can't *get into* the house.
How is he *getting on* in his new job? (How is he progressing?)
Get on with your work. (Continue . . .)
He's so difficult, I can't *get on with* him. (We are not on good terms.)
Tom was punished, but Jim *got off* lightly. (He escaped punishment.)
I can't *get* the cap of this pen *off*. (I can't remove it.)
He has now *got over* his illness. (He has recovered.)
I want to *get* this interview *over* as quickly as possible. (I want to finish it.)
He *got through* his exams. (He succeeded in passing his exams.)
He *got through* a huge amount of food. (He succeeded in eating . . .)

Exercise
Supply the missing words in the following sentences:

1. He has never got . . . his wife's death.
2. How did the thief manage to get . . . the house?
3. Did you get . . . your driving test?
4. The lid is stuck. I can't get it . . .
5. He gets . . . very well . . . all his new colleagues.
6. 'Please stop talking and get . . . . . . your work,' she said.

b No Camping. (l. 19)
On public notices we write *No Camping* instead of *Do not camp.*

Exercise
How would these appear on public notices:

1. Do not smoke in this compartment.
2. Do not park.
3. Do not wait on this side of the street today.

75 SOS

When a light passenger plane flew off
course some time ago, it crashed in the
mountains and its pilot was killed. The
only passengers, a young woman and her
5 two baby daughters, were unhurt. It was
the middle of winter. Snow lay thick on
the ground. The woman knew that the
nearest village was miles away. When it
grew dark, she turned a suit-case into a
10 bed and put the children inside it, covering them with all the clothes she could
find. During the night, it got terribly
cold. The woman kept as near as she
could to the children and even tried to get
15 into the case herself, but it was too small.
Early next morning, she heard planes

*She turned a suit-case into
a bed*

passing overhead and wondered how she could send a signal. Then she had an
idea. She stamped out the letters 'SOS' in the snow. Fortunately, a pilot saw
the signal and sent a message by radio to the nearest town. It was not long before
20 a helicopter arrived on the scene to rescue the survivors of the plane crash.

Précis

In not more than 80 words, describe what happened. Write two different paragraphs
using the points and connections given below.

CONNECTIONS	POINTS	CONNECTIONS
	1. Plane crashed—mountains.	*When*
but	2. Only passengers—woman, baby daughters not hurt.	
and	3. Mid-winter—extremely cold.	*However, and*
so	4. Put children in case.	*After putting*
	5. Covered them—clothes.	*and*
and	6. Kept close all night.	*the woman*
When	7. Planes—next morning.	*On hearing*
	8. Stamped 'SOS'—snow.	*the woman*
This	9. Seen by pilot.	*which*
who	10. Message sent.	
and	11. Rescued—helicopter.	*and*

Composition

Write two paragraphs in about 150 words using the ideas given below:
1. A light aeroplane with a heavy cargo—sudden storm—high winds—the pilot made
   a crash landing in the snow.
2. The pilot was unhurt—roped the plane to a rock—spent the night in a tent—next
   morning—found that the plane had been swept away by the wind—smashed to
   pieces—cargo and wreckage in the snow.

Letter-writing

Write a suitable *Purpose* in about 50 words to follow this introductory paragraph:

Forgive me for not writing earlier to thank you for the lovely scarf you sent me for my birthday, but I have been in bed with 'flu.

Key Structures

What happened? Review: **KS 17, 76, 132.**

Exercises

A. Underline all the verbs in the passage that tell us *what happened*.

B. Give the correct form of the verbs in brackets. Do not refer to the passage until you finish the exercise.

When a light passenger plane (fly) off course some time ago, it (crash) in the mountains and its pilot (kill). The only passengers, a young woman and her two baby daughters (be) unhurt. It (be) the middle of winter. Snow (lie) thick on the ground. The woman (know) that the nearest village (be) miles away. When it (grow) dark, she (turn) a suit-case into a bed and (put) the children inside it, covering them with all the clothes she (can) find. During the night, it (get) terribly cold. The woman (keep) as near as she could to the children and even (try) to get into the case herself, but it (be) too small. Early next morning, she (hear) planes passing overhead and (wonder) how she (can) send a signal. Then she (have) an idea. She (stamp) out the letters 'SOS' in the snow. Fortunately, a pilot (see) the signal and (send) a message by radio to the nearest town. It (not be) long before a helicopter (arrive) on the scene to rescue the survivors of the plane crash.

Special Difficulties

When it grew dark . . . (ll. 8–9)
Study the verbs in italics. They are all used in the sense of the verb *become*.
He *grew* (or *got*) angry when I told him about it.
The leaves *are turning* (or *getting*) yellow.
This apple *has gone* bad.
Coal *got* scarce last winter.
Everything you said *came* true.
She *fell* ill while she was on holiday.

Exercise

Supply the correct verbs in the following sentences:
1. During the night it . . . terribly cold.
2. He was so tired, he . . . asleep.
3. When the teacher left the classroom, the children . . . noisy.
4. If you do not put the milk in the refrigerator, it will . . . sour.
5. This knob has . . . loose.
6. The children . . . quiet when he entered the room.
7. Even though I am . . . older, I am not . . . wiser.
8. She's . . . so fat you won't recognize her.
9. This post . . . vacant last year.
10. Don't worry, everything will . . . right in the end.

76   April Fools' Day

'To end our special news bulletin,' said the voice of the television announcer, 'we are taking you to the macaroni fields of Calabria. Macaroni has been grown in
5 this area for over six hundred years. Two of the leading growers, Giuseppe Moldova and Riccardo Brabante, tell me that they have been expecting a splendid crop this year and harvesting has begun earlier
10 than usual. Here you can see two workers who, between them, have just finished cutting three cart-loads of golden brown macaroni stalks. The whole village has been working day and night gathering
15 and threshing this year's crop before the September rains. On the right, you can

golden brown macaroni stalks

see Mrs Brabante herself. She has been helping her husband for thirty years now. Mrs Brabante is talking to the manager of the local factory where the crop is processed. This last scene shows you what will happen at the end of the harvest:
20 the famous Calabrian macaroni-eating competition! Signor Fratelli, the present champion, has won it every year since 1961. And that ends our special bulletin for today, Thursday, April 1st. We are now returning you to the studio.'

Précis

In not more than 85 words write an account of the television programme. Write two different paragraphs using the points and connections given below.

CONNECTIONS	POINTS	CONNECTIONS
	⌈ 1. End of news bulletin.	
		2. Television announcer showed viewers fields—Calabria.	
where	⌊ 3. Grown—six hundred years.	*Here*
	⌈ 4. Harvesting earlier this year.	*This year*
and		5. Whole village working hard.	
before	⌊ 6. September rains.	*before*
	⌈ 7. Crop: processed—factory.	*so that the crop*
		8. After harvest—famous competition.	
which		9. Signor Fratelli—since 1961.	*This*
That	⌊10. End of bulletin—April 1st.	*With that*

Composition

Write an imaginary account of a macaroni-eating competition. Write two paragraphs in about 150 words using the ideas given below:
1. The appearance of the six competitors—all very fat—their past achievements— huge quantity of macaroni prepared, weighed and served.
2. Quantity, not speed was the important thing—competitors eating for three hours— only one man left—he asked for more!

Letter-writing

Write a suitable *Purpose* of about 50 words to follow this introductory paragraph:

I have just heard that Tom Blake will be staying with you for a week. I would love to meet him again as I haven't seen him for years.

Key Structures

What has happened? What has been happening?
Review: **KS 19, 77, 133.**

Exercises

A. Underline all the verbs in the passage which tell us *what has happened* and *what has been happening*.

B. Give the correct form of the verbs in brackets. Do not refer to the passage until you finish the exercise:

Macaroni (grow) in this area for over six hundred years. Two of the leading growers, Giuseppe Moldova and Riccardo Brabante, tell me that they (expect) a splendid crop this year and harvesting (begin) earlier than usual. Here you can see two workers who, between them, just (finish) cutting three cart-loads of golden brown macaroni stalks. The whole village (work) day and night gathering and threshing this year's crop before the September rains. On the right, you can see Mrs Brabante herself. She (help) her husband for thirty years now. This last scene shows you what will happen at the end of the harvest: the famous Calabrian macaroni-eating competition! Signor Fratelli, the present champion, (win) it every year since 1961.

Special Difficulties

Words Often Confused.

a Usual and Usually. Study these examples:
Harvesting has begun earlier than usual. (ll. 9–10)
He usually gets up at 6 o'clock.

b Between and Among. Study these examples:
Here you can see two workers who, between them, have just finished cutting·three cart-loads of macaroni. (ll. 10–13)
Tom sat between Jill and Jennifer.
The Prime Minister was among those present.
You'll find it somewhere among those newspapers.

c Manager, Director, Headmaster. Study these examples:
Mrs Brabante is talking to the manager of the local factory. (l. 18)
Mr Jones is the director of several companies.
Who is the headmaster of this school?

Exercise

Supply any of the above words in the following sentences:
1. I found your pipe. It was . . . those things on the table.
2. As . . ., he asked the same silly questions.
3. The lady in the shop asked to see the . . .
4. He has been . . . of this school for seventeen years.
5. It seems to be warmer than . . . this month.
6. Everybody dreams of living like a company . . . with a large expense account.
7. She stuck the flower . . . the pages of a book.
8. He . . . returns from work about this time, but he is late today.

77 A Successful Operation

The mummy of an Egyptian woman who died in 800 B.C. has just had an operation. The mummy is that of Shepenmut who was once a singer in the Temple of
5 Thebes. As there were strange marks on the X-ray plates taken of the mummy, doctors have been trying to find out whether the woman died of a rare disease. The only way to do this was to operate.
10 The operation, which lasted for over four hours, proved to be very difficult because of the hard resin which covered the skin. The doctors removed a section of the mummy and sent it to a laboratory. They
15 also found something which the X-ray plates did not show: a small wax figure of the god Duamutef. This god which has the head of a cow was normally placed inside a mummy. The doctors have not yet decided how the woman died. They feared that the mummy would fall to pieces when they cut it open, but for-
20 tunately this has not happened. The mummy successfully survived the operation.

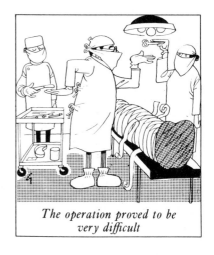

The operation proved to be very difficult

Précis

Write a summary of the passage *in not more than 70 words*.
Write two different paragraphs using the points and connections given below.

CONNECTIONS	POINTS	CONNECTIONS
	⌈ 1. Doctors operated—mummy: Egyptian woman.	
who	⌊ 2. Died 800 B.C.	*who*
whether	⌈ 3. Wanted to find out—died rare disease.	*in order . . . if*
After removing	⌈ 4. Removed section.	
	⌊ 5. Sent it to laboratory.	*which*
During the operation	⌈ 6. Unexpectedly found figure—god. ⌉	*Inside the mummy*
Though	⌈ 7. Afraid mummy fall to pieces.	
	⌊ 8. Survived operation. ⌋	*but*

Composition

Write two paragraphs in about 150 words using the ideas given below:
1. A mummy disappeared from a museum—newspaper reports—strange stories about the mummy—the public got alarmed.
2. An official announcement was issued from the museum—scientists were studying the mummy—it would be back in its place soon.

Letter-writing

Write a suitable *Purpose* of about 50 words to follow this introductory paragraph:
   I am afraid I will not be able to come with you to next Thursday's concert. I have had to change my plans because something quite unexpected has happened.

Key Structures

What happened? What has happened? What has been happening?
Review: KS 21, 80, 135.

Exercises
A. Underline all the verbs in the passage which tell us *what happened*, *what has happened*, and *what has been happening*.

B. Give the correct form of the verbs in brackets. Do not refer to the passage until you finish the exercise:
The mummy of an Egyptian woman who (die) in 800 B.C. just (have) an operation. As there (be) strange marks on the X-ray plates taken of the mummy, doctors (try) to find out whether the woman (die) of a rare disease. The only way to do this (be) to operate. The operation which (last) for over four hours (prove) to be very difficult. The doctors (remove) a section of the mummy and (send) it to a laboratory. They also (find) something which the X-ray plates not (show). The doctors not (decide) yet how the woman (die). They (fear) that the mummy would fall to pieces when they (cut) it open, but fortunately this not (happen). The mummy successfully (survive) the operation.

C. Supply *since*, *for* or *ago* in the following sentences:
1. He stayed with us . . . two weeks.
2. She arrived two weeks . . .
3. I have not seen him . . . Monday.
4. He has been ringing up continually . . . lunch time.
5. We waited . . . ages.
6. He left a month . . . and I have not seen him . . . then.
7. It has not rained . . . March.
8. My grandparents lived here a long time . . .
9. I have not heard from him . . . 1959.
10. We have been working on this new plane . . . over a year now.

Special Difficulties

Words Often Confused.
a B.C. and A.D. Study these examples:
The mummy of an Egyptian woman who died in 800 B.C. . . . . (ll. 1–2)
Julius Caesar died in 44 B.C.
William the Conqueror invaded Britain in A.D. 1066.

b Skin, Leather, Complexion. Study these examples:
Hard resin covered the skin. (l. 12)
This briefcase is made of leather.
Look at her rosy cheeks. She has a lovely complexion.

c Wax and Candle. Study these examples:
A small wax figure of the god Duamutef. (ll. 16–17)
The lights went out so we lit candles.

Exercise
Choose the correct words in the following sentences:
1. Even though she is old, she still has a good (skin) (complexion).
2. These seat-covers are made of (skin) (leather).
3. A baby's (skin) (leather) is very soft.
4. It is pleasant to have a meal by (candle) (wax) light.
5. Homer lived around 800 (A.D.) (B.C.)

78　The Last One?

After reading an article entitled 'Cigarette Smoking and Your Health' I lit a cigarette to calm my nerves. I smoked with concentration and pleasure as I was sure
5 that this would be my last cigarette. For a whole week I did not smoke at all and during this time, my wife suffered terribly. I had all the usual symptoms of someone giving up smoking: a bad tem-
10 per and an enormous appetite. My friends kept on offering me cigarettes and cigars. They made no effort to hide their amusement whenever I produced a packet of sweets from my pocket. After seven days
15 of this I went to a party. Everybody around me was smoking and I felt ex-

My friends kept on offering me cigarettes

tremely uncomfortable. When my old friend Brian urged me to accept a cigarette, it was more than I could bear. I took one guiltily, lit it and smoked with satisfaction. My wife was delighted that things had returned to normal once more.
20 Anyway, as Brian pointed out, it is the easiest thing in the world to give up smoking. He himself has done it lots of times!

Précis

In not more than 80 words, describe the writer's experiences. Write two different paragraphs using the points and connections given below.

CONNECTIONS	POINTS	CONNECTIONS
Having read	1. Read article—smoking.	*The writer*
	2. Writer smoked last cigarette.	*and*
	3. Did not smoke—week.	
and	4. Wife suffered.	*and*
because	5. Bad temper—large appetite.	*because of her husband's*
Meanwhile	6. Friends offered cigarettes.	*Whenever*
and . . . to see	7. Amused—sweets.	*because*
When	8. Went to party.	*However, at a . . .*
	9. Accepted cigarette.	
which	10. Offered by friend.	*from*
and since then	11. Returned to normal.	*Now*

Composition

Write two paragraphs in about 150 words using the ideas given below:
1. Two young boys wanted to smoke—took two cigarettes from father's packet—went and hid in the garage.
2. They lit the cigarettes—smoke and coughing—father saw smoke coming from garage—rushed down—smiled when he saw boys—offered them cigars—the boys accepted them—both very sick.

Letter-writing

Arrange the following heading in the correct order. Put in full stops and commas where necessary:

Brisbane/15 Gower St/24th April 19—/Australia/Queensland

Key Structures

A and The. Review: **KS 23, 81, 138.**

Exercises

A. Put in *a(n)* or *the* where necessary. Do not refer to the passage until you finish the exercise:

After reading . . . article entitled '. . . Cigarette Smoking and Your Health' I lit . . . cigarette to calm my nerves. I smoked with . . . concentration and . . . pleasure as I was sure that this would be my last cigarette. For . . . whole week I did not smoke at all and during this time my wife suffered terribly. I had all . . . usual symptoms of someone giving up . . . smoking: . . . bad temper and . . . enormous appetite. My friends kept on offering me . . . cigarettes and . . . cigars. They made no effort to hide their amusement whenever I produced . . . packet of . . . sweets from my pocket. After seven days of this I went to . . . party.

B. Write sentences using *a*, *the*, *some* or *any* with the following:

1. Making coffee. Do you want . . .? 2. Exports/increase/this year. 3. Afraid/thunder/lightning. 4. Boy/sent/school/deaf. 5. Tax laws/help/rich. 6. Spend/evening/listen/music. 7. Crime/not pay. 8. Like/apple or orange? 9. Are you/artist or musician? 10. Take/sugar/tea?

Special Difficulties

The verb *keep* has a different meaning in each of these sentences. Study them carefully:
My friends *kept on* offering me cigarettes. (ll. 10–11) (Continued.)
Please *keep off* the grass. (Do not walk on it.)
He *kept away from* the party. (He did not come.)
Under my essay, the teacher wrote, 'Good work! *Keep it up!*' (Continue making an effort.)
He ran so fast, I could not *keep up with* him. (I could not remain beside him.)
A big notice on the door said, '*Keep out!*' (Do not come in.)
The boy was *kept in* after school. (He was made to remain behind as a punishment.)

Exercise
Supply the missing words in the following sentences:
1. I think he kept . . . . . . the meeting on purpose.
2. Keep . . . the floor. I have just finished scrubbing it.
3. He has just begun a diary. I wonder how long he will keep it . . .
4. He kept . . . making the same mistake.
5. We keep Tim . . . of the room because Betty has measles.
6. Most people spend their lives trying to keep . . . . . . their neighbours.
7. Three children were kept . . . yesterday afternoon because they had misbehaved during the music lesson.

79 By Air

I used to travel by air a great deal when I was a boy. My parents used to live in South America and I used to fly there from Europe in the holidays. An air-hostess would take charge of me and I never had an unpleasant experience. I am used to travelling by air and only on one occasion have I ever felt frightened. After taking off, we were flying low over the city and slowly gaining height, when the plane suddenly turned round and flew back to the airport. While we were waiting to land, an air-hostess told us to keep calm and to get off the plane quietly as soon as it had touched down. Everybody on board was worried and we were curious to find out what had happened. Later we learnt that there was a very important person on board. The police had been told that a bomb had been planted on the plane. After we had landed, the plane was searched thoroughly. Fortunately, nothing was found and five hours later we were able to take off again.

I used to travel by air a great deal

Précis

In not more than 80 words describe what happened from the moment the plane took off. Write two different paragraphs using the points and connections given below.

CONNECTIONS	POINTS	CONNECTIONS
	1. Plane took off.	*After having*
and	2. Flew low—city.	
When	3. Gaining height.	*Although*
	4. Had to return—airport.	
Meanwhile	5. Told to keep calm.	*During this time*
After	6. Disembarked.	*until*
	7. Learnt—important person.	
Someone had told	8. Police—bomb.	*Because*
but though	9. Searched.	
	10. Found nothing.	*However*
	11. Five hours later took off.	*so*

Composition

Write two paragraphs in about 150 words using the ideas given below:
1. Plane took off—a passenger threw a lighted cigarette into an air-vent—he thought it was an ash-tray.
2. Smoke—panic—the plane returned to the airport—fire-engines, ambulances—no one was hurt—the fire was put out—the plane took off again.

Letter-writing

Write a suitable *Purpose* of about 50 words to follow this introductory paragraph:

You will be surprised to hear that your uncle Peter has unexpectedly returned from South America. He is staying with us at present and I know that he would very much like to see you.

Key Structures

What happened? What was happening? What used to happen? Review: **KS 25, 83, 139.**

Exercises

A. Underline all the verbs in the passage that tell us *what happened, what was happening,* and *what used to/would happen.*

B. Give the correct form of the verbs in brackets. Use *would* in place of *used to* where possible. Do not refer to the passage until you finish the exercise:
I (travel) by air a great deal when I (be) a boy. My parents (live) in South America and I (fly) there from Europe in the holidays. An air-hostess (take) charge of me and I never (have) an unpleasant experience. I am used to travelling by air and only on one occasion have I ever felt frightened. After taking off, we (fly) low over the city and slowly (gain) height, when the plane suddenly (turn) round and (fly) back to the airport. While we (wait) to land, an air-hostess (tell) us to keep calm and to get off the plane quietly as soon as it had touched down.

C. Explain the difference in meaning between these two sentences:
1. I *used to* fly there from Europe in the holidays. (ll. 3–4)
2. I *am used to* travelling by air. (ll. 6–7) (**SD 140**)

Special Difficulties

The verb *take* has a different meaning in each of these sentences. Study them carefully:
After *taking off*, we were flying over the city . . . (ll. 9–10)
He *took off* his coat.
He is always *taking off* his teacher. (He is always making fun of him by imitating him.)
Young Tom *takes after* his father. (He resembles his father.)
That wardrobe *takes up* a lot of space. (It occupies a lot of space.)
He has *taken up* French. (He has begun to learn French.)
When his wife died, he *took to* drinking. (He started drinking and it became a habit.)
He was so persuasive that I *was taken in*. (I was deceived.)
The reporter *took down* everything I said. (The reporter wrote . . .)
That business was doing very badly until Jones *took over*. (He became in charge of it.)

Exercise
Supply the missing words in the following sentences:
1. Who will take . . . when the present director leaves?
2. As soon as he got into the lift he took his hat . . .
3. You shouldn't be taken . . . by stories like that.
4. Last year he took . . . Russian; now he's taking . . . Chinese.
5. None of my children takes . . . me.
6. The new rocket will take . . . from Cape Kennedy.
7. 'Please take . . . this letter for me, Miss Ray,' the manager said.
8. He takes . . . people so well he ought to go on the stage.

80 The Crystal Palace

Perhaps the most extraordinary building of the nineteenth century was the Crystal Palace, which was built in Hyde Park for the Great Exhibition of 1851. The
5 Crystal Palace was different from all other buildings in the world, for it was made of iron and glass. It was one of the biggest buildings of all time and a lot of people from many countries came to see
10 it. A great many goods were sent to the exhibition from various parts of the world. There was also a great deal of machinery on display. The most wonderful piece of machinery on show was
15 Nasmyth's steam hammer. Though in those days, travelling was not as easy as it is today, steam boats carried thousands of visitors across the Channel from

The most wonderful piece of machinery

Europe. On arriving in England, they were taken to the Crystal Palace by train.
20 There were six million visitors in all, and the profits from the exhibition were used to build museums and colleges. Later, the Crystal Palace was moved to South London. It remained one of the most famous buildings in the world until it was burnt down in 1936.

Précis

Give an account of the history of the Crystal Palace *in not more than 85 words*. Write two different paragraphs using the points and connections given below.

CONNECTIONS	POINTS	CONNECTIONS
	1. The Crystal Palace.	
which	2. Built—exhibition.	
	3. Different—others.	*Made of . . . it*
because	4. Iron and glass.	
	5. Goods—world.	*. . . not only . . .*
as well as	6. Machinery.	*but . . . as well*
So many	7. Visitors: boat, train.	*This attracted . . . who*
that it was possible	8. Colleges—museums.	*Later*
from	9. Profits.	*from*
After the exhibition	10. Moved—South London.	*The Crystal Palace*
where	11. Remained.	*and . . . until*
until	12. Burnt down 1936.	*when*

Composition

Write two paragraphs in about 150 words using the ideas given below:
1. A visit to a modern exhibition—how I got there—the exhibition attracted large crowds.
2. My first impressions—the things on display—a walk round the exhibition hall—the exhibits that I liked best—tired at the end of the day.

Letter-writing

Write a suitable *Purpose* of about 50 words to follow this introductory paragraph:

I have some wonderful news for you. I have at last managed to get two tickets for the Football Cup.

Key Structures

The best and the worst. Review: **KS 27, 86, 141.**

Exercises

A. How many comparisons can you find in the passage? Underline as many as you can.

B. Supply the missing words in the following. Do not refer to the passage until you finish the exercise:

Perhaps the . . . extraordinary building of the nineteenth century was the Crystal Palace which was built in Hyde Park for the Great Exhibition of 1851. The Crystal Palace was different . . . all other buildings . . . the world, for it was made of iron and glass. It was one of the . . . (big) buildings . . . all time and a . . . of people from . . . countries came to see it. A great . . . goods were sent to the exhibition from various parts of the world. There was also a great . . . of machinery on display. The . . . wonderful piece of machinery on show was Nasmyth's steam hammer. Though in those days, travelling was not . . . easy . . . it is today, steam boats carried thousands of visitors across the Channel from Europe. The Crystal Palace remained one of the . . . famous buildings . . . the world until it was burnt down in 1936.

Special Difficulties

Phrases with On. Compare **SD 108.**
Study these examples:
There was also a great deal of machinery *on display*. (ll. 12–13)
The most wonderful piece of machinery *on show* . . . (ll. 13–14)
He has gone to Frankfurt *on business*.
I didn't catch the bus. I came here *on foot*.
I asked to see the officer *on duty*.
On the whole, it has been a very successful year.
Look at that smoke. That building must be *on fire*.
I don't think it was an accident. He did it *on purpose*.
On the average, I make six telephone calls a day.
You mustn't *on any account* sign the contract before you read it.
I know I had agreed to let you go to the cinema, but *on second thoughts*, you should stay at home and finish your homework.

Exercise
Supply phrases with *on* in the following sentences:
1. While the guard was . . ., he heard a shot.
2. I've changed my mind. . . . I'll go by plane instead.
3. I think you dropped your handkerchief . . . so that he could pick it up.
4. You must be exhausted! Did you come all that way . . . ? You should have taken a taxi.
5. I'm not always pleased with his work, but . . . it is satisfactory.
6. You must not, . . ., leave this room.
7. . . ., 250,000 tourists visit this town each year.

81 Escape

When he had killed the guard, the prisoner
of war quickly dragged him into the
bushes. Working rapidly in the darkness,
he soon changed into the dead man's
5 clothes. Now, dressed in a blue uniform
and with a rifle over his shoulder, the
prisoner marched boldly up and down in
front of the camp. He could hear shouting in the camp itself. Lights were blazing
10 and men were running here and there:
they had just discovered that a prisoner
had escaped. At that moment, a large
black car with four officers inside it,
stopped at the camp gates. The officers
15 got out and the prisoner stood to attention
and saluted as they passed. When they

*The prisoner marched boldly
up and down*

had gone, the driver of the car came towards him. The man obviously wanted
to talk. He was rather elderly with grey hair and clear blue eyes. The prisoner
felt sorry for him, but there was nothing else he could do. As the man came near,
20 the prisoner knocked him to the ground with a sharp blow. Then, jumping into
the car, he drove off as quickly as he could.

Précis

In not more than 85 words describe what the prisoner did. Write two different paragraphs using the points and connections given below.

CONNECTIONS	POINTS	CONNECTIONS
After having	⎡ 1. Prisoner of war killed guard. ⎤	*As soon as he*
	⎢ 2. Dragged—bushes. ⎥	*and*
and	⎣ 3. Changed into clothes. ⎦	*the prisoner of war*
Then he	⎡ 4. Rifle over shoulder. ⎤	*With*
and	⎣ 5. Marched—camp. ⎦	
A short time afterwards	⎡ 6. Four officers—car. ⎤	*when*
so . . . and	⎣ 7. Attention—saluted. ⎦	*and*
When they had gone	⎡ 8. Driver—towards him. ⎤	*When the driver*
and after	⎢ 9. Knocked out. ⎥	
	⎢ 10. Jumped into car. ⎥	*Then, jumping*
and	⎣ 11. Drove away. ⎦	

Composition

Write two paragraphs in about 150 words using the ideas given below:
1. Dark night—a prisoner of war who had escaped was dressed as a guard—he was
   still in the camp—took part in the search for the 'missing' prisoner.
2. He went out in a lorry with the other guards—into the countryside—the guards
   went into the forest—the prisoner escaped.

Letter-writing

The Conclusion: The last paragraph of a letter should take the form of a polite wish. Learn the following phrases by heart:
Please give my love/regards to . . .
I hope you will be well again soon.

Exercise
Write five opening sentences which could be used in letters to friends or relations.

Key Structures

At, In, To, With etc. Review: **KS 29, 87, 143.**
A. Underline the words *into*, *in*, *with*, *at*, and *to* in the passage. Note how they have been used.

B. Supply the missing words in the following. Do not refer to the passage until you finish the exercise:
1. When he had killed the guard, the prisoner of war quickly dragged him . . . the bushes. Working rapidly . . . the larkness, he soon changed . . . the dead man's clothes. Now, dressed . . . a blue uniform and . . . a rifle over his shoulder, the prisoner marched boldly up and down in front of the camp. He could hear shouting . . . the camp itself.
2. . . . that moment, a large black car . . . four officers inside it, stopped . . . the camp gates. The officers got out and the prisoner stood . . . attention.
3. He was rather elderly . . . grey hair and clear blue eyes.
4. As the man came near, the prisoner knocked him . . . the ground . . . a sharp blow. Then, jumping . . . the car, he drove off as quickly as he could.

Special Difficulties

Words Often Confused.
a Cloth, Clothing, Clothes. Study these examples:
I wanted to have a suit made so I bought three and a half yards of cloth.
You should give all this old clothing away.
He soon changed into the dead man's clothes. (ll. 4–5)

b Salute, Greet. Study these examples:
He stood to attention and saluted as they passed. (ll. 15–16)
He went to the station to greet his friend.

c Clear, Clean. Study these examples:
He was rather elderly with clear blue eyes. (l. 18)
The water in the stream was very clear.
His instructions were very clear. (They were easy to understand.)
We can cross now. The road is clear.
She keeps her house very clean.

Exercise
Supply any of the above words in the following sentences:
1. The guard . . . the general.
2. When the canal was . . . the ship went through.
3. I bought a piece of . . . to make a dress.
4. I haven't bought any new . . . for years.
5. The soldier . . . his mother with a kiss.

82 Monster or Fish?

Fishermen and sailors sometimes claim
to have seen monsters in the sea. Though
people have often laughed at stories told
by seamen, it is now known that many of
5 these 'monsters' which have at times
been sighted are simply strange fish.
Occasionally, unusual creatures are
washed to the shore, but they are rarely
caught out at sea. Some time ago, how-
10 ever, a peculiar fish was caught near
Madagascar. A small fishing-boat was
carried miles out to sea by the powerful
fish as it pulled on the line. Realizing that
this was no ordinary fish, the fisherman
15 made every effort not to damage it in any

rarely been seen alive by man

way. When it was eventually brought to shore, it was found to be over thirteen
feet long. It had a head like a horse, big blue eyes, shining silver skin, and a
bright red tail. The fish, which has since been sent to a museum where it is being
examined by a scientist, is called an oarfish. Such creatures have rarely been seen
20 alive by man as they live at a depth of six hundred feet.

Précis
Give an account of what happened *in not more than 80 words*. Write two different
paragraphs using the points and connections given below.

CONNECTIONS	POINTS	CONNECTIONS
	1. Strange fish caught—Madagascar.	
after having pulled	2. Fishing-boat—out to sea.	*Though*
Making	3. Effort—damage.	
	4. Fisherman—brought it to shore.	*On being brought*
The fish, which	5. Thirteen feet.	*the fish*
with	6. Head like horse.	*and*
	7. Sent museum.	*Now that*
It . . . who said	8. Examined—scientist.	
	9. Oarfish.	*It*
and	10. Six hundred feet.	*and*

Composition
Write two paragraphs in about 150 words using the ideas given below:
1. A man in a bar—explaining to others how he caught a big fish—rough seas—great
   difficulty—boat carried out to sea.
2. After several hours he pulled the fish up—never seen before—its size, appearance
   and colours—but it got away.

Letter-writing
The Conclusion. Learn the following phrases by heart:
I shall be looking forward to hearing from/seeing you soon.
I hope you will settle down in your (new job, school etc.).

Write a suitable *Purpose* for a letter in about 50 words. The letter has as its conclusion:
'I hope you will be well again soon.'

Key Structures

A peculiar fish was caught near Madagascar. Review: **KS 31, 89, 146.**

Exercises
A. Underline the verbs in the passage and study their form.

B. Give the correct form of the verbs in brackets. Do not refer to the passage until
you finish the exercise.
Though people have often laughed at stories told by seamen, it . . . now (know) that
many of these 'monsters' which . . . at times (sight) are simply strange fish. Occasionally, unusual creatures (wash) to the shore, but they . . . rarely (catch) out at sea. Some
time ago, however, a peculiar fish (catch) near Madagascar. A small fishing-boat
(carry) miles out to sea by the powerful fish as it pulled on the line. When it . . .
eventually (bring) to shore, it (find) to be over thirteen feet long. The fish, which . . .
since (send) to a museum where it (examine) by a scientist, (call) an oarfish. Such
creatures . . . rarely (see) alive by man as they live at a depth of six hundred feet.

Special Difficulties

Words Often Confused.
a Laugh and Laugh at. Study these examples:
Everybody laughed when the circus clown made his appearance.
Though people have often laughed at stories told by seamen . . . (ll. 2–4) (People have
made fun of . . .)
b Wash and Wash up. Study these examples:
I must wash my hands. They are very dirty.
Have you ever seen a cat washing itself?
Unusual creatures are washed to the shore. (ll. 7–8) (They are carried to the shore by
water.)
The man was washed overboard by a big wave.
I'll wash up tonight. (I'll wash the dishes.)

Exercise
Supply any of the above words in the following sentences:
1. What a lot of dirty plates! Who is going to . . .?
2. Don't wear that hat. People will . . . you.
3. The bridge was . . . away by the river.
4. We all . . . when he told us a funny story.
5. The boy was told to . . . his hands before sitting at table.

83 After the Elections

The former Prime Minister, Mr Wentworth Lane, was defeated in the recent elections. He is now retiring from political life and has gone abroad. My friend,
5 Crawley, has always been a fanatical opponent of Mr Lane's Radical Progressive Party. After the elections, Crawley went to the former Prime Minister's house. When he asked if Mr Lane lived
10 there, the policeman on duty told him that since his defeat, the ex-Prime Minister had gone abroad. On the following day, Crawley went to the house again. The same policeman was just walking
15 slowly past the entrance, when Crawley asked the same question. Though a little

retiring from political life

suspicious this time, the policeman gave him the same answer. The day after, Crawley went to the house once more and asked exactly the same question. This time, the policeman lost his temper. 'I told you yesterday and the day before
20 yesterday,' he shouted, 'Mr Lane was defeated in the elections. He has retired from political life and gone to live abroad!'

'I know,' answered Crawley, 'but I love to hear you say it!'

Précis

Give an account of what happened *in not more than 80 words*. Write two different paragraphs using the points and connections given below.

CONNECTIONS	POINTS	CONNECTIONS
After having	1. Defeated—election.	*Since*
	2. Prime Minister retired abroad.	
who	3. Crawley—fanatical opponent—Party.	*As*
	4. Went—house—three times.	
and	5. Asked policeman.	*Each time*
whether	6. Mr Lane's house.	*if*
When	7. Third time—angry policeman.	
	8. Told—defeat, retirement.	*he was told*
	9. Crawley said—something he loved to hear.	*but*

Composition

Write two paragraphs in about 150 words using the ideas given below:
1. A politician was giving a pre-election speech: big promises: more houses, schools etc.—better foreign policy.
2. Members of the audience asked rude questions—the politician lost his temper—said that the audience did not deserve more houses etc.—walked off angrily—defeated in the election.

Letter-writing

The Conclusion. Learn the following phrases by heart:
I am very sorry for all the trouble this has caused you.
I wish you good luck/every success in . . .

Exercise
In about 50 words write the *Purpose* for a letter which has one of the above phrases as its conclusion.

Key Structures

Review: KS 188–204
What is happening? What always happens? (KS 188)
What happened? (KS 190)
What has happened? What has been happening? (KS 192)
What was happening? (KS 198)
A peculiar fish was caught near Madagascar. (KS 204)

Exercises
A. Underline all the verbs in the passage noting carefully how they have been used. Revise any Key Structures you have forgotten.

B. Give the correct form of the verbs in brackets. Do not refer to the passage until you finish the exercise:
The former Prime Minister, Mr Wentworth Lane, (defeat) in the recent elections. He now (retire) from political life and (go) abroad. My friend, Crawley, always (be) a fanatical opponent of Mr Lane's Radical Progressive Party. After the elections, Crawley (go) to the former Prime Minister's house. When he (ask) if Mr Lane (live) there, the policeman on duty (tell) him that since his defeat, the ex-Prime Minister had gone abroad. On the following day, Crawley (go) to the house again. The same policeman just (walk) slowly past the entrance, when Crawley (ask) the same question. Though a little suspicious this time, the policeman (give) him the same answer. The day after, Crawley (go) to the house once more and (ask) exactly the same question. This time, the policeman (lose) his temper. 'I (tell) you yesterday and the day before yesterday,' he (shout), 'Mr Lane (defeat) in the elections. He (retire) from political life and (go) to live abroad!'
'I (know),' (answer) Crawley, 'but I (love) to hear you say it!'

Special Difficulties

Temper and Mood.
Study these examples:
This time the policeman *lost his temper*. (ll. 18–19) (He got angry.)
Keep your temper! (Don't get angry!)
After what happened last night I was surprised to find that he was *in* such *a good temper* this morning. (He was not angry.)
You should apologize to him. He's *in a very bad temper*. (He is angry.)
I enjoyed myself at the party. I was *in a very good mood*. (I was cheerful.)
Don't disturb him. He's *in a very bad mood*. (He is not cheerful, but not necessarily angry.)
I'm *in the mood for* a drive into the country. (I would very much like to go for a drive into the country.)

Exercise
Use each of the above italicized phrases in sentences of your own.

84 On Strike

Busmen have decided to go on strike next week. The strike is due to begin on Tuesday. No one knows how long it will last. The busmen have stated that the strike
5 will continue until general agreement is reached about pay and working conditions. Most people believe that the strike will last for at least a week. Many owners of private cars are going to offer 'free
10 rides' to people on their way to work. This will relieve pressure on the trains to some extent. Meanwhile, a number of university students have volunteered to drive buses while the strike lasts. All the
15 young men are expert drivers, but before they drive any of the buses, they will have to pass a special test. The students are going to take the test in two days' time. Even so, people are going to find it difficult to get to work. But so far, the public has expressed its gratitude to the students in letters to the Press. Only one or
20 two people have objected that the students will drive too fast!

. . . people on their way to work

Précis

In not more than 80 words, describe what will happen next week. Write two different paragraphs using the points and connections given below.

CONNECTIONS	POINTS	CONNECTIONS
which	1. Busmen's strike begins Tuesday. 2. May last a week.	*Because . . . which*
Because of this	3. Car-owners—rides. 4. People going—work.	
, too,	5. University students—volunteered—buses.	*who*
but	6. Pass special test.	
Though	7. Difficult to get to work. 8. Public grateful.	*Despite the fact that*
Only	9. One or two objected.	*except for . . . who*
that	10. Too fast.	*that*

Composition

Write two paragraphs in about 150 words using the ideas given below:
1. The strike began—the students drove badly—the buses were seldom on time—often crowded—the public complained—the busmen were pleased.
2. The students threatened to go on strike—they did so—this angered the busmen who returned to work.

Letter-writing

The Conclusion. Complete the following sentences:
1. I shall be looking . . . 2. I am very sorry for . . . 3. I hope you will . . . 4. I wish you . . . 5. Please give my . . .

Key Structures

What will happen? Review: **KS 35, 93, 149.**

Exercises

A. Underline all the verbs in the passage which tell us what will happen.

B. Give the correct form of the verbs in brackets. Do not refer to the passage until you finish the exercise:

Busmen have decided to go on strike next week. The strike is due to begin on Tuesday. No one knows how long it (last). The busmen have stated that the strike (continue) until general agreement (reach) about pay and working conditions. Most people believe that the strike (last) for a week. Many owners of private cars (offer) 'free rides' to people on their way to work. This (relieve) pressure on the trains to some extent. Meanwhile, a number of university students have volunteered to drive buses while the strike (last). All the young men are expert drivers, but before they (drive) any of the buses, they (have to) pass a special test. The students (take) the test in two days' time. Even so, people (find) it difficult to get to work. But so far, the public has expressed its gratitude to the students in letters to the Press. Only one or two people have objected that the students (drive) too fast!

Special Difficulties

Study the word order in the following sentences:
People are going to find it difficult to get to work. (l. 18)
He thought it easy to pass the examination.
He considered it wrong that she should have to wait.
I feel it right that he should be punished.
I think it wrong for people to behave like that.

Exercise

Supply the missing parts in the following sentences. Your sentences must be similar in form to those given above.
1. He thought it . . .
2. He finds it unnecessary . . .
3. . . . to find a job.
4. She thinks it important . . .
5. . . . for him to wait so long.
6. . . . a good thing that . . .

85 Never too Old to Learn

I have just received a letter from my old school informing me that my former headmaster, Mr Reginald Page, will be retiring next week. Pupils of the school, old and
5 new, will be sending him a present to mark the occasion. All those who have contributed towards the gift will sign their names in a large album which will be sent to the headmaster's home. We
10 shall all remember Mr Page for his patience and understanding and for the kindly encouragement he gave us when we went so unwillingly to school. A great many former pupils will be attending a
15 farewell dinner in his honour next Thursday. It is a curious coincidence that the day before his retirement, Mr Page will have been teaching for a total of forty years. After he has retired, he will devote himself to gardening. For him, this will be an entirely new hobby. But this does not matter, for, as he has often
20 remarked, one is never too old to learn.

one is never too old to learn

Précis

Make a summary of the passage *in not more than 80 words*. Write two different paragraphs using the points and connections given below.

CONNECTIONS	POINTS	CONNECTIONS
Now that	1. Former headmaster, Mr Page, retiring.	*After twenty-eight years as*
	2. Pupils—gift.	*not only*
and . . . with	3. Album—signatures.	*but also*
	4. Attending farewell dinner in honour.	
After having	5. Completed forty years as teacher.	*of a man who*
	6. Devote—gardening.	*Now*
which for him	7. New hobby.	*Though*
but	8. Never too old.	*because*

Composition

Write two paragraphs in about 150 words using the ideas given below:
1. The headmaster's speech—he thanked the pupils—he remembered pupils past and present—many successful careers—humorous incidents.
2. His own future—memories—he welcomed old pupils to come and visit him—how he would spend his time—it would take him forty years to put his garden in order.

Letter-writing

How to end a letter. Study this example:
> I am looking forward to seeing you soon.
> Yours sincerely,
> Tom

This is how we usually end letters to friends. We may end 'Yours very sincerely,' 'Yours,' or 'Love,'.

Exercise
How would you end letters to each of the following:
Your mother; your best friend; an acquaintance.

Key Structures

What will happen? What will be happening? What will have been happening?
Review: **KS 37, 96, 151.**

Exercises
A. Study the use in the passage of all the verbs which express the future.

B. Give the correct form of the verbs in brackets. Do not refer to the passage until you finish the exercise.
I have just received a letter from my old school informing me that my former head-master, Mr Reginald Page, (retire) next week. Pupils of the school, old and new, (send) him a present to mark the occasion. All those who have contributed towards the gift (sign) their names in a large album which (send) to the headmaster's home. We all (remember) Mr Page for his patience and understanding and for the kindly encourage-ment he gave us when we went so unwillingly to school. A great many former pupils (attend) a farewell dinner in his honour next Thursday. It is a curious coincidence that the day before his retirement, Mr Page (teach) for a total of forty years. After he (retire) he (devote) himself to gardening. For him, this (be) an entirely new hobby.

Special Difficulties

Too and Enough.
Study the following sentences:
One is never too old to learn. (l. 20)
It is too difficult for me to understand.
It is easy enough for me to understand.

Exercise
Join the sentences below in the way shown in these examples:
a The wall is high. I cannot climb it. (too)
   The wall is too high to climb.
   The wall is too high for me to climb.
b The wall is low. I can climb it. (enough)
   The wall is low enough to climb.
   The wall is low enough for me to climb.

1. This car is expensive. I cannot buy it. (too)
2. This car is cheap. I can buy it. (enough)
3. The tea is hot. I cannot drink it. (too)
4. This piece of music is difficult. I cannot play it. (too)
5. This piece is easy. I can play it. (enough)

86 Out of Control

As the man tried to swing the speed-boat round, the steering-wheel came away in his hands. He waved desperately to his companion, who had been water-skiing
5 for the last fifteen minutes. Both men had hardly had time to realize what was happening when they were thrown violently into the sea. The speed-boat had struck a buoy, but it continued to move very
10 quickly across the water. Both men had just begun to swim towards the shore, when they noticed with dismay that the speed-boat was moving in a circle. It now came straight towards them at tremendous
15 speed. In less than a minute, it roared past them only a few feet away. After it

. . . swam on quickly

had passed, they swam on as quickly as they could because they knew that the boat would soon return. They had just had enough time to swim out of danger when the boat again completed a circle. On this occasion, however, it had slowed
20 down considerably. The petrol had nearly all been used up. Before long, the noise dropped completely and the boat began to drift gently across the water.

Précis
In not more than 80 words describe what happened from the moment the men were thrown into the sea. Write two different paragraphs using the points and connections given below.

CONNECTIONS	POINTS	CONNECTIONS
The moment	⌈ 1. Speed-boat struck buoy. ⌉	*Because*
	⌊ 2. Both men—water. ⌋	
As	⌈ 3. It moved off. ⌉	
	⌊ 4. Men—shore. ⌋	*and while*
Turning	⌈ 5. Circle—towards them.	
After	6. Just missed them. ⌋	*and only just*
until	⌊ 7. Swam—out of danger. ⌉	*no sooner . . . than*
When	8. Boat returned. ⌋	
	⌈ 9. Lost speed. ⌉	*This time, however*
Soon . . . and	⌊ 10. Petrol used up—floated. ⌋	*because . . . and*

Composition
Write two paragraphs in about 150 words using the ideas given below:
1. A speed-boat was out of control—no one was in it—it was moving towards a small fishing-boat—the fishermen tried to row away.
2. The speed-boat came nearer—the fishermen dived into the sea—the speed-boat ran out of petrol—stopped just before it reached the fishermen.

Letter-writing
Which of the following endings are correct:
Yours sincerely, Your's sincerely, Yours sincerely, yours sincerely, Yours Sincerely, Your's, Yours, Yours Very Sincerely.

Key Structures

What had happened? What had been happening? Review: **KS 39, 97, 153.**

Exercises

A. Underline the verbs in the passage which tell us *what happened*, *what had happened* and *what had been happening*.

B. Give the correct form of the verbs in brackets. Do not refer to the passage until you finish the exercise:

As the man tried to swing the speed-boat round, the steering-wheel came away in his hands. He (wave) desperately to his companion who (water-ski) for the last fifteen minutes. Both men hardly (have) time to realize what was happening when they (throw) violently into the sea. The speed-boat (strike) a buoy, but it (continue) to move very quickly across the water. Both men just (begin) to swim towards the shore, when they (notice) with dismay that the speed-boat was moving in a circle. It now (come) to-wards them at tremendous speed. In less than a minute, it (roar) past them only a few feet away. After it (pass), they (swim) on as quickly as they could because they (know) that the boat would soon return. They just (have) enough time to swim out of danger when the boat again (complete) a circle. On this occasion, however, it (slow) down considerably. The petrol nearly all (use) up. Before long, the noise (drop) completely and the boat (begin) to drift gently across the water.

Special Difficulties

Words Often Confused.
a Enough and Fairly. Study these examples:
Your work is not good enough. (Compare **SD 210**)
I missed the train this morning. I didn't get up early enough.
They had just had enough time to swim out of danger. (l. 18)
I didn't buy enough sugar.
There are enough flowers in that vase.
George is a fairly tall person but still not tall enough to get into the police force.
I know he's a fairly good player, but he doesn't play well enough to get into the team.

b Petrol and Benzine. Study these examples:
The petrol had nearly all been used up. (l. 20)
Driving a car is becoming an expensive business. The price of petrol has gone up again.
Those stains might come off if you use benzine.

Exercise
Supply the missing words in the following sentences:
1. It's . . . cold today, but not really cold . . . to light a fire.
2. This book was . . . interesting, but I didn't enjoy it as much as I expected to.
3. What type of . . . do you use in your car?
4. This class has given me . . . trouble so far.
5. You haven't put . . . flowers in that vase.
6. This stain would not come out even after I had used . . .
7. Is that suit-case large . . . to take all these clothes?

87 A Perfect Alibi

'At the time the murder was committed, I was travelling on the 8 o'clock train to London,' said the man.

'Do you always catch such an early 5 train?' asked the inspector.

'Of course I do,' answered the man. 'I must be at work at 10 o'clock. My employer will confirm that I was there on time.'

10 'Would a later train get you to work on time?' asked the inspector.

'I suppose it would, but I never catch a later train.'

'At what time did you arrive at the 15 station?'

'At ten to eight. I bought a paper and waited for the train.'

'And you didn't notice anything unusual?'

'Of course not.'

'I suggest you are not telling the truth'

20 'I suggest,' said the inspector, 'that you are not telling the truth. I suggest that you did not catch the 8 o'clock train, but that you caught the 8.25 which would still get you to work on time. You see, on the morning of the murder, the 8 o'clock train did not run at all. It broke down at Ferngreen station and was taken off the line.'

Précis

In not more than 80 words show how the inspector proved that the man's alibi was false. Write two different paragraphs using the points and connections given below.

CONNECTIONS	POINTS	CONNECTIONS
At	1. Time of murder.	*When the murder*
that	2. Man claimed—travelling.	*that*
	3. 8 o'clock train, London.	
and	4. Arrived work on time.	*He said that*
When	5. Inspector asked—later train, work on time.	*Then*
	6. Man agreed it would.	*Though*
but	7. Always travelled early.	
	8. Inspector suggested: lying.	*In reply*
because	9. 8 o'clock train—broke down.	*as*
so	10. Man caught 8.25.	*and therefore*

Letter-writing

Continue the conversation begun in the passage. Write about 150 words using the ideas given below:

The man suddenly 'remembered' that he had caught the later train—didn't he notice anything unusual?—not unusual for a train to be late—how did he spend the time?— waited on the platform for 25 minutes—read a newspaper—the inspector suggested that the man was lying—a neighbour saw him leave the house at 8.15, just after the murder—the man was arrested.

Letter-writing

The Signature. How you sign your name depends on how well you know the person you are writing to. You may use your full name, your first name, or even a nickname. Your signature must be readable. It must come under the letter-ending.

Exercise
Write suitable letter-endings and signatures to the following:
Your sister; your wife or husband; your employer; a close friend.

Key Structures

He said that . . . He told me . . . He asked . . . Review: **KS 41, 99, 155.**

Exercises
A. Imagine that your are writing a newspaper report of the conversation that took place between the man and the inspector. Answer these questions on the passage. Where necessary, use the words given in brackets:
Lines 1–3 What did the man say he was doing at the time the murder was committed?
Lines 4–5 What did the inspector ask him?
Lines 6–9 Did the man say that he did or that he didn't? At what time did he have to be at work? (*because*) What would his employer confirm?
Lines 10–11 What did the inspector ask him then?
Lines 12–13 What did the man suppose? Did he ever catch a later train? (*but*)
Lines 14–15 What did the inspector ask?
Line 16 At what time did the man say he had arrived at the station? What did he do there? (*He added that he . . .*)
Lines 18–19 What did the inspector ask him? Did the man say that he had or that he hadn't? (*When the inspector asked him . . . the man . . .*)
Lines 20–21 What did the inspector suggest?
Lines 22–24 What did the inspector point out?

B. Here is part of a report that appeared in a newspaper. Write the actual conversation that took place between the man and the inspector. (**SD 74**) Do not refer to the passage until you finish the exercise.
At the time the murder was committed, the man said that he was travelling on the 8 o'clock train to London. The inspector asked if he always caught such an early train. The man answered that he did. He had to be at work at 10 o'clock. His employer would confirm that he was there on time. Then the inspector asked him if a later train would get him to work on time. The man supposed that a later train would get him to work on time but he never caught a later train. The inspector asked him what time he arrived at the station. The man said that he had arrived there at ten to eight. He added that he bought a paper and waited for the train. When the inspector asked him if he had noticed anything unusual, the man said that he had not.

88   Trapped in a Mine

Six men have been trapped in a mine for seventeen hours. If they are not brought to the surface soon they may lose their lives. However, rescue operations are
5 proving difficult. If explosives are used, vibrations will cause the roof of the mine to collapse. Rescue workers are therefore drilling a hole on the north side of the mine. They intend to bring the men up
10 in a special capsule. If there had not been a hard layer of rock beneath the soil, they would have completed the job in a few hours. As it is, they have been drilling for sixteen hours and they still have a long
15 way to go. Meanwhile, a microphone, which was lowered into the mine two

the men are cheerful

hours ago, has enabled the men to keep in touch with the closest relatives. Though they are running out of food and drink, the men are cheerful and confident that they will get out soon. They have been told that rescue operations are
20 progressing smoothly. If they knew how difficult it was to drill through the hard rock, they would lose heart.

Précis

Make a summary of the passage *in not more than 80 words*. Write two different paragraphs using the points and connections given below.

CONNECTIONS	POINTS	CONNECTIONS
who	1. Six men—trapped—seventeen hours	
	2. May lose lives.	*and*
because	3. Rescue difficult.	
Since	4. Explosives—collapse.	*as*
	5. Drilling—hard rock.	*Because of this*
but	6. Progress slow.	*yet*
Two hours ago	7. Microphone lowered.	*Now that*
and	8. In touch—relatives.	
	9. Running short—food.	*Though*
but	10. Good spirits.	

Composition

Continue the above passage. Write two paragraphs in about 150 words using the ideas given below:

1. During the rescue operations there was a loud noise—collapse of mine—microphone silent—the men's voices were heard an hour later—they were all right.
2. Drilling began again—the collapse had made things easier—the men were brought to the surface—the scene on their return.

Letter-writing

The Postscript. If you wish to add something to your letter after you have finished it, you may do so under your signature. Whatever you write must be preceded by the letters 'P.S.' which stand for 'Postscript'. Study this example:

Yours sincerely,

Tom

P.S. I'll send you a copy of the book by separate post.

Exercise

Write two letter-endings followed by postscripts.

Key Structures

If. Review: **KS 43, 101, 158.**

Exercises

A. How many sentences in the passage contain the word *if*? Study the form of the verbs in these sentences.

B. Give the correct form of the verbs in brackets. Do not refer to the passage until you finish the exercise.
1. If they (not bring) to the surface soon they may lose their lives.
2. If explosives are used, vibrations (cause) the roof of the mine to collapse.
3. If there had not been a hard layer of rock beneath the soil, they (complete) the job in a few hours.
4. If they knew how difficult it was to drill through the hard rock, they (lose) heart.

C. Give the correct form of the verbs in brackets:
1. If he had fitted safety belts to his car he (not injure).
2. The man would have been saved if a helicopter (be) available.
3. If you come home late, you (find) the key under the mat.
4. I would have found the house easily if he (give) me the correct address.
5. If smoking (forbid), illnesses will be reduced.

Special Difficulties

The verb *run* has a different meaning in each of these sentences. Study them carefully:
They are *running out of* food (l. 18) (They have nearly used up all their supplies.)
A crowd of boys *ran after* the beggar. (They chased the beggar.)
That boy was nearly *run over* by a car. (The car nearly hit him.)
Don't drive so fast. This car hasn't been *run in* yet. (The car must be driven slowly so as not to damage the new engine.)
I *ran into* Helga while I was in Sweden. (I met her by accident.)

Exercise

Supply the missing words in the following sentences:
1. I ran . . . an old friend of mine in a restaurant yesterday.
2. While driving to work yesterday, I ran . . . . . . petrol and had to walk to a garage.
3. This car will have to be serviced as soon as it has been run . . .
4. She's been taken to hospital. She was run . . . by a car.
5. I ran . . . him, but I could not catch him.

89 A Slip of the Tongue

People will do anything to see a free show—even if it is a bad one. When the news got round that a variety show would be presented at our local cinema by the
5   P. and U. Bird Seed Company, we all rushed to see it. We had to queue for hours to get in and there must have been several hundred people present just before the show began. Unfortunately, the
10 show was one of the dullest we have ever seen. Those who failed to get in need not have felt disappointed as many of the artistes who should have appeared did not come. The only funny things we heard
15 that evening came from the advertiser at the beginning of the programme. He was

He was obviously very nervous

obviously very nervous and for some minutes stood awkwardly before the microphone. As soon as he opened his mouth, everyone burst out laughing. We all know what the poor man *should* have said, but what he *actually* said was:
20 'This is the Poo and Ee Seed Bird Company. Good ladies, evening and gentlemen!'

Précis

Make a summary of the passage *in not more than 80 words*. Write two different paragraphs using the points and connections given below.

CONNECTIONS	POINTS	CONNECTIONS
	⌈ 1. Local cinema—packed. ⌉	
because	│ 2. P. & U. Bird Seed Co. │	
	⌊ 3. Presenting free variety show. ⌋	
As . . . who	⌈ 4. Many artistes should . . . ⌉	*but . . . who*
	│ 5. Failed to turn up. │	
	⌊ 6. Show very dull. ⌋	*Because of this*
	⌈ 7. Funniest thing— ⌉	
who	│ 8. Advertiser introduced programme │	*who at the beginning*
	│ saying: │	
	⌊ 9. 'This . . . gentlemen.' ⌋	

Composition

Write a newspaper report of the event described in the passage. Write two paragraphs in about 150 words using the ideas given below:

1. There was a long queue of people outside the cinema—many people failed to get in—they were the lucky ones.
2. A description of the stage—there was a large, ugly model of a yellow bird—free packets of bird-seed for the audience—the advertiser's mistake—how the audience reacted—the rest of the show: a disappointment.

Letter-writing

Write three letter-endings followed by postscripts.

Key Structures

Must, Have to, Need, Should. Review: **KS 45, 104, 160.**

Exercises

A. Note how the verbs *have to, must, need* and *should* have been used in the passage.

B. Supply the correct form of *have to, must, need* and *should* in the following. Do not refer to the passage until you finish the exercise:
1. We . . . queue for hours to get in and there . . . (be) several hundred people present just before the show began. Unfortunately, the show was one of the dullest we have ever seen. Those who failed to get in . . . not (feel) disappointed as many of the artistes who . . . (appear) did not come.
2. As soon as he opened his mouth, everyone burst out laughing. We all know what the poor man . . . (say), but what he *actually* said was: 'This is the Poo and Ee Seed Bird Company . . .'

C. Supply *must not* or *need not* in the following sentences:
1. You . . . open the door of the compartment until the train has stopped. It is very dangerous.
2. You . . . bother to post those letters for me. I'll be going out myself soon.

D. Supply the correct form of *have to* or *should* in the following sentences:
1. I'm sorry I couldn't get here on time. I (. . . go) to the bank.
2. I (. . . go) to the dentist yesterday but I forgot all about it.
3. We (. . . begin) work at 9 o'clock but we never do.

Special Difficulties

Words Often Confused and Misused.
a Free and Single. Study these examples:
People will do anything to see a free show. (ll. 1–2)
The people are free to choose who will govern them.
Is she still single? I thought she was going to get married last April.

b Queue and Row. Study these examples:
We had to queue for hours to get in. (ll. 6–7)
There was a long queue outside the cinema.
I enjoyed the performance because I had a very good seat in the fifth row.

c Funny. Study these examples:
The only funny things we heard that evening . . . (ll. 14–15)
There's something funny about this house. (Something peculiar.)

Exercise

A. Choose the correct words in the following sentences:
1. I joined the (queue) (row) at the bus-stop.
2. He's still (free) (single) even though he's over forty. I don't think he'll ever marry.

B. Write two sentences bringing out the meanings of the word *funny*.

90 Brasilia

Though Brazil is one of the richest countries in the world, much of it has not yet been developed. It was mainly for this reason that the Brazilian government decided to have a new city built 600 miles north-west of Rio de Janeiro. Designed by the great architect Lucio Costa, the new city, Brasilia, replaced Rio de Janeiro as the capital of Brazil in 1960. Brasilia has been carefully planned for modern living. Its wide roads, which can take fourteen lanes of traffic, have been kept away from living areas. Children do not have to cross busy streets to go to school. Housewives can visit shopping centres on foot, for in these specially designed living

great difficulty in persuading people

areas, cars are unnecessary. At first, the government had great difficulty in persuading people to leave Rio and to settle in Brasilia. Since 1960, however, the population has been growing all the time. Brasilia has quickly established itself as the capital of the country. The idea to have the capital moved so far inland will have a great effect on the future of Brazil.

Précis

Make a summary of the passage *in not more than 80 words*. Write two different paragraphs using the points and connections given below.

CONNECTIONS	POINTS	CONNECTIONS
Because	1. Brazil needs to be developed.	
	2. New city, Brasilia, built 600 miles, Rio.	*which was built*
It	3. Designed Lucio Costa.	*and which*
and	4. Became capital 1960.	
Though	5. Planned for modern living.	*It*
	6. People at first reluctant to go.	*but*
Since ... not	7. 1960—population increasing.	*However, with the increase*
only		
but also	8. Established as capital.	

Composition

Write two paragraphs in about 150 words on 'Cities of the Future'. Use the ideas given below:

1. Cities of the present—unsuited to modern living—unhealthy—traffic—noise—time wasted travelling.
2. Cities of the future—no private houses and private gardens—blocks of flats—all comforts—away from traffic—schools and shops near—no transport problems—designed for living.

Letter-writing

Write your address, the date and the opening paragraph of a letter to a friend. Your letter should begin, 'I have just . . .'

Key Structures

Have. Review: **KS 47, 105, 161.**

Exercises

A. Note how the verb *have* has been used in the passage.

B. Write these sentences again using *have* with the verbs in italics. Do not refer to the passage until you finish the exercise.
1. The Brazilian government decided *to build* a new city.
2. The idea *to move* the capital so far inland will have a great effect on the future of Brazil.

C. Use a construction with *have* in place of the words in italics:
1. At first, the government *found it very difficult to persuade* people to leave Rio.
2. The idea to have the capital moved so far inland *will greatly affect* the future of Brazil.

D. In which of these sentences can we put *got* after *have*:
1. We have to increase our exports.
2. The police have been inquiring into the matter.
3. This car has a new engine.
4. We had a telegram from Aunt Mabel this morning.
5. This play has a large cast.
6. They are having a music festival in Salzburg next year.
7. He has a haircut once a fortnight.

E. Write these sentences again using *have* with the verbs in italics:
1. He *has published* the book. He has had . . .
2. We *have not sent* the letter to his new address.
3. 'I *shall deliver* the parcel,' said the shop-assistant.
4. Are you going *to clean* this suit?
5. When will you *dye* this jacket?

Special Difficulties

Note how these two sentences have been joined:
Brasilia was designed by Lucio Costa. It replaced Rio de Janeiro as the capital of Brazil.
Designed by Lucio Costa, Brasilia replaced Rio de Janeiro as the capital of Brazil. (See ll. 6–9)

Exercise
Join the sentences below in the same way:
1. The debate was attended by two hundred people. It was one of the most interesting in the series.
2. The swimmer was encouraged by his success. He entered a competition.
3. It was completed in 1644. It is one of the most famous cathedrals ever built.
4. He was born in 1895. He fought in two World Wars.

91 Three Men in a Basket

A pilot noticed a balloon which seemed to be making for a Royal Air Force Station nearby. He informed the station at once, but no one there was able to explain
5 the mystery. The officer in the control tower was very angry when he heard the news, because balloons can be a great danger to aircraft. He said that someone might be spying on the station and the
10 pilot was ordered to keep track of the strange object. The pilot managed to circle the balloon for some time. He could make out three men in a basket under it and one of them was holding
15 field-glasses. When the balloon was over the station, the pilot saw one of the men

someone might be spying

taking photographs. Soon afterwards, the balloon began to descend and it landed near an airfield. The police were called in, but they could not arrest anyone, for the basket contained two Members of Parliament and the Commanding
20 Officer of the station! As the Commanding Officer explained later, one half of the station did not know what the other half was doing!

Précis

In not more than 80 words, explain what happened from the time the pilot was ordered to keep track of the balloon. Write two different paragraphs using the points and connections given below.

CONNECTIONS	POINTS	CONNECTIONS
While circling	1. Pilot circled balloon.	*under which there was*
	2. Saw three men—basket.	*. . . containing*
one of whom	3. Field-glasses.	*one of whom*
When	4. Flew station.	*Before landing on*
	5. Took photographs.	*and*
Then	6. Landed—airfield.	
but	7. Police—arrest.	*As two of the men were . . . and the*
because	8. Two Members of Parliament and Commanding Officer.	*other was . . . the police . . .*
Afterwards.	9. One half—the other half.	*The mystery was explained when*

Composition

Imagine that the police did not believe the three men and arrested them. Write two paragraphs in about 150 words using the ideas given below:
1. The men struggled—they explained who they were—they were not believed—taken to the police station.

2. The police questioned the men—they refused to answer—the Commanding Officer telephoned the station—a senior officer arrived—he identified the C.O.—the police apologized.

Letter-writing

Write opening sentences which would be suitable for letters to the following:
1. A friend who has not written to you for a long time.
2. A friend who has been expecting to hear from you for a long time.
3. An aunt who entertained you to dinner and a visit to the theatre.
4. A friend who has successfully passed a difficult examination.

Key Structures

Can, Able to, Manage to. Review: **KS 49, 107, 163.**

Exercises
A. Underline the verbs *can*, *able to* and *manage to* in the passage. Note how they have been used.

B. Supply the correct forms of *can*, *able to* and *manage to* in this paragraph. Do not refer to the passage until you finish the exercise:
He informed the station at once, but no one there . . . explain the mystery. The officer in the control tower was very angry when he heard the news, because balloons . . . be a great danger to aircraft. He said that someone might be spying on the station and the pilot was ordered to keep track of the strange object. The pilot . . . circle the balloon for some time. He . . . make out three men in a basket under it and one of them was holding field-glasses.

C. Supply the correct form of *can* or *able to* in the following:
1. . . . you show me the way to the station please?
2. I gave him a few lessons and he . . . soon swim.
3. They . . . jump into the sea before the boat sank.
4. You . . . not leave this room until you get permission.

Special Difficulties

The verb *make* has a different meaning in each of the following sentences. Study them carefully.
A balloon seemed to be *making for* a Royal Air Force Station. (ll. 1–3) (It seemed to be travelling towards . . .)
He could *make out* three men in a basket. (ll. 12–13) (He could see.)
I could not *make out* what he said. (I could not understand.)
Please *make out* a fresh copy. (Write out another one.)
He *made up* a story about two men and a horse. (He invented.)
She spends hours *making up* in front of the mirror. (She uses cosmetics.)
I must *make up for* the time I lost this morning. (I must compensate for . . .)

Exercise
Supply the missing words in the following sentences:
1. I lost my lecture notes and had to make . . . a new set.
2. I can't make . . . what you've written.
3. When it got dark we made . . . home.
4. My daughter often makes . . . stories of her own.
5. How can you make . . . . . . all those lessons you missed?

92 Asking for Trouble

It must have been about two in the morning when I returned home. I tried to wake up my wife by ringing the door-bell, but she was fast asleep, so I got a ladder
5 from the shed in the garden, put it against the wall, and began climbing towards the bedroom window. I was almost there when a sarcastic voice below said, 'I don't think the windows need cleaning at this
10 time of the night.' I looked down and nearly fell off the ladder when I saw a policeman. I immediately regretted answering in the way I did, but I said, 'I enjoy cleaning windows at night.'

'I'd prefer to stay here'

15 'So do I,' answered the policeman in the same tone. 'Excuse my interrupting you. I hate to interrupt a man when he's busy working, but would you mind coming with me to the station?'

'Well, I'd prefer to stay here,' I said. 'You see, I've forgotten my key.'
20 'Your what?' he called.

'My key,' I shouted.

Fortunately, the shouting woke up my wife who opened the window just as the policeman had started to climb towards me.

Précis

In not more than 80 words describe what happened from the moment the writer returned home. Write two different paragraphs using the points and connections given below.

CONNECTIONS	POINTS	CONNECTIONS
	⌈ 1. The writer returned home—2.0 a.m. ⌉	*On*
and	⌊ 2. Rang door-bell.	
Having	⌈ 3. Failed to wake wife.	*but*
	⌊ 4. Put ladder—wall.	*After having*
and	⌊ 5. Climbed—bedroom window.	
Suddenly	⌈ 6. Policeman called out.	*when*
but	⌊ 7. Answered rudely.	*Answering*
	⌊ 8. Told him—key.	
	⌈ 9. Shouting woke wife.	
	⌈ 10. Opened window.	*who*
just as	⌊ 11. Policeman climbing ladder after him.	*at the moment when*

Composition

Continue the above passage. Write two paragraphs in about 150 words using the ideas given below:

1. At first my wife did not recognize me—thought I was a thief—saw the policeman—called for help.
2. The policeman pulled me down the ladder—my wife realized her mistake—she explained who I was—she apologized to the policeman—the policeman apologized to me.

Letter-writing

Address an envelope to a married woman who lives abroad.

Key Structures

I don't think the windows need cleaning. Review: **KS 51, 110, 166**.

Exercises

A. Give the correct form of the verbs in brackets. Do not refer to the passage until you finish the exercise.

I tried to wake up my wife by (ring) the door-bell, but she was fast asleep, so I got a ladder from the shed in the garden, put it against the wall, and began (climb) towards the bedroom window. I was almost there when a sarcastic voice below said, 'I don't think the windows need (clean) at this time of the night.' I looked down and nearly fell off the ladder when I saw a policeman. I immediately regretted (answer) in the way I did, but I said, 'I enjoy (clean) windows at night.'

'So do I,' answered the policeman in the same tone. 'Excuse my (interrupt) you. I hate (interrupt) a man when he's busy (work), but would you mind (come) with me to the station?'

'Well, I'd prefer (stay) here,' I said. 'You see, I've forgotten my key.'

'Your what?' he called.

'My key,' I shouted.

Fortunately, the (shout) woke up my wife who opened the window just as the policeman had started (climb) towards me.

B. Complete the following sentences:
1. I am accustomed to . . .
2. Fancy . . .!
3. I always avoid . . .
4. He accused me of . . .

Special Difficulties

'I enjoy cleaning windows at night.'
'So do I,' answered the policeman. (ll. 13–15)
Study these examples:
He reads a lot and so do I.
He doesn't read much and neither do I.
He can swim and so can I.
He can't swim and neither can I.

Exercise

Join each of these pairs of sentences using *so* or *neither*.
1. He likes classical music. I like classical music.
2. He has had breakfast. I have had breakfast.
3. He doesn't like classical music. I don't like classical music.
4. She will buy a new dress. I will buy a new dress.
5. He hasn't had breakfast. I haven't had breakfast.
6. They ran quickly. We ran quickly.
7. She won't buy a new dress. I won't buy a new dress.
8. You are late. I am late.
9. They didn't run quickly. We didn't run quickly.
10. He could speak French. I could speak French.
11. He couldn't speak French. I couldn't speak French.

93 A Noble Gift

One of the most famous monuments in the world, the Statue of Liberty, was presented to the United States of America in the nineteenth century by the people
5 of France. The great statue, which was designed by the sculptor Auguste Bartholdi, took ten years to complete. The actual figure was made of copper supported by a metal framework which had
10 been especially constructed by Eiffel. Before it could be transported to the United States, a site had to be found for it and a pedestal had to be built. The site chosen was an island at the entrance of New York
15 Harbour. By 1884, a statue which was 151 feet tall, had been erected in Paris.

One of the most famous monuments

The following year, it was taken to pieces and sent to America. By the end of October 1886, the statue had been put together again and it was officially presented to the American people by Bartholdi. Ever since then, the great monu-
20 ment has been a symbol of liberty for the millions of people who have passed through New York Harbour to make their homes in America.

Précis

In not more than 80 words describe how the Statue of Liberty came to be built in New York Harbour. Write two different paragraphs using the points and connections given below.

CONNECTIONS	POINTS	CONNECTIONS
which	1. Statue—presented U.S.A.	
	2. French people—19th century.	
	3. Designed—Bartholdi.	*Though*
and	4. Built on metal frame—Eiffel.	
where	5. Site chosen—island—New York Harbour.	
	6. Pedestal built.	*and*
and	7. The statue erected Paris 1884.	*The statue was first*
	8. Re-erected two years later—America.	*but*
	9. October 1886—presented.	*and*

Composition

Imagine you are entering New York Harbour by ship. Write two paragraphs in about 150 words using the ideas given below:
1. Sailing into N.Y. Harbour between Long Island and Staten Island: the Statue of Liberty: first impressions.
2. A first glimpse of New York—Manhattan—skyscrapers: the Empire State building —the United Nations building—great ships in the harbour—bridges, traffic and people.

Letter-writing

Write five sentences which could be used to begin letters to friends.

Key Structures

The Statue of Liberty was presented to the United States of America. Review: KS 53, 111, 167.

Exercises

A. Underline the verbs in the passage and study their form.

B. Give the correct form of the verbs in brackets. Do not refer to the passage until you finish the exercise.

One of the most famous monuments in the world, the Statue of Liberty, (present) to the United States of America in the nineteenth century by the people of France. The great statue, which (design) by the sculptor Auguste Bartholdi, took ten years to complete. The actual figure (make) of copper (support) by a metal framework which . . . especially (construct) by Eiffel. Before it (could/transport) to the United States, a site had (to find) for it and a pedestal had (to build). The site (choose) was an island at the entrance of New York Harbour. By 1884, a statue which was 151 feet tall, (erect) in Paris. The following year it (take) to pieces and (send) to America. By the end of October 1886, the statue (put) together again and it . . . officially (present) to the American people by Bartholdi.

Special Difficulties

Stress.

Read these two sentences aloud:

The Statue of Liberty was a present from the French people.

It was presented to the United States of America.

In the first sentence, *present* is a noun and the accent falls on the first syllable: présent.

In the second sentence, *present* is a verb and the accent falls on the second syllable: presént.

Here are some common words which are stressed in the same way: accent, conduct, contest, contrast, export, import, increase, insult, produce, protest, record, and transport.

Exercise

Read these sentences aloud. Mark in the correct stress of the words in italics:

1. This year we have *exported* more than we have *imported*.
2. Our *records* show that *exports* have gone up.
3. Everybody *protested* against the *increase* in income tax.
4. He was *insulted* when I criticized his *accent*.
5. Please *conduct* yourselves properly when you are in the museum.
6. He entered for the *contest* and broke a *record*.

94 Future Champions

Experiments have proved that children can be instructed in swimming at a very early age. At a special swimming pool in Los Angeles, children become expert at
5 holding their breath under water even before they can walk. Babies of two months old do not appear to be reluctant to enter the water. It is not long before they are so accustomed to swimming that they
10 can pick up weights from the floor of the pool. A game that is very popular with these young swimmers is the underwater tricycle race. Tricycles are lined up on the floor of the pool seven feet under
15 water. The children compete against each other to reach the other end of the pool.

future Olympic champions

Many pedal their tricycles, but most of them prefer to push or drag them. Some children can cover the whole length of the pool without coming up for breath even once. Whether they will ever become future Olympic champions, only
20 time will tell. Meanwhile, they should encourage those among us who cannot swim five yards before they are gasping for air.

Précis

In not more than 80 words describe what goes on at the children's swimming pool in Los Angeles. Write two different paragraphs using the points and connections given below.

CONNECTIONS	POINTS	CONNECTIONS
	1. Swimming pool—Los Angeles.	
	2. Children taught—hold breath—walk.	*who*
	3. Begin learning: two months old.	*often begin*
and, in time	4. Weights—bottom of pool.	*Though*
	5. Game they enjoy—race.	
which	6. Takes place seven feet under water.	*This*
Some . . . others	7. Pedal—push—pull.	*and*
and	8. A few get across—without coming up for air.	

Composition

Imagine witnessing the sort of underwater tricycle race described in the passage. Write two paragraphs in about 150 words using the ideas given below:
1. The children dived into the water—found their tricycles—started off.
2. A child was pulling his tricycle—dropped it—hindered two others—got it out of the way—another child was pedalling hard—won the race—rose to surface dragging up his tricycle.

Letter-writing

Write suitable conclusions which could be used in letters to:
1. A friend who has got a new job.
2. A friend you will be meeting soon.
3. A friend who has been ill.

Key Structures

Review: **KS 55, 114, 170.**

Exercise
Study these examples:
Children can be instructed *in* swimming . . . (ll. 1–2)
Children become expert *at* holding their breath . . . (ll. 4–5)
They do not appear to be reluctant *to* enter the water. (ll. 7–8)
They are so accustomed *to* swimming . . . (ll. 8–9)
The children compete *against* each other . . . (ll. 15–16)
Supply the missing words in the following sentences:
1. Many people do not approve . . . blood-sports. 2. He was found guilty . . . murder and condemned . . . death. 3. Has it ever occurred . . . you that those twins are quite different . . . each other in many ways? 4. I consulted my lawyer . . . the matter and I shall act . . . his advice. 5. It is impossible to prevent them . . . quarrelling . . . each other. 6. He is responding . . . treatment and will soon be cured . . . his illness. 7. Even though he is thirty-five, he lives . . . his mother and is completely dependent . . . her. 8. I tried to reason . . . him, but he was very rude . . . me. 9. I am grateful . . . you for being so patient . . . him. 10. He might be good . . . his job, but you can't rely . . . him. 11. I am thinking . . . looking . . . a new job. 12. If you interfere . . . other people's affairs, you will regret it. 13. Do you believe . . . all that nonsense? 14. It should be obvious . . . you that if you persist . . . bothering him, he will get angry . . . you. 15. You demand too much . . . him; he is not really equal . . . the task. 16. Don't be so sure . . . yourself! 17. He has provided . . . every emergency. 18. I was afraid . . . mentioning it . . . him. 19. Don't blame him . . . this; I am responsible . . . what has happened. 20. He is so keen . . . learning, you should encourage him . . . his efforts. 21. Beware . . . people who appear to be enthusiastic . . . your success. 22. I appealed . . . him for help. 23. I am sorry . . . having asked him. I was shocked . . . his refusal. 24. Are you interested . . . opera? 25. Are you aware . . . the difficulties that lie ahead . . . you? 26. He's entitled . . . a pension, but he won't dream . . . retiring yet. 27. Who is going to pay . . . the damage? 28. This car is inferior . . . the one I bought last year. 29. I'm afraid I can't comment . . . your work just yet. 30. She may pride herself . . . her abilities, but she's not capable . . . bringing up children. 31. We are accustomed . . . bad weather. 32. How can you agree . . . such an idea when you are ignorant . . . the basic facts? 33. He confessed . . . me that he had just been converted . . . some strange religion. 34. She wanted to borrow the record . . . me but she was shy . . . asking. 35. If you fail . . . this attempt, don't count . . . me for help.

95 A Fantasy

When the Ambassador of Escalopia returned home for lunch, his wife got a
shock. He looked pale and his clothes
were in a frightful state.

5 'What has happened?' she asked.
'How did your clothes get into such a
mess?'

'A fire-extinguisher, my dear,' answered
the Ambassador drily. 'University stu-
10 dents set the Embassy on fire this morning.'

'Good heavens!' exclaimed his wife.
'And where were you at the time?'

'I was in my office as usual,' answered
15 the Ambassador. 'The fire broke out in
the basement. I went down immediately,

*set the Embassy on fire
this morning*

of course, and that fool, Horst, aimed a fire-extinguisher at me. He thought I was
on fire. I must definitely get that fellow posted.'

The Ambassador's wife went on asking questions, when she suddenly noticed
20 a big hole in her husband's hat.

'And how can you explain *that*?' she asked.

'Oh, that,' said the Ambassador. 'Someone fired a shot through my office
window. Accurate, don't you think? Fortunately, I wasn't wearing it at the time.
If I had been, I would not have been able to get home for lunch.'

Précis

In not more than 80 words write an account of what had happened at the Escalopian
Embassy. Write two different paragraphs using the points and connections given below.

CONNECTIONS	POINTS	CONNECTIONS
While	1. Ambassador, Escalopia—in office.	
	2. Students—basement—fire.	*when*
When	3. Ambassador—went to investigate.	*After*
	4. Man called Horst—fire-extinguisher.	
because	5. Thought Ambassador on fire.	*under the impression*
Moreover	6. Hole—Ambassador's hat.	*In addition to this*
which	7. Made when someone fired shot—window.	*It*
	8. Ambassador lucky.	
for	9. Not wearing it.	*that*

Composition

In about 150 words, write an imaginary account of the scene in the basement when the
Ambassador went down to investigate. Use the ideas given below:
The Ambassador shouted—Horst explained: the Ambassador *was* on fire—the
Ambassador denied it—Horst insisted—aimed the fire-extinguisher at him—the
Ambassador very angry—will send Horst to the South Pole—Horst explained that

Escalopia has broken off diplomatic relations with the South Pole—the Ambassador went out angrily—Horst was pleased with himself.

Letter-writing

Write a letter to a friend inviting him or her to come to a party. Supply a suitable Introduction and Conclusion. Use the following ideas to write your *Purpose*: the reason for the party—time and place—many old friends will be there.

Key Structures

Review of verb-forms. **KS 149, 167.**

Exercises

A. Imagine that you are writing a newspaper report of the conversation that took place between the Ambassador and his wife. Write the passage again using the notes given below:

Lines 5–11 When she asked what . . . and how . . ., the Ambassador answered drily that a fire-extinguisher had been responsible. He then told her that . . .

Lines 12–13 His wife was most surprised and asked him where . . .

Lines 14–17 The Ambassador answered that he . . . When the fire broke out . . . he . . . Omit: 'of course'.

Lines 17–18 Horst thought the Ambassador . . . The Ambassador said that he must . . .

Lines 19–21 . . . big hole in her husband's hat and asked him how . . .

Line 22 Omit: 'Oh, that,' The Ambassador said that someone had . . .

Line 23 The shot was accurate, but fortunately he had not been wearing his hat at the time. If he . . .

B. Give the correct form of the verbs in brackets:

'We just (receive) a report,' (say) the radio announcer, 'that rioting (break) out in Umgolia. Students, who (demonstrate) outside the Escalopian Embassy during the day, (break) into the building last night and (set) it on fire. The students (protest) against the new tax on beer mugs which recently (impose) by the Escalopian government. A spokesman (say) that the beer mug industry in Umgolia seriously (affect). The Escalopian Ambassador, who (say) to have been slightly injured, bravely (defend) by his servant, Mr Flugel Horst. Mr Horst (keep) off the students with a fire-extinguisher. The Premier of Umgolia (announce) this evening that, in future, steps (take) to prevent further incidents.'

C. Give the correct form of the verbs in brackets. Do not refer to the passage until you finish the exercise:

1. 'What (happen)?' she asked. 'How . . . your clothes (get) into such a mess?'
2. 'Oh, that,' said the Ambassador. 'Someone (fire) a shot through my office window. Accurate, . . . n't you think? Fortunately, I not (wear) it at the time. If I had been, I not (able) to get home for lunch.

96   The Dead Return

A Festival for the Dead is held once a year in Japan. This festival is a cheerful occasion, for on this day, the dead are said to return to their homes and they are welcomed by the living. As they are expected to be hungry after their long journey, food is laid out for them. Specially-made lanterns are hung outside each house to help the dead to find their way. All night long, people dance and sing. In the early morning, the food that had been laid out for the dead is thrown into a river or into the sea as it is considered unlucky for anyone living to eat it. In towns that are near the sea, the tiny lanterns which had been hung in the streets the night before,

a cheerful occasion

are placed into the water when the festival is over. Thousands of lanterns slowly drift out to sea guiding the dead on their return journey to the other world. This is a moving spectacle, for crowds of people stand on the shore watching the lanterns drifting away until they can be seen no more.

Précis

In not more than 80 words give an account of the Festival for the Dead. Write two different paragraphs using the points and connections given below.

CONNECTIONS	POINTS	CONNECTIONS
	1. Japanese annual festival—cheerful occasion.	
As	2. Dead return home.	*for*
	3. Food laid out.	*Food is not only*
and	4. Lanterns lit—guide them.	*but . . . as well*
	5. People dance, sing all night.	*while*
and	6. Uneaten food—sea, river, next morning.	
	7. Some places: lanterns: sea.	
and	8. People watch—shore.	
until	9. Drift out of sight.	*as*

Composition

Imagine witnessing the sort of festival described in the passage. Write two paragraphs in about 150 words using the ideas given below:

1. Preparations: the making of the lanterns; preparing food—description of the streets at night; people dancing and singing.
2. The following morning—food was thrown away—lanterns on the sea—people watching—the lanterns disappeared—the sun rose.

Letter-writing

Write a letter to a friend refusing an invitation to a party. Supply a suitable Introduction and Conclusion. Use the following ideas to write your *Purpose*: you regret you cannot come—reason why—you bought tickets for a play a month ago—you have arranged to go with several friends.

Special Difficulties

Review SD 188–222.

Exercises

A. Words Often Confused.

Choose the correct words in the following sentences:

1. He came to see me yesterday as (usually) (usual). (**SD 192a**)
2. There was no one I knew (between) (among) those present. (**SD 192b**)
3. The (headmaster) (manager) of this store is kept very busy. (**SD 192c**)
4. Children's (cloths) (clothes) are difficult to choose. (**SD 202a**)
5. He never (greets) (salutes) anyone in the morning. (**SD 202b**)
6. Your hands are not very (clean) (clear), are they? (**SD 202c**)
7. Mary's in the kitchen. She's (washing) (washing up) the plates. (**SD 204b**)
8. If you lose your (temper) (mood) you will regret it. (**SD 206**)
9. This problem is (enough) (too) difficult for me. (**SD 210**)
10. He is (enough) (fairly) good at his work. (**SD 212a**)
11. He is trying hard but his work is still not good (enough) (fairly). (**SD 212a**)
12. It will be more expensive to run a car now that (benzine) (petrol) has gone up. (**SD 212b**)
13. Young people should remain (free) (single) for a few years before they marry. (**SD 218a**)
14. There was a long (row) (queue) at the bus-stop. (**SD 218b**)

B. *Get* (**SD 188a**); *keep* (**SD 196**); *take* (**SD 198**); *run* (**SD 216**); *make* (**SD 222**).

Complete these sentences by adding any of the following words: into, in, after, out, out of, down, up, away, for, over, from.

1. His lies would not take . . . anybody but a fool.
2. The explorers returned because they had run . . . . . . food.
3. He is very good at making . . . stories for children.
4. It took him a long time to get . . . his illness.
5. Mrs Jones told her daughter to keep . . . . . . the stove.
6. During the storm, the ship made . . . the nearest harbour.
7. Has this car been run . . . yet?
8. The bird accidentally flew into the room and couldn't get . . .
9. I don't believe that children should be kept . . . after school.
10. He spoke so quickly, I didn't have time to take . . . what he said.
11. Though we all ran . . . the thief, we could not catch him.
12. I hadn't seen him for years and I accidentally ran . . . him in the street this morning.
13. Ronald will take . . . the family business now that his father has died.
14. Can you make . . . the address on this envelope?
15. I've taken . . . painting in my spare time.